Advanced Photography

Fifth Edition

Advanced Photography

Fifth Edition

Michael Langford FBIPP, HonFRPS
Royal College of Art, London

Focal Press
London and Boston

Focal Press
is an imprint of Butterworth Scientific

 PART OF REED INTERNATIONAL P.L.C.

First published 1969
Second edition 1972
Third edition 1974
Fourth edition 1980
Fifth edition 1989

© Michael Langford, 1989

British Library Cataloguing in Publication Data

Langford, Michael, 1933–
   Advanced photography.—5th ed.
   1. Photography
   I. Title
   770

   ISBN 0-240-51088-7

Library of Congress Cataloging-in-Publication Data

Langford, Michael John, 1933–
   Advanced photography/Michael Langford.—5th ed.
     p. cm.
   Includes index.
   ISBN 0-240-51088-7
   1. Photography.   I. Title.
TR145.L3175 1989
770–dc 19   88-24153

Typeset by BC Typesetting, Exeter EX2 8PN
Printed and bound in Great Britain by
Butler & Tanner, Frome, Somerset

Contents

Introduction

This book is for students who understand the basic equipment and techniques of photography. It takes you on beyond basics in both depth and breadth — explaining the technical background to practice for serious enthusiasts and students of professional photography. Like the companion textbook *Basic Photography*, it approaches technical matters as a means to a practical end, rather than a separate area of study. Depth of content is determined by the need to understand the kind of data presented by manufacturers in selling lenses, lighting, films, processing equipment etc. to experienced users. The book's breadth includes differences between amateur and professional photography; wide-ranging subject problems; audio-visual production and presentation; and the reproduction of photographs in print.

For the most part, however, chapters are designed as modules — to be read individually and not necessarily in sequence. Each one is planned to increase your technical control in a particular area. For example, the chapter on tone control gathers together all the factors which influence the tonal qualities of your picture, from original subject contrast through exposure, processing, printing, to the way you finally display results. The lighting control chapter discusses colour, contrast, the mixing of sources such as flash and incandescent lamps, the use of IR or UV illumination, and choosing and buying lighting to set up a studio. Processing is looked at from an organization and management point of view, as well as the techniques themselves.

Photographic films are reviewed over two chapters. The first 'takes apart' modern published data, to help weigh up the details of one type of material against another. The following chapter takes a wider look at how films work in relation to how we see; here and elsewhere you will notice electronic photography (still video) growing as a rival to conventional chemical photography materials. Colour printing from negatives and from slides is explained in detail from first principles, on the basis that so far you have only tackled printing in black and white. Throughout, the book complements rather than repeats the contents of *Basic Photography*. Each chapter ends with a summary, designed as a quick guide to coverage as well as for topic revision.

Today's dominance of colour, in commercial photography and amateur snapshot photography at least, is heavily supported by the service on offer from colour laboratories. For routine, stereotyped work you can now get by with little technical knowledge, provided you have a well programmed automatic camera and use a good lab. But lack of understanding limits you in all sorts of ways — when picking equipment and materials, for example, or using subtle forms of lighting and camerawork to interpret subjects, or when creatively printing. Technical ignorance is also an obvious handicap in dealing with other professionals such as art directors, the staff of labs or print repro houses, and clients themselves. The fact remains today that having a sound technical knowledge coupled with visual imagination and self-discipline puts you firmly in the driving seat. You can then decide with some certainty which way you want to go.

M.L.

1

Amateur and professional photography

This chapter reviews photography as an occupation – whether you are amateur or professional or take pictures which are anything from strictly functional illustrations to expressive works of art. It looks broadly at the qualities you need for success in widely differing fields, and it discusses markets for all kinds of professional photography, comparing work as an employee with being a self-employed freelance or managing a business with staff of your own. Most of the types of photography outlined here are discussed further in greater organizational and technical detail in Chapter 8.

Differences in approach

Amateur

People often describe themselves as 'only' amateurs, as if apologizing for this status. After all, the word *amateurish* suggests the second rate. However, amateur simply means that you earn your living doing something else. Do not assume that amateur photography must always be inferior to professional photography. Each requires an attitude of mind which differs in several ways – but is not necessarily 'better' or 'worse'.

As an amateur, you may envy the professional, wishing you could combine business with pleasure into a kind of full-time hobby, using professional equipment and facilities. However, the professional knows that the hidden advantage of being amateur is the freedom you have to shoot what and when you like. You can develop your own ideas – experiment in approach, subject and technique – without much concern over how long any of this might take. You can be self-indulgent. (Throughout the history of photography many amateurs have been the visual innovators, such as J. M. Cameron, Robert Demachy, Paul Strand and J. H. Lartigue.)

As an amateur, you can work for an exhibition or a competition of your choice – or just for yourself or family. You can also enjoy the equipment and techniques as a refreshing change from your daily work. On the other hand, you lack the pressure of deadlines, the

1

Fig. 1.1 The main areas of photography. Many other divisions are possible and sometimes work spans more than one area

challenge of commissions and commercial competition to keep you on your toes. It is easy to become complacent or set targets too low to be much of a challenge. After all, the world is not bounded by the judge's view of photography at the local camera club. If you want to take your hobby seriously you should find the time to keep yourself aware of trends by looking at published photographs and visiting galleries. In this way you can widen your knowledge of how different people use photography to express ideas and communicate information.

Professional

A professional photographer must be reliable. He or she also needs financial and organizational skills, just as much as visual and technical expertise, in order to stay in business. People rely on you as a professional to produce some sort of result, always. Failure does not simply mean you receive no fee – most work is commissioned, so you have let someone down. A client's money invested in models, props, special locations, etc. is thrown away, a publication deadline may be missed or an unrepeatable event remains undocumented.

You therefore have to ensure – as far as humanly possible – that everything in the chain between arriving to shoot and presenting the finished work functions without fail. You need to be an effective organizer of people, locations, transport, etc., able to make the right choice of time and day, and, of course, arrive punctually yourself. You must be able to anticipate hold-ups and avoid them. As a last resort, you should know how to act if a job has to be abandoned or re-shot. Pressures of this kind are both a worry and a stimulus – but, of course, they make a successful result all the more worthwhile. See page 43.

Working professionally also means that you have to produce results at an economical speed and cost. You must think of overheads such as rent and taxes, and equipment depreciation, as well as direct costs such as photographic materials and fuel. It is seldom possible to linger longingly over a job as if it was a leisure occupation. You also need to know how to charge – how to cost out a commission accurately and balance a reasonable profit margin against client goodwill (will they come again?), bearing in mind the competition and the current going rate for the job.

Equipment is no more or less than a set of tools from which you select the right 'spanner' for the picture you have in mind. Every item must give highest quality results but also be rugged and reliable – vital gear may need duplicate back-up. The cost of fouling up an assignment because of equipment failure can be greater than the photographic equipment itself, so it is a false economy to work with second-rate tools.

One of the challenges of professional work is to make interesting, imaginative photographs within the limitations of a dull commercial brief. For example, how do you make a strong picture out of a set of ordinary plastic bowls – to fill an awkward-shaped space on a catalogue page? Eventually you should be able to refuse the more dead-end work, but at first you will need every commission you can find. In the same way, you must learn how to promote yourself and build up a range of clients who provide you with the right subject opportunities and freedom to demonstrate your ways of seeing, as well as income.

Photography is still one of the few occupations in which you can create and make things as a one-person business or department. It suits the individualist – one reason why the great majority of professional photographers are self-employed. There is great satisfaction in a job which demands daily use of visual and technical skills. The experience you build up daily as a professional increases your confidence and dexterity and permits the use of short cuts, knowing which routines are really important.

'Independent'

Photography does not just divide neatly into amateur and professional categories. After all, it is a *medium* – of communication, expression, information, even propaganda – and as such can be practised in hundreds of different ways. You can shoot pictures purely to please yourself and develop your style; for example, working for one-person exhibitions, books, and sponsored projects, awards and scholarships. It is possible to build up a national or international reputation in this way if your photography is good enough. You can sell pictures through galleries or agents as works of art.

Most of these so-called 'independent' photographers make their living from another occupation such as teaching, writing or some other kind of photographically related full- or part-time job. Independent photography relies on the growing number of galleries, publications and industrial and government sponsors of the arts interested in our medium. In this, photography follows long-established patterns in painting, poetry, music, etc. If you are sufficiently motivated, then working for yourself free of commercial pressures can lead to *avant-garde* results of the highest standard. Some independent photographers work for political or other ideological beliefs. Outlets here include pressure groups, trade unions, charities, arts centres, local community associations, specialist publishing houses and archives. It is one of the great strengths of photography that so many of these options are open to be explored.

How photographs are read

If you are really going to progress as any kind of photographer, in addition to technical expertise you need a strong visual sense (something you develop as an individual). This should go beyond composition and picture structuring to include some understanding of why people see and react to photographs in different ways. The latter can

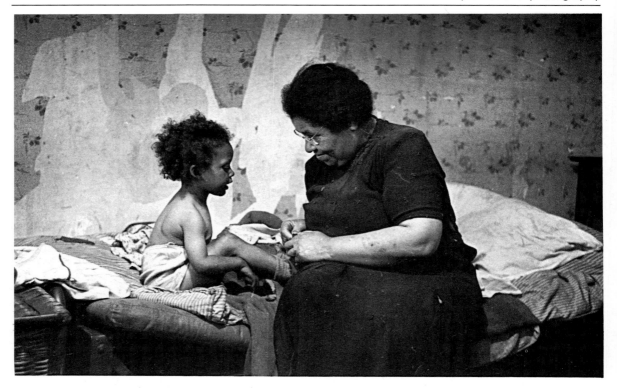

Fig. 1.2 This picture was taken by Bert Hardy in 1949, for the weekly magazine *Picture Post*. See text

be a lifetime's study, because so many changing influences are at work. Some aspects of reading meaning from photographs are blindingly obvious, others much more subtle. However, realizing how people tend to react to pictures helps you to predict the influences of your own work – and then to plan and shoot with this in mind.

The actual physical act of *seeing* first involves the lens of your eye forming a crude image on the retina. Second, it concerns your brain's perception and interpretation of this image. You might view exactly the same scene as the next person but differ greatly in what you make of what you see. In the same way, two people may look at the same photographic print but read its contents quite differently.

Look at Figure 1.2, for example. Some people might see this picture primarily as a political document, evidence of life under a particular regime. For others it is a statement documenting the subjugation of women. Still others would just enjoy the shot for its composition – the visual structures it contains – seeing the subject as secondary. Again, the same picture could be read as containing historical information on dress or decor of a particular period, or it might even simply be seen as demonstrating the effect of a particular camera, lens or film.

None of us is wholly objective in interpreting photographs – everyone is influenced by their own background. Experience so far of life (and pictures) may make you approach every photograph as a work of art . . . or some form of political statement . . . or a factual record for measurement and research, etc. This kind of tunnel vision, or just general lack of experience, confuses visual communication between photographer and viewer. In a similar way, it is difficult to imagine a colour you have not actually seen or to speak words you have never heard.

A shot like Figure 1.3, for example, which happens to be a leaf section magnified ×165 would probably be viewed as an abstract pattern by someone unused to seeing electron photomicrographs. A scientist might recognize and look 'through' the picture as if seeing into the microscope eyepiece itself, picking on the subject's factual detail. A sculptor, architect or industrial designer might file it as a reference for particular three-dimensional forms it shows. The point is that none of us work entirely in a vacuum. Unless you are uncompromisingly working to please yourself you must think to whom your photography is directed and how it is likely to be received. This will help to clarify your aims in approaching subject and presentation.

Sometimes your visual communication must be simple, direct and clear – as in most product advertising. This may be aimed at known groups of receivers identified because they are readers of a particular journal, drivers past billboards or people buying at art store counters. Other photographs may be more successful and mind-provoking when they *suggest* rather than *state* things – see Figure 4.8, for example. The more obscure your image, the more likely it is to be interpreted in different ways – but maybe this is your intention?

Much also depends on the way your pictures are physically presented – how they relate to any adjacent pictures, whether they appear on pages you turn or are isolated in frames hung on the wall. Some photographers add slogans, quotations or factual or literary captions when presenting their work to clarify it, to give an extra 'edge' by posing questions, or even purposely to confuse the pictures. They often rate word and image as equally important. It is an approach which has worked well in the past (see examples by Duane Michals and Jim Goldberg). In less able hands literary additions can become a gimmick or a sign of weakness, patching up an inability to express yourself through pictures. They can easily seem pretentious (flowery titles) or patronizing (rhetoric emphasizing something viewers are well able to appreciate for themselves). It is significant that in the advertising world copywriting is a very skilled profession, heavily

Fig. 1.3 Electron micrograph of a fractured turnip leaf, showing the cell structure. Magnification (in this reproduction) ×170. (Dr Jeremy Burgess/Science Photo Library)

market-researched. Pictures and words are planned together, adding a great deal to total message impact.

Markets for professional photography

At one time second-rate 'professional' photographers could make a good living simply out of the mystique of working the equipment. They knew what exposure to give and how to use camera movements, and they employed much better lenses than were available to amateur photographers. Improvements in equipment and simplification of processes today allow talented amateurs to equal or surpass this level, while top professionals – with flair, imagination and business sense – reach greater heights than ever before. You can still find mediocre professional photography, of course. Some is produced by transients, people who drift into photography and just as quickly disappear again. Some professionals do stay in business but only by clinging to rock-bottom prices, which stunts growth.

Professional photography, being a loose collection of individuals, small units or departments, is structured mostly by the markets for pictures. The main markets are commercial and industrial; portraits and weddings; press and photojournalism; advertising and editorial illustration; and technical and scientific applied photography. These are only approximate categories – they often merge and overlap. A photographer in 'general practice', for example, might tackle several of them to meet the requirements of his or her local community. On the other hand, there are a few specialist photographers working in quite narrow fields – fashion, architecture or natural history, for example – who operate internationally and compete with similar specialists in other countries for worldwide markets.

Commercial and industrial photography

This covers the general photographic needs of commerce and industry, often businesses in your immediate area but sometimes spread quite widely, as when serving companies within a widely dispersed group. Clients range from solicitors, real estate agents, local light industry and town councils up to very large manufacturing or construction organizations working on an international scale.

Your photography might be used to spread a good public relations image of the company. It will be needed to record processes, products and new building developments. Some pictures issued with 'press releases' will be reproduced on editorial pages of magazines (often specialist publications). Others are used in catalogues, brochures and internal company reports. Photographs may be an essential element in a staff training scheme, or needed as legal evidence or for archival records. Work will extend beyond supplying prints and transparencies, and is likely to include video work and sequences for presentation in audiovisual form. See Chapter 11.

Large commercial/industrial studios dealing with a lot of public relations commissions may offer a total communications 'package'. This teams up photographers, graphic designers, advertising and marketing people, and writers. The result is that a complete campaign, perhaps from the launching conference (announcing a new product to the client's sales force), through press information, general and specialist advertising to brochures and instruction manuals for the client's customers, can all be handled in a coordinated way 'in-house'.

A few industrial organizations run their own small photographic departments employing two or three staff photographers. Such departments may be general-purpose or form part of a larger public relations unit. The advantage to management is that they always have photographers available who are familiar with the company's personnel, its geographical layout and general publicity policy. However, an in-house photographic department is uneconomic if there is an uneven pattern to projects and contracts. Workflow may then be so erratic that salaried staff either have too little to do or are over-whelmed so that assistance must be bought outside.

Portrait and wedding photography

Professional businesses of this kind deal with the public directly. Some operate out of High Street studios, but because so much of the work is now shot on location (for example, portraits 'at home') special premises are not essential. Other portrait and wedding photographers work from businesses inside departmental stores. In all instances it is important to have the right form of display/shop window/reception area where your best work can be admired by people of the income group you are aiming to attract.

To succeed in photography of this type you need an absorbing interest in people and the ability to flatter their appearance rather

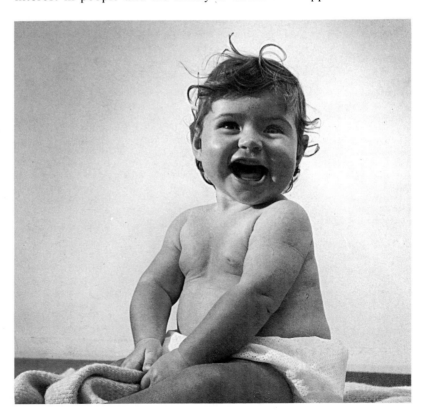

Fig. 1.4 Portrait taken in the child's home using a pair of flash units. A camera with waist-level finder makes it easier to shoot at floor level

than reveal harsh truths about them. After all, it is the clients or their closer associates who pay your bill – unlike photojournalism or advertising pictures commissioned by magazines or agencies. The people you arrange in front of the camera require sympathetic but firm direction. It helps to have an extrovert, buoyant personality and the ability to put people at their ease (especially in the unfamiliar environment of a studio) to avoid selfconscious or 'dead'-looking portraits.

The work typically covers formal portraits of executives for business purposes; family groups; weddings; animal portraits; and sometimes social events and front-of-house pictures for theatrical productions. See Chapter 7.

Press photography and photojournalism

Press photography differs from photojournalism in the same way that single newspaper pictures differ from picture magazine features. Both are produced for publication and therefore have to meet firm deadlines. However, as a press photographer you usually have to sum up an event or situation in one final picture. You need to know how to get quickly into a newsworthy situation, seek out its essence without being put off by others (especially competitors) and always bring back technically acceptable results, even under near-impossible conditions.

Most press photographers work for local newspapers. Where there is relatively little 'hard' news you work through an annual calendar of

Fig. 1.5 Shooting pictures at a press conference often means tough competition from fellow photographers and television. It's difficult to get something striking and different. Showing the whole situation like this is one approach. (By John Downing/*Daily Express*)

hand-shaking or rosette-waving local events, plus general-interest feature material which you generate yourself. Other press photographers work as staff on national or international papers where there is keen competition to cover public events. (See Figure 1.5, for example.) However, most 'hot' news events are now covered by television, with its unassailable speed of transmission into people's homes. Electronic still-image transmission (page 276) helps to get press photographs back to base, but newspapers still lose out due to the time needed to print and distribute them.

More photographers are employed by or work freelance for press agencies. These organizations often specialize – in sport, travel, personalities, etc. – or handle general-interest material. The agency's job is to slant the picture and written material to suit the interests of a very wide range of different publications and sell material to them at home and abroad.

Photojournalism is a smaller market. However, here your work can form more of an in-depth picture essay and be shot over a longer period than press photography, aiming to fill several pages in a picture magazine or newspaper colour supplement. Other outlets include corporate house journals and prestige publications from leading names in oil, finance, shipping, etc.

As a photojournalist you should be able to provide a well-rounded coverage of your story or theme. For example, bold start-and-finish pictures, sequence shots, comparative pairs and strong single images all help a good art editor to lay out pages which have variety and impact. (On the other hand, a bad art editor can ruin your set of pictures by insensitive hacking to fit them into available space.)

Occasionally a photojournalist will cover the story entirely, using pictures with captions or even writing the text as well. Mostly, however, you work independently of the journalist producing the text, having both been briefed by the editor. Photojournalism is difficult to break into as an unknown photographer. One way round this is to find and complete a really strong project on your own initiative and take it to editors of appropriate publications for their opinions and advice.

Editorial and advertising photography

Editorial illustration means photography (often single pictures) to illustrate magazine features on subjects as diverse as food, gardening, make-up, fashion, etc. A lot of this kind of work is handled in the studio. You have less scope to express your own point of view than in photojournalism, yet it allows more freedom of style than most advertising photography. Editorial photography in prestigious magazines and books is a good 'shop window' for your work and can provide a steady income, although it is not usually well paid.

Advertising photography is much more restrictive than outsiders might expect. At the top end of the market, however, it offers very high fees (and is therefore very competitive). The work tends to be a team effort, handled for the client by an advertising agency. You must expect to shoot to some form of sketched layout, specifying the height-to-width proportions of the final picture and the placing of any superimposed type. Ideally, you will be drawn into one of the initial planning stages with the creative director, graphic designer and client,

Fig. 1.6 An editorial still-life shot like this looks deceptively simple. It takes skill and patience to suggest the differences in decoration, shape and size, and also achieve a strong grouping. (By Annie Morris)

to contribute ideas. Sometimes the layout will be loose and open – a mood picture, perhaps – or it might be a tight 'pack shot' of a product, detailed down to the placing of individual highlights. At the unglamorous lower end of the market advertising merges into commercial photography, with income to match.

Whether or not you are chosen as a photographer for a particular campaign depends on several factors. For example, is your approach in tune with the essential spirit required – romantic, camp, straight and direct, humorous? Depending on the subject, do you have a flair for fashion, an obsession for intricate still-life shots, skill in organizing people or in grabbing pictures from real-life situations? Have you done pictures (published or folio specimens) having this kind of 'feel' or 'look' before, even though for some totally different application? Do you have any special technical skills which are called for, and are you careful and reliable enough – without lacking visual imagination? Can you work constructively with the team, without clashes of personality? Finally, are your prices right?

Most of these questions, of course, apply to the choice of a professional photographer for any assignment. However, in top advertising work the financial investment in models, locations, stylists and designers (as well as the cost of the final bought advertising space) is so high that choosing the wrong photographer could be a disaster.

Technical and scientific photography

This is a very different area, where meticulous technical skills and accuracy are all-important. Any expressionism or original personal style of your own will tend to get in the way of clearly communicating information. Photographs are needed as factual, analytical documents, perhaps for forensic or medical evidence, military or industrial research and development. You will probably be a staff photographer, employed by the government, a university or an industrial research institute. Photographic skills required include photomacro and photomicro still photography, high-speed recording and other forms of photo-instrumentation, including video. There is also a great deal of routine straight photography on location and in the laboratory.

You will be expected to have more than just photographic know-how. As a medical photographer you need a working knowledge of anatomy and an understanding of medical terms as well as concern for patients and an interest in medicine generally. As a scientific photographer you should have a sufficiently scientific background to understand advanced equipment and appreciate clearly what points scientist colleagues want to show in their reports and specialist papers. As a police photographer you should know what is or is not admissible in law and how to present evidence efficiently to a court. On top of this, you must assess the potential of all new photographic materials and processes which might be applicable to your field. You will also be expected to improvise techniques for tackling unusual requirements.

To be a good 'applied' photographer you should therefore enjoy a methodical, painstaking approach to solving technical challenges. You will probably be paid according to a fixed, national salary scale which is not particularly high. However, there is better job security than offered by many other branches of professional photography.

Roles within a photographic business

Perhaps you are a one-person freelance or one of the team in an independent studio or in-house photographic department. Every professional photography business must combine a number of skills, and for each skill you might require an individual employee, either on

Fig. 1.7 Above: technical record of a fractured metal die, to illustrate an equipment failure report

Fig. 1.8 Right: an informational picture showing preparation of the sand core for an engine casting. This was shot for education and training purposes

the payroll or 'bought in' (by using an outside custom laboratory, for example). For the lone freelance several or all of the following roles have to be filled by one person.

Manager/organizer

Managing means making sure photography goes on efficiently and economically. You must hire any necessary staff and/or outside services, check that quality control and reliability are maintained, watch finances. Like any other administrator, you will be concerned with safety; premises; insurances (including Model Release, page 287); and best-value purchase of equipment and materials. You must know when to buy and when to hire items. Every assignment must be costed and charged for accurately, remembering the competition and producing the work as economically as possible without dropping standards. As manager, you must understand essential book-keeping and copyright, and be able to liaise with the accountant, bank manager, tax inspector and lawyer. If you employ staff you must be able to direct and motivate them, creating a team spirit and pride in the photography produced.

Photographer

Ideally, a photographer should be free to take photographs. In practice, apart from being technically reliable and visually imaginative you must be a good organizer and also be able to liaise directly with the client. Dealing with whoever is paying for your services is harmonious enough if you both see eye to eye, but, unfortunately, clients have odd quirks of their own. When it is obvious that this will lead to disaster (for which the photographer will eventually be blamed) considerable tact and persuasiveness are needed.

At a pre-briefing you should identify what the client has in mind, or at least the purpose of the picture and how and where it will be used. If the brief is very open-ended, float some ideas of your own and see how cooperatively these are received. If still in doubt, do the job, photographing the way you would like to see it done but cover yourself by shooting additional (for example, more conventional?) versions the client might expect. Often in this way you can 'educate' clients, bring them around to using more distinctive photography. But never experiment at the clients' expense, so that they end up with results they cannot use. As a photographer, you should carry through each of your jobs whenever possible – if not printing yourself then at least supervising this stage. Finally, discuss the results directly with whoever briefed you in the first place.

Technicians

Technicians provide the photographer's back-up – processing, printing, special effects, finishing – to turn camera work into final photographs. Technical staff are employed full time or hired as and when required for jobs – through use of a custom laboratory, for example, or hiring a freelance retoucher. Technicians have specialized knowledge and skills highly developed by long practice in their particular area. They can give photographers valuable advice before shooting, and sometimes bail them out afterwards if some technical blunder has been made. Printing staff are also kept busy producing reprints of previous negatives, which helps to give the unit a steady cash flow.

Working as a technician is sometimes creative but more often routine. You must produce work fast, and to highest professional standards. In return, there is more security and often better pay in being a first-class technician than an ordinary photographer. Too many people want to be photographers, overlooking equally satisfying jobs of this kind.

Ancillary roles

In major cities where there is plenty of work you can set yourself up as a freelance assistant, hired by the day or job by freelance photographers, just as they might hire a studio or camera equipment. Other supporting roles include photographer's agent – someone who gets commissions for you by taking and showing your work to potential clients. Agents seek out jobs, promote you and handle money negotiations. In return, they are paid a percentage of your fees. Stylists can be hired to find suitable locations for shots, furnish a studio set or lay on exotic props. Model agencies supply male and female models – attractive, ugly, 'characterful', young and old. Specialist photographic/theatrical sources hire trained animals, uniforms or antique cars for you – everything from a stuffed hyena to a military tank.

Turning professional

There is no strictly formal way into professional photography. You do not have to be registered or certified, or, for most work, belong to a union. Most young photographers go through an art college or technical college photography course. Some come into photography from design, fine art or some form of science course. Others go straight into a professional business as a junior member of staff and work their way up, perhaps with part-time study.

College photographic programmes range from basic technician certificate courses to national diplomas and Bachelor's (BA) and Master's (MA) degrees. Certificate courses tend to train you for the technical procedures and processes which make you immediately useful today as an employee. Diploma courses are also craft based but are more broadly professional. Most degree courses aim to help develop you as an individual – they are academic, like humanities courses, encouraging original ideas and approaches which pave the way to tomorrow's photography. However, certificates, diplomas and degrees themselves are only pieces of paper. Unless you are applying for a government-type photographic job with a pay scale formally linked to paper qualifications your best proof of ability is a portfolio of outstanding work. Organizations such as the Royal Photographic Society and various professional photographers' associations offer fellowships to individuals submitting pictures considered to reach a suitable standard of excellence. Make sure that your commercial portfolio contains not only photographs but also cuttings showing how your photography has been used in print. Pages from magazines, brochures, etc. all help to promote confidence in you in the eyes of potential clients.

Summary: Amateur and professional photography

- Amateur photography allows you greater freedom than professional work, but being a pro makes commercial factors – reliability, fast economic working methods and good organization – as important as your photographic skills. Often you have to create interesting pictures within a quite restrictive brief.
- In the same tradition as other creative arts, some fine *avant-garde* photographers operate as 'independents'. They build up international reputations through exhibitions, books, direct sale of prints, etc., yet earn their living at least in part at another job.
- To progress beyond a certain level in photography you need to learn how people read meaning into photographs. Everyone is influenced by their own background and attitude to life, in seeing significant things in pictures. You can also influence reaction through the way sequences or single pictures are presented. Understanding how your work is likely to be received will help you to decide the best approach to your subject.
- Professional photography is mostly market structured – commercial and industrial, portraits and weddings, press and photojournalism, advertising and editorial, and technical and scientific.
- Commercial/industrial work covers promotional and record photography for firms and institutions. Your photography may be part of a complete communications 'package', including brochure design. Portrait/wedding photography is aimed directly at the public. You need to be good at flattering people through your photography and general manner.
- Press photography, very time based and competitive, means summing up a newsworthy event. Photojournalism allows space for more in-depth visual essays. You can therefore think in terms of sequence – supply the art editor with a full coverage containing strong potential start-and-finish shots.
- Editorial/advertising photography often means close working with designers. Advertising work is heavily planned – you usually work to a layout within a team including a creative director, a graphic designer and a copywriter.
- Technical/scientific applications of photography call for factual, analytical records. You are likely to be an employed staff photographer, either working on industrial/university research projects or at a forensic or medical centre.
- There are several key roles in any photographic business or department. A manager administrates quality control, accounts, safety, equipment and materials. One or more photographers organize shoots, liaise with clients and carry out jobs efficiently, imaginatively and economically. Technicians follow through the photographers' work and service reprint orders. Ancillary roles include freelance assistant; agent; stylist; and agencies for models, props, etc.
- Most people get into professional photography by taking an appropriate full-time college course, or they start in a studio and study part-time. However, 'getting on' depends more on evidence of your practical achievements than on paper qualifications.

2
Choosing lenses

Fine image quality depends a great deal on having a good lens, but you will find that even good lenses are only intended for a limited range of working conditions. Optics which excel under one set of circumstances can give quite poor results under another. This chapter explains some of the problems faced by lens designers and manufacturers, and shows how every product is a compromise between what today's technology will allow and what we as photographers will actually buy. It also helps you to understand the lens quality data in manufacturers' technical literature, and what to look for when buying a lens, new or second-hand. Special types of lenses are discussed too, in terms of practical handling and suitability for different kinds of photography.

The lens designer's problems

We all tend to take a modern lens for granted. It is just accepted as an image-forming collection of glass elements, somewhat overpriced and easily damaged. In fact, every good lens is really a skilfully solved set of problems concerning the control of light. Designing a lens means juggling image quality, the picture area covered, consistency over a wide range of subject distances, an acceptably wide aperture – and finally coming up with something which is not too large, heavy or expensive to manufacture.

Glass

The designer's raw material is optical glass, which starts as a molten mixture of chemicals, including barium, lanthanum and tantalum oxides. According to its chemical content, each type of glass has a particular (1) refractive index and (2) dispersive power (Abbe number).

Refractive index (RI) means the glass's light-bending power, measured for a wavelength of light near the middle of the spectrum (typically, 590 nm yellow-green, see Figure 2.1). The higher the RI,

Substance	Mean RI*
Vacuum	1.000
Water	1.333
Magnesium fluoride	1.378
Fused silica	1.458
Hard crown optical glass	1.519
Common window glass	1.528
Lead crystal drinking glass	1.538
Dense flint optical glass	1.927
Diamond	2.419

*Measurement at wavelength 590 nm

Fig. 2.1 Some refractive index values

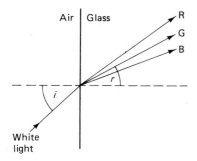

Fig. 2.2 Refraction and dispersion. Mean refractive index with this glass is sine *i* divided by sine *r*. Dispersion (exaggerated here) is shown by the different RI for red and blue light. Glass dispersive power is given an Abbe number: the greater the dispersion the lower the number

the more steeply oblique light entering the glass is changed in direction. The 'dispersive power' of the glass means the difference between its refractive indexes for red and blue light (see Figure 2.2). The greater this difference, the more white light is split into a wide spectrum of colours, just as a prism or droplets of rain disperse sunlight into a rainbow. Dispersion is an important factor in glass for photographic lenses because your subject matter is often multi-coloured and lit by a white-light mixed-wavelength source.

Mean refractive index and dispersive power are fairly independent. You can have two glasses which have the same refractive index but different dispersive power, and glasses which differ in refractive index but which have identical dispersive power. Figure 2.3 shows how this makes over 150 different kinds of optical glass available for the designer to choose. Glass used for lenses must also have the right physical properties to be machined and polished to the designer's chosen shapes without breaking. It must be completely colourless, unlike ordinary window glass, which shows a green tinge when you look through it end-on. Other requirements include freedom from defects such as bubbles; general stability; and resistance to atmospheric conditions and reasonable handling during day-to-day use.

Design and manufacture

A photographic lens is built up from a series of lens elements. The designer works by calculating the necessary front and back surface contours of each element, its appropriate glass and the spacing of one element relative to another in the lens barrel (allowing for the aperture diaphragm and perhaps shutter). The aim in all this is to correct the mixture of optical errors – 'aberrations' – which always occur in images of a scene formed by simple lens elements alone.

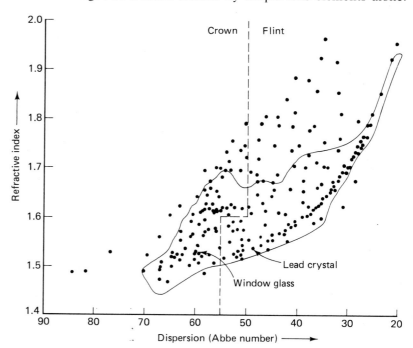

Fig. 2.3 The 150 or so optical glass types produced for lenses by Schott, Germany. Glass for windows and lead crystal tableware are included for comparison. Enclosed zone defines the limits to manufacture 50 years ago

Fig. 2.4 Internal structure of a regular *f*/1.4 50 mm lens for a 35 mm SLR camera. Lens design is a complex, mathematical combination of different lens elements, precisely located in the barrel along with aperture and focusing mechanism

Glass Types, curvatures, number of elements, separation, coating; size and weight

Engineering Centring, spacing, focusing, zooming or floating of elements, aperture

Closely check the image of a scene formed by a single-element magnifying glass and you will see the slightly fuzzy, distorted, low-contrast picture which is the collective effect of aberrations.

Some of the main aberrations are shown in Figures 2.5 to 2.10. It is not too difficult to reduce or eliminate each one *individually* by some means. For example, Figure 2.11 shows how the designer can correct chromatic aberration by combining a converging shape lens made in high refractive index medium-dispersion glass with a diverging shape lens of glass having less refractive index but matching dispersion. The dispersion effects of converging and diverging elements then almost exactly cancel each other out, although together they still converge light and so form an image.

Some aberrations are corrected by similar 'equal-but-opposite' combinations, some by stopping down, others by mathematical ratio of surface curvatures or an equal arrangement of elements in front of and behind the aperture. The handicap every designer faces is that the best way to correct one optical fault often worsens another. Matters can be helped by adding further lens elements (each offers a choice of two further surface curvatures and different glass), or you can fit a smaller aperture, or limit lens coverage to a narrower angle of view to cut out the worst aberrations which tend to appear away from the centre of the image field. However, as elements are added light scatter builds up at every extra glass surface, and this gradually reduces image brilliance, despite the anti-reflective coating given to all modern optics. The lens also becomes heavy and expensive because of the cost of machining so many elements. Again, photographers want wider, not smaller, aperture lenses and optics which have generous covering power, especially for camera movements.

Using highly sophisticated computing equipment, the designer calculates the paths of hundreds of light rays from a test subject to each part of the picture format the lens is being designed to cover. Compromises have to be made. Ideally, image quality should remain excellent whether the lens is focused for close or for distant subjects

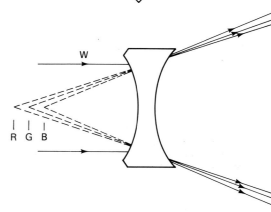

Fig. 2.5 Spherical aberration. Above: rays refracted by outer zones of a spherically shaped lens come to focus (F) nearer the lens than rays refracted through central zones

Fig. 2.6 Chromatic aberration. Right: dispersion of white light in simple converging and diverging lens elements causes different points of focus for each colour

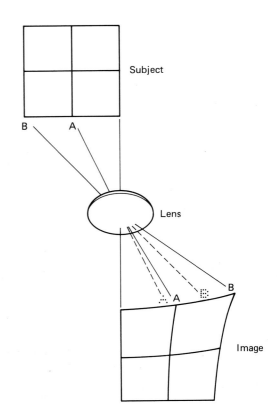

Fig. 2.7 Curvature of field. Above: A is further from the lens centre than B. So sharp image A_1 forms closer to the lens than B_1. The focal plane is saucer shaped: centre and edges cannot both be focused on a flat surface at any one setting

Fig. 2.8 Curvilinear distortion. Right: the rays most off-axis make too large an angle with the axis, 'strectching' the image of a square into a curved, pincushion shape. When refracted rays make too small an angle the opposite effect, barrel distortion, results. See Figure 2.22

Fig. 2.9 Coma. Each circular zone of the lens focuses oblique rays from an off-axis point at a different position relative to lens and lens axis. The patch of light formed (drawn as it appears at point of focus C) is pulled out like a comet. An oblique form of spherical aberration (Figure 2.5)

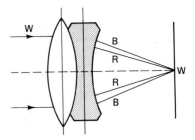

Fig. 2.11 Correcting chromatic aberration by combining positive and negative elements of different glass types. See text

Fig. 2.10 Astigmatism. Light from an off-axis subject point is imaged spread out as either a radial line (at focal plane B) or a tangential line (plane A). Best compromise image is at intermediate plane X. Other off-axis points image as lines A_2 or B_2 etc.

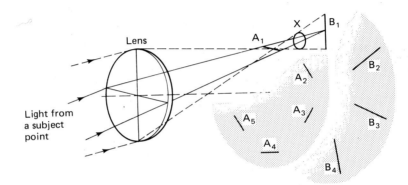

when used at any of its aperture settings, and with no difference between the centre and corners of the picture format. At the same time, it is no good if the designer pursues ideal aberration correction if the resulting lens is uneconomic to make.

Each advance in lens manufacturing helps the designer. For example, you can have groups of 'floating' elements which mechanically alter their position in the lens barrel as the lens is focused for different distances. Elements can be given 'aspheric' instead of spheric surface contours (see Figure 2.12) or, in the case of small elements, be made in glass which has a graduated refractive index between centre and edges. These developments allow lenses with a better and more consistent performance, using fewer rather than more lens elements. So the trend is towards lighter and more compact lenses, as well as more extreme focal lengths and wider maximum apertures.

Fig. 2.12 Various lens elements, each having one aspheric shaped surface (A). S shows how one of these contours would be if given a normal and more easily produced spherical surface

Checking lens image quality

Lens quality is difficult to pin down by something simple such as a number. Sharpness is subjective – clarity judged by human vision –

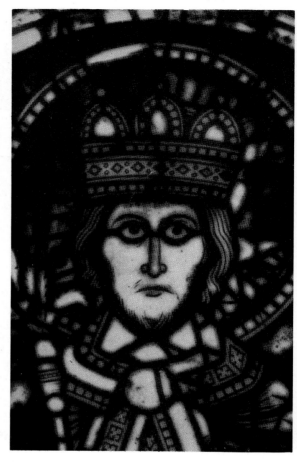

Fig. 2.13 Image sharpness is subjective, depending on contrast as much as fine detail. Left-hand picture (A) was shot with a lens giving poor resolution but good image contrast. Right-hand picture (B) used a lens corrected to resolve finer detail but giving lower contrast. Viewed carefully from normal reading distance, (B) looks sharpest. But from two metres away (A) seems sharpest – your eyes no longer see the fine detail reproduced in (B) so this factor no longer matters. Courtesy Carl Zeiss

and has to include image contrast as well as how much fine detail is actually present. Look carefully at Figure 2.13, for example. You can do simple practical tests yourself to get an idea of the quality of a lens. This is helpful if you are trying out a second-hand lens before buying. On the other hand, manufacturers do much more sophisticated tests and publish typical performance as figures or graphs for each of their lens range.

D-I-Y lens tests

Irrespective of whether the lens is for small-, medium- or large-format photography, try to test it mounted in some larger-format camera which has a fine-etched focusing screen. A 35 mm or rollfilm format lens can be fitted onto a 4 × 5 inch viewcamera or a 4 × 5 inch camera lens on an 8 × 10 inch camera. Use bag bellows or a recessed lens panel if necessary to allow the lens close enough to focus. Have the lens axis dead centre and at true right angles to the enlarged focusing screen, which you trace out with the vertical and horizontal outlines of the format your lens must cover. Acceptable image quality outside this area will prove how much you could use the lens off-centre – by shift or swing movements, for example. Have a focusing magnifier to examine the appearance of the image on the screen.

Some image qualities are best checked if you use a large-area, detailed subject. Pin up several sheets of newspaper at right angles to the lens axis at, say 4 metres away (for a general-purpose lens) or any other distance you know you will often use. Have this improvised 'test chart' brightly and evenly lit. Then with the lens at widest aperture, focus for the centre of the format and examine image quality over parts of the screen further away from the axis. As you increase this distance the image may look less sharp, due to various off-axis aberrations and curved field. The latter is proved by refocusing – see if the outer zone grows sharper at the expense of the centre.

Slight curved field is a problem with some wide-aperture lenses, but is overcome when stopped down one to two stops. The position of sharp focus for the screen centre should be quite definite. If you have any uncertainty about this position, or see it change as you stop down, this suggests residual spherical aberration (Figure 2.5). You can also check for curvilinear distortion by having straight lines in the subject imaged well out in the image field and comparing these against a ruler laid flat across the screen.

Other faults are best seen using a rear-illuminated pinhole as a subject. Set this up at an appropriate distance and sharply focused centre frame, then slide it sideways, parallel to the screen until imaged well out in the field. A change in the *shape* of the spot of light and any colour fringing that appears could be the combined effects of astigmatism, coma and lateral colour. Some of this will disappear when you stop down.

Try altering the focusing when the spot is imaged well off centre. If you see reduced aberration fringes on two parts of the spot's circumference (in line with a line drawn outwards from the lens axis) at one focusing position, and on parts at right angles to these at another focusing position, astigmatism is probably present. A damaged lens may show no dents but still have one or more elements de-centred. (It only takes a few thousandths of a millimetre misalignment between the axis of some lens elements to produce noticeable loss of image quality.) To check this, image the pinhole centre-format. When you move either lens or screen forwards or back through the position for sharp focus the spot of light should widen to a truly *circular* patch, not any other shape. Tests like this are interesting to do but really require more critical analysis than is possible by just looking at a camera focusing screen, however fine-grained it may be.

Understanding modulation transfer function

Modern lens manufacturers put their products through far more extensive tests than you can do yourself and publish what they call 'modular transfer function' (MTF) information. Do not be intimidated by this jargon, which comes from electronics rather than photography. Once you know how to read them, MTF data give plenty of practical information to judge lens quality against price. Unfortunately, graphs often appear in technical brochures without much explanation of terms, so it is worth looking at how they are drawn and what they mean.

MTF test procedure is somewhat like checking a hi-fi system, where you feed in signals covering a range of known sound frequencies then

Fig. 2.14 Typical test chart pattern for lens testing. The limit of good image sharpness is taken to be the point at which you can no longer tell whether bars are oriented horizontally or vertically. (Test it with your eyes at various distances)

compare each one against its purity of output. However, for lens testing the 'subject' is a patchwork chart of grids (Figure 2.14), each grid having a number of equal-width black and white lines. One black and one white line is considered a pair, so you can quote the number of line pairs per millimetre (lp/mm) to describe the fineness or coarseness of the grid subject. High numbers of lp/mm mean fine detail, which scientists call high spatial frequency. Low lp/mm represent coarse detail or low spatial frequency.

The next bit of terminology is *modulation,* which basically means the change between light and dark values. A microscope/computer system scans across the lens's image of chosen bars and the resulting signals are compared against direct readings off the chart. A perfect lens would image the grid with black lines perfectly black and white lines white. In practice, because of remaining aberrations and diffraction black lines become lighter and white lines darker, and original contrasty boundaries between the two appear more graduated when the light from the subject is *transferred* through the lens. Modulation is therefore always less than 100%, and could even drop

Fig. 2.15 Basic elements of an MTF graph for a camera lens designed to cover a 4 × 5 inch negative, allowing ample movements. The higher and straighter the plots the more consistent the image quality. (Note that image diagonal distances from the centre are in log values, which expand central area data relative to edges)

to the point where bars are completely indistinguishable from spaces (zero modulation).

What MTF graphs mean

The usual kind of lens modulation transfer function graph (Figure 2.15) shows modulation 0–100% on the left-hand axis. On the base line it maps out distance across the image patch, from the lens axis (left-hand end) out to some appropriate radius point to the right. For a lens designed to cover 35 mm format without movements this might be 22 mm. For a 6 × 6 cm format lens the equivalent would be 40 mm, and for 4 × 5 inch format about 80 mm. However, if your camera offers movements which shift or tilt the lens axis away from the centre of the film it is important to have information 'further out' than a circle only just covering the format. For example Figure 2.15, for a 4 × 5 inch viewcamera lens, shows performance out to a radius of 177 mm, with a marker showing the acceptable limit of off-axis use as about 155 mm.

Lens performance is plotted for a particular frequency of patterns – perhaps 20 lp/mm. As you move further from the lens axis towards corners of the picture, performance (percentage modulation) drops. The better the lens, the less this drop-off will be. You also find that the plot line splits into two. One is marked S for sagittal, meaning response when the grid has its lines parallel to a line drawn outwards from the axis. The other, T for tangential, is for when the grid pattern is turned 90°. Any remaining aberrations such as astigmatism (Figure 2.10) cause differences in the two results. Again, the less they differ, the better the lens.

Plots for 35 mm format lenses are usually shown for 40 lp/mm. This figure is related to the resolution assumed necessary for the final image you view. For example, a 24 × 36 mm format picture shot with a 50 mm lens, then enlarged onto 8 × 10 inch paper 25 cm wide (magnification ×7) and seen from 30 cm typical normal viewing distance, looks natural in subject scale and perspective (see *Basic Photography*). However, at this reading distance the human eye can resolve, at best, about 5–6 lp/mm. Try it yourself looking at a ruler. (It is a stark reminder that limited eye ability forms the whole basis of depth of field.) So referring back to 35 mm format, eye resolution ×7 gives about 40 lp/mm necessary in the camera for the final image to look sharp.

Fig. 2.16 MTF graphs separately plot patterns running parallel to a line running from the lens axis, and others at right angles to these. Far right: performance over an image field at least 22 mm radius must be shown for a lens intended to cover 35 mm format

Sironar-N 1:5.6 f = 150 mm
MTF on image area   Magnification ratio 1:20 f/11

Sironar-N 1:5.6 f = 150 mm
MTF on image area   Magnification ratio 1:20 f/22

Geronar-WA 1:8 f = 90mm
MTF on image area   Magnification ratio 1:30 f/16

Fig. 2.17 MTF graphs for two large-format camera lenses. The Sironar-N is a high quality six-element lens. Graphs show changes when lens is at f/11 (top) and f/22 (middle graph). Image quality across the film becomes more consistent as stopping down reduces aberrations. However, the general level deteriorates slightly due to diffraction from the smaller aperture. The Geronar lens (bottom graph) is a budget-priced four-element wide-angle. Courtesy Rodenstock

50 mm $f/1.8$ lens for 35 mm SLR at 1 : 50

f-no.	Axis	Corner
1.8	45 lp/mm	40 lp/mm
2.8	50	45
4	56	50
5.6	63	56
8	70	63
11	63	56
16	56	50
22	50	45

Average resolution figures* at widest aperture

Lens type	Axis	Corner
4 × 5 in (all)	28 lp/mm	22 lp/mm
6 × 6 cm (80 mm)	32	25
35 mm (50 mm)	40	30

* Just-distinguishable lines before modulation drops to unacceptable level.

Fig. 2.18 Lines per mm resolution performance of typical camera lenses. The top table shows how image quality peaks at f-numbers about the middle of the range

On larger formats this is different again – an 8 × 10 inch print from a 4 × 5 inch negative is enlarged ×2. About 20 lp/mm on the film will give a result which looks sharp to the eye. So MTF graphs for large-format lenses seldom show plots for spatial frequency finer than about 20 lp/mm. Clearly, these taking and viewing assumptions can be upset if you are to enlarge from only a part of the negative or make giant enlargements to be seen close up. The brightness of illumination on the final print also greatly influences eye resolution.

Most MTF graphs plot extra lines showing performance at 30 or 20 lp/mm or even (large-format lenses) 10 and 5 lp/mm. Do not ignore them. With a good lens it is important that broad detail also maintains contrast across the image. Some of the finer detail is lost by the graininess of the light-sensitive material you expose it on (page 66) or the dot pattern of a half-tone screen (page 269). In these instances it is the lower frequencies that communicate most of your image. When comparing MTF graphs for different lens brands remember that manufacturers tend to present performance in the most favourable way. Compare carefully the scaling of graphs, such as spacings between figures on the modulation axis relative to those on the image field axis. Some manufacturers label the latter 'image height'.

Checking the small print

Alongside the graph should be the f-number used during testing. Often this is $f/5.6$ or $f/22$ for 35 mm and large-format lenses, respectively. If a MTF curve *is* shown for the widest aperture it will show poorer performance because of more pronounced aberrations; at smallest aperture it will again deteriorate mostly due to diffraction. In the case of a large-format camera lens, comparing graphs at different apertures tells you how the limits of coverage change. For example, stopped down appropriately, a normal lens for 4 × 5 inch format might well cover 5 × 7 inches or even 8 × 10 inches (both as a wide-angle lens), provided you do not use movements. Alternatively, the same graphs show how far movements on a 4 × 5 inch camera can bring the lens off-centre on the film before image quality suffers on one side of your picture. See also Figure 3.4.

Graphs should also state the distance of the subject test chart, usually as a ratio (typically, 20 : 1 for a 4 × 5 inch format lens, but for a macro lens 1 : 1, and for a 35 mm format enlarging lens 1 : 10). You should expect to see a macro lens giving best performance at around 1 : 1, whereas a general-purpose lens image would deteriorate when used so close. Enlarging lenses need characteristics similar to macro lenses (see page 33). However, do not expect any lens to give 100% modulation, even with a coarse frequency subject like 10 lp/mm, imaged on-axis and at optimum f-number. This is because the aperture always creates some diffraction, varying with different lens designs. Often plots for 40 lp/mm start on-axis at less than 50% modulation and then get worse.

Other MTF graphs

Another type of MTF graph (Figure 2.19) allows you to compare two lenses in a different way, plotting percentage modulation against a wide range of lp/mm. It does not tell you anything about image

Fig. 2.19 MTF plots (axial image) from two lenses, for different fineness of detail. Lens A is most suitable for a video camera — X denotes the cut-off frequency of 625-line television systems. See text. Lens B is more suitable for chemical film photography, where acceptable modulation is needed down to about 40–50 lp/mm. Bottom: type of test chart used. For photographs of a subject taken with these lenses, see Figure 2.13

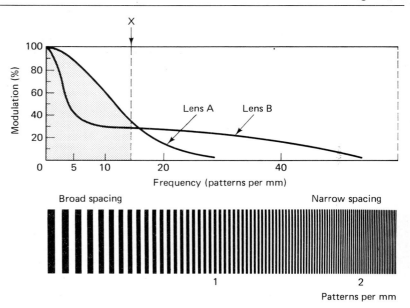

quality *across the image field*, but makes it easy to see how response worsens as detail becomes finer. As with previous MTF graphs, the greater the area shown *under* the plot line, the better the lens. One lens plotted on Figure 2.19 has its aberration corrections biased in such a way that the most contrasty, best-quality image occurs with *broad* detail, then it rapidly deteriorates with finer detail. A lens designed with these priorities is ideal for a video camera, where the limitations of the television medium (traditionally, 625 or 525 lines) are so crude that anything finer would be lost in the system. The other lens is designed for regular photography. Priority here has been given to corrections which give generally lower but more consistent percentage modulation down to much finer patterns, because silver halide systems are more able to record such detail. The graph proves again how lenses can be closely designed for a set function.

MTF graphs scaled in the same way are also published for different kinds of photographic films. As explained in Chapter 4, the resolving power limits of films range between about 200 lp/mm and 25 lp/mm, according to speed, grain, level of exposure and type of development. So you can combine the performance of your camera lens and your film to get one graph plot representing the complete imaging system – from subject to processed result. This is about the closest anyone can get to representing photographic image quality through diagrams or figures (see pages 70–71).

Buying lenses

Each manufacturer sets its own minimum quality image acceptance standards, but every lens – even though one of hundreds of the same design – is also an individual product. Glasses, shaping, spacing and centring can differ in minute ways as lenses come off the production line. So although quality control should ensure that no lens giving *less* than a minimum standard gets through, some lenses may in fact be considerably better. You will also find two manufacturers offering lenses of similar specification at quite different prices. One significant reason may be that the cheaper manufacturer sets slightly lower standards and operates less strict quality control. The result is more of a 'lucky dip' from which you may (or may not) draw a good lens.

Understanding some of the lens designer's problems shows you the importance of using a lens only within its intended performance range. A telephoto lens with a long extension tube added *may* focus close enough for 1:1 copying, but your results will probably be poor quality. (This is not the same as a lens, such as a zoom, designed to offer 'macro mode' which shifts internal floating elements to correct for close working.) Again, some true macro lenses give indifferent results when focused for distant landscapes.

Most lenses give their best image quality stopped down to about the middle of their f-number range. The wider you open up, the less certain aberrations are corrected; but too much stopping down begins to lose quality because of diffraction (Figure 2.18). So the upper and lower ends of the f-number scale are limited by lens design and what the manufacturers regard as the limits of acceptable image quality. Sometimes two lenses of the same brand and with identical focal lengths are radically different in structure and price, because one opens up an additional stop or covers a larger area (allowing camera movements) without worsening quality.

When you are choosing a new lens read as much of the manufacturer's technical specification as possible. Lenses for specialized purposes have their aberration corrections biased in a particular direction. For example, a lens for an aerial survey camera must give optimum quality for distant subjects and avoid any distortion of shape because results are used for measurement purposes. A lens for enlarging or copying has its corrections balanced to give best quality when subjects are close. A shift lens, or any lens for a camera offering shift movements, needs generous covering power (and to achieve this will probably not have a very wide maximum aperture). A lens for 35 mm press photography or surveillance work may barely cover its format, because all the design emphasis is directed towards widest possible aperture. As Figure 2.19 shows, do not expect a lens specially designed for a different recording medium such as limited-resolution video to perform quite as well taking silver halide photographs.

Second, choose a lens remembering handiest size and weight for your expected shooting conditions. This is especially important with long focal length lenses to be used on different locations. Do not go for maximum apertures wider than you will ever need – it only increases bulk. Lens condition is especially important if you are buying second-hand. Elements with scratches (perhaps from excessive cleaning?) will more seriously affect image quality than a speck of black or even a bubble in the glass. A lens which has been dropped may show no obvious external sign of damage yet have internal elements mis-centred, giving general deterioration of image quality. So if you must buy a second-hand lens always try it out first under your own typical working conditions or invest in a professional test (available from most major camera repairers).

Fig. 2.20 A zoom lens design showing groups of 'floating elements' which are re-positioned during zooming to alter focal length and maintain best correction of aberrations

Fig. 2.21 One basic form of zoom lens construction in which two sets of components are movable. Top: movement backwards to give inverted telephoto setting. Bottom: movement forwards for the telephoto setting. Rear nodal point (N) becomes progressively further from the focal plane, giving longer focal length and larger image detail. Converging components (+) remain static. See also Figure 2.31

Special lens types

Zoom lenses

New optical glasses with novel combinations of refractive index and dispersive properties, plus better lens design, mean that the best modern zoom lenses give really good image quality. To understand how a zoom lens works, remember that the focal length of a complete lens depends on the focal lengths of its component elements and the distances by which they are separated (affecting their 'throw'). In a zoom lens groups of elements move within the lens barrel when you alter the focal length control. This zooming action therefore 'restructures' the lens – for example, from inverted telephoto through to telephoto (shown schematically in Figure 2.21).

Zooming should alter focal length and therefore image magnification, without disturbing focus. At the same time, the designer has to arrange that aberration corrections also adjust to keep pace with your focal length changes as well as your focusing. It is particularly difficult to hold corrections for curvilinear distortion (Figure 2.8). The tendency in a poor-quality zoom is for square-shaped subjects to be imaged pincushion-shaped at one end of the zoom range and barrel-shaped at the other (see Figure 2.22).

Ideally, a zoom should also maintain the f-number you set throughout its zooming range. In practice, to keep down cost and size, many zooms slightly change the amount of light they pass. Whatever f-number you have set at longest focal length becomes up to one stop wider when you change to shortest focal length setting. You will find that these 'variable aperture' zooms have two colour-coded setting marks for the aperture ring, one for the shortest and one for the longest focal length. As for exposure, automatic through-the-lens camera

Inverted telephoto

Normal

Telephoto

Barrel

Pincushion

Fig. 2.22 Barrel and pincushion distortion, shown here in exaggerated form

metering takes care of any changes as you zoom. However, if you use manual TTL metering, a non-dedicated flashgun or a separate exposure meter, be prepared to re-adjust the aperture ring at different zoom settings.

Because of their complexity, and a very competitive market, zoom lenses vary more in image quality than any other lens type. Some zooms fully match the standards of fixed focal length lenses. Others are much worse. It is true to say that the greater the zoom range (ratio of shortest to longest focal length), the less likely image quality generally will match that of a fixed focal length lens. A zoom with a ×5 or ×6 range, for example, is unlikely to be as good as one of ×3 or ×4. Similar reservations apply to the quality of zooms when set to macro mode. Unlike a good fixed macro lens, sharpness often deteriorates towards the corners of the picture. The answer is to tread warily, read the technical specifications and, when possible, make practical tests to check whether a particular zoom gives you good enough results.

Mirror lens designs

A photographic lens can be combinations of glass elements and curved mirrors. Figure 2.23 shows a typical mirror lens layout; it has a characteristic squat drum shape and an opaque circular patch in the centre of the front lens (the back of the inward-facing second mirror). The advantage of mirrors is that a long focal length lens becomes physically much shorter – its optics are 'folded up'. Mirrors do not suffer from chromatic aberration because they *reflect* instead of refract light. So the designer needs fewer correcting elements and this, plus the lightweight mirrors, makes the complete lens far less heavy than the same focal length in conventional optics.

However, a mirror lens has three disadvantages:

1. It cannot be stopped down – having a diaphragm would vignette corners of the picture. So you cannot alter depth of field, and exposure has to be controlled by fitting grey neutral density filters or by relying on the shutter alone. Mirror lenses do not therefore suit auto-exposure cameras using shutter priority or programme modes – only aperture priority or manual modes will work.
2. Any bright out-of-focus highlights spread into doughnut-ring shapes (see the front cover picture) instead of the usual discs of light we accept as similar to eyesight. The dark shape is due to the front mirror.
3. Aberrations increase to unacceptable levels away from the lens axis, so mirror designs are limited to narrow angle, long focal lengths. Typically, they come as 500 mm, or 1000 mm lenses for 35 mm format, with a fixed aperture of about $f/8$ or $f/11$.

Fig. 2.23 Typical 500 mm mirror lens and internal structure. C: corrector plate. M: primary converging mirror. S: secondary mirror. L: weak secondary correctors for aberration control. N: neutral density filter (changeable) for exposure control

Fig. 2.24 Extreme fisheye lenses produce circular pictures, but together with the distortion of shapes they give this can suit some subjects. Chris Harris set up a remote camera to shoot Richard Branson in his hot air balloon, using an 8 mm Nikon fisheye. It was triggered by an IR release in Branson's left hand

Fig. 2.25 Wide-angles, unlike fisheyes, are formally corrected for distortion. But extreme wide-angles still 'pull' shapes furthest from the picture centre. This is especially obvious with shots of human figures, least with plain areas such as floor or sky. (By Ilkay Mehmet)

Fig. 2.26 A 16 mm f/3.5 fisheye lens

Relatively few mirror lenses are available (they are described as 'catadioptric' or 'reflex' types in some brochures). Nevertheless, their light weight and handy shape make them convenient to use, especially for natural history or sports photography on location.

Fisheye lens designs

Fisheyes are special wide-angle lenses in which correction of curvilinear (barrel) distortion is sacrificed in order to give extreme angle of view. Angles of 180° or 220° are quite common, but to achieve this, image magnification varies greatly across the picture, producing strange fishbowl results (see Figure 2.24). In all other respects a good fisheye gives excellent image quality.

The lens has wide-diameter, bulbous front elements, which diverge light – similar in principle to a normal type lens looking through a concave window. This large expanse of front glass makes a fisheye vulnerable to damage when carrying or using the lens. You cannot add a lens hood or external filters because they cut into the angle of view, so light-shading tabs and 'dial-in' filters are built into the barrel itself.

Depth of field is phenomenal, typically stretching from 30 cm to infinity at f/8. Maximum aperture is often about f/5.6. A few wider-aperture (f/2.8) fisheye lenses are also made, but some need front elements 20 cm or more in diameter, which makes them extremely heavy and expensive. Most are designed for 35 mm format cameras, and one or two for rollfilm types. You can also fit a 'fisheye converter' over the front of a regular lens. The best of these give excellent quality results, provided your camera lens is stopped down.

A fisheye is best used sparingly, for spectacular industrial, advertising or editorial shots. They give novel geometry but you soon find that this dominates each and every subject you shoot, giving repetitive results. Some fisheyes are intended for special purposes such as surveillance work in confined spaces, photographs inside architectural models or all-sky photography for meteorology. In technical photography an orthographic grid can be laid over the final image to help you to make direct measurements.

Soft-focus lens designs

When you focus a soft-focus lens it images any point of light from the subject as a sharp core overlaid with a 'halo' of spread illumination. The resulting softness of outline works well for atmospheric landscapes, portraits (weddings, children, etc.), especially in colour. The effect is most noticeable with contrasty subject lighting. Large tonal areas appear less softened than fine detail. In portraits, for example, skin blemish detail is suppressed and yet facial features in general remain much clearer than an image that is out of focus. See also Figure 2.27.

Soft-focus lenses differ in detail, but all tend to be highly corrected for optical errors with the exception of spherical aberration. As Figure 2.5 showed, retaining this error gives the mixture of sharp and unsharp characteristics of a soft-focus image.

You must be able to control the degree of 'softness', to suit your subject. With some lenses this is crudely achieved by stopping down – the aperture ring shows symbols for softest focus at widest setting,

Fig. 2.27 Left to right: normal lens in focus; normal lens out of focus; soft-focus lens. Soft-focus gives a combination of sharp and unsharp detail, and lowered contrast. See also Figure 4.7

down to sharpest focus fully stopped down. Better designs have floating elements which shift to increase or decrease spherical aberration when you turn an extra control ring. You can then control softness independently of depth of field.

A few soft-focus lenses, undercorrected for spherical aberration, accept interchangeable multi-perforated aperture discs (Figure 2.28). Each disc makes image points consist of a hard core (central aperture) surrounded by overlapping smaller patches of light which form a halo effect. For different effects you change discs. One disadvantage of this system is that, like a mirror lens, every bright unsharp subject highlight takes on the frontal appearance of the lens – a central patch surrounded by smaller patches. Each disc is marked with an 'equivalent *f*-number' for exposure purposes.

It is advisable to focus a soft-focus lens at the actual aperture to be used for shooting. If possible, use a plain matt focusing screen so you

Fig. 2.28 Near right: (a) regular lens, image out of focus; (b) soft-focus lens image — each point on the subject records as a nebulous halo with a hard core. Far right: soft-focus lens for a large-format camera. This has interchangeable perforated discs to give different amounts of light spread

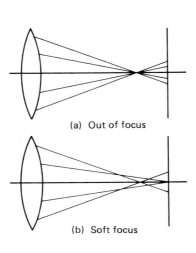

(a) Out of focus

(b) Soft focus

Macro numbers

Focusing distance (m)

Fig. 2.29 Macro lens, showing extra macro numbers on focusing scale relating to magnification. To find your subject magnification on film, divide the macro number into 1 (e.g. 10 means magnification of ×0.1)

can then judge precise effects. Split-screen SLR manual focus aids and autofocus may not function. Where possible, measure exposure through the lens using the camera in manual or aperture priority mode.

You can produce superficially similar soft-focus results using a diffusing attachment over a regular lens. (A finely etched 'anti-Newton's rings' transparency cover glass is cheapest.) However, close comparison of results from an attachment against a good soft-focus lens will soon convince you of the subtleties of the latter. As an alternative technique, you can shoot on reversal film with a normal lens and enlarge this onto reversal paper (such as Cibachrome) using a soft-focus lens or attachment on the enlarger. Do not try this when printing from negatives, because the lens will then spread *shadows* rather than highlights, giving a very different atmospheric effect.

Macro lenses

The aberration corrections in a macro lens are balanced to give optimum image quality when the subject is relatively close. Focal length is usually normal or slightly long for the format it covers (for example, 50 mm or 100 mm for 35 mm cameras). The lens is designed to have a relatively modest maximum aperture such as $f/3.5$ or $f/4$, but often stops down as far as $f/32$. Smaller apertures are helpful to improve the shallow depth of field you get when working close.

Most macros for 35 mm and rollfilm cameras have extended focusing barrels so that you can continuously focus out from infinity setting to image close subjects ×0.5 (half-size). As Figure 2.29 shows, the focusing ring has an extra scale of 'macro' numbers, typically from 10 down to 2. These are handy for precise record photography – by noting the number you are using for a particular shot the subject size and magnification can be accurately calculated later for captioning your picture. You can also use the scale to set a predetermined ratio, then move the camera nearer or further until the image is sharp.

Of course, any macro lens will focus still closer subjects if you add on extension tubes or bellows between lens and camera body. However, at magnifications greater than about ×2.0 you may find image quality gradually deteriorating, because you are outside the design limits of aberration corrections. For finest quality you can then change to a more expensive 'true' macro (or 'macro bellows') lens, each one corrected for optimum results at a particular magnification (for example, ×5, ×10, etc.). Such lenses come without a focusing mount, because they are intended for use with adjustable bellows. Scientific and natural history photographers often work with sets of these true macros, changing them in the same way as microscope objectives.

Always remember that through-the-lens metering is the most accurate way of measuring exposure when shooting close up, using extended lens-to-film distances. Image brightness dims considerably, and is not automatically taken into account if you are using a separate meter or a non-dedicated flashgun. It is especially easy to overlook this when working with studio flash using a separate flash meter (see page 149).

Converter lens attachments

You can buy attachments containing multi-elements to add to your main lens and convert its focal length. The most common types are teleconverters, containing predominantly diverging lens elements and designed to fit behind a specific camera lens of long focal length. Typically, a ×2 teleconverter doubles the prime lens's focal length, re-correcting aberrations so that the same image performance is maintained. It also reduces aperture by two stops, and if used with a zoom lens in macro mode it doubles previous magnification. Similarly, a ×1.4 converter multiplies focal length, macro magnification and *f*-number by 1.4 (in other words, aperture is reduced one stop). Teleconverters are most often made for particular 35 mm format camera lenses of 300 mm and longer or zoom equivalents, and effectively give you two lenses from one. However, do not mix brands, and beware of converters claimed to be 'universal'.

A few converters are designed to fit over the *front* of a normal focal length lens. They form shorter focal length inverted telephoto lenses, giving a wide angle of view yet keeping the lens-to-film distance unchanged. A typical wide-angle converter changes a 50 mm lens to 30 mm, or a 35 mm lens to 21 mm. Often image quality deteriorates and in no way matches a fully corrected wide-angle lens of this focal length. An exception is some front-fitting converters designed to transform normal angle lenses into fisheyes (page 31).

Fig. 2.30 Specifications for a range of 35 mm format lenses. Notice the greater complexity of construction in wide-angle and zoom lens types. Long focal lengths are less able to focus close subjects (macro lenses excepted). Similarly telephoto lens size increases greatly with focal length, and many are heavy and costly

Focal length and max. aperture	Construction: groups–elements	Angle of view	Min. f-stop	Closest marked distance (m)	Size: diameter × length (mm)
Wide-angle					
13 mm *f*/5.6	12–16	118°	22	0.3	115 × 99
18 mm *f*/3.5	10–11	100°	22	0.25	75 × 72
20 mm *f*/2.8	9–12	94°	22	0.25	65 × 54
24 mm *f*/2.8	9–9	84°	22	0.3	63 × 57
Normal					
50 mm *f*/1.2	6–7	46°	16	0.5	68 × 59
50 mm *f*/1.8	5–6	46°	22	0.6	63 × 36
Telephoto					
105 mm *f*/1.8	5–5	23°	22	1	78 × 88
200 mm *f*/2	8–10	12°	22	2.5	138 × 222
300 mm *f*/4.5	5–6	8°	32	3.5	78 × 202
600 mm *f*/5.6	6–7	4°	32	5.5	134 × 382
1000 mm *f*/11	8–9	2°	32	14	134 × 577
Reflex					
500 mm *f*/11	6–6	5°	—	1.5	89 × 116
1000 mm *f*/11	5–5	2°	—	8	119 × 241
Zoom					
28–85 mm *f*/3.5/4.5	11–15	74–28°	22	0.8	67 × 97
35–135 mm *f*/3.5/4.5	14–15	62–18°	22	0.4	68 × 112
80–200 mm *f*/4	9–13	30–12°	32	1.2	73 × 162
Fisheye					
6 mm *f*/2.8	9–12	220°	22	0.25	236 × 171
16 mm *f*/2.8	5–8	180°	22	0.3	63 × 66
Macro					
105 mm *f*/2.8	9–10	23°	32	0.11	66 × 91

A completely different type of converter, which fits between lens and camera body, adapts a manually focused lens to autofocus, provided that the body contains autofocus drive. You leave the regular lens set for infinity. The camera's autofocus mechanism engages with the converter and then moves focusing elements within it until a sharp image is sensed. The result is a fully autofocused system.

Influences on image sharpness

Good lens quality is of vital importance, but for the best possible sharpness in your final print you have to take care at every key stage on the way. The following checklist contains all the main influences on image detail:

1. *Lens quality.* Use the highest-quality modern lens you can afford. Its covering power must match or exceed your camera's picture format. The correction of aberrations must suit your typical subject distance. The lens should be multicoated to minimize scattered light.
2. *Lens condition.* Do not use a lens with scratches, grease, dust, condensation or misalignment of elements (for example, due to physical mishandling). Avoid inferior filters, converters or close-up lenses.
3. *Camera.* Focusing must be completely accurate on the film – beware of non-registration of focusing screen, and also autofocus errors. Do not overuse movements (especially viewcamera shift movements which can position the picture format excessively off-

Fig. 2.31 Bulk and weight increase with focal length. However, differences are made less by telephoto and retrofocus (inverted telephoto) designs. Rear diverging elements give a telephoto a greater focal length than its back focus. Front diverging elements give retrofocus designs shorter focal length than back focus. Without this the larger lens here would be 25 times longer than the wide-angle axis). Sometimes focus or zoom control slips when the camera is pointed vertically. Mechanical faults include SLR mirror movement vibration, shutter bounce or film starting to wind-on before the shutter has fully reclosed, etc.

4. *Shooting conditions.* The atmosphere may contain dust, ripples of warm air, pollution, moisture particles. Avoid shooting through even clear glass windows, *especially* with a long focal length lens. Prevent vibration or movement of camera or subject during exposure.

5. *The light-recording material.* Its ability to resolve fine detail; film speed, grain and emulsion thickness; degree of exposure and development; also the type of developer.

6. *Enlarging.* Image magnification, type of light source, quality and condition of enlarging lens; the flatness of the film in the carrier and accuracy of focusing; movement during exposure; the contrast and surface texture of your printing paper.

7. Finally, there are the conditions under which you view your result, especially the brightness of the lighting and your viewing distance.

No-one can control all these factors all the time, of course, but at least try to use equipment and routines which minimize the pitfalls if optimum sharpness is important in your work.

Summary: Choosing lenses

● Lenses begin with optical glasses, manufactured with precise refractive index and dispersive qualities (Abbe Number). Glass should be colourless, offer the right machining qualities, yet be tough and stable.

● The designer works to satisfy a given lens specification (focal length, coverage, maximum aperture, focusing range, etc.). The challenge is to avoid optical aberrations by combining elements of different glasses, deciding their shapes and spacing. Developments such as new glasses with extreme combinations of RI and dispersion, aspheric shaping and 'floating elements' extend design possibilities, but a balance always has to be found between optimum performance and economic price.

● Lens image quality is difficult to express, depending on contrast as well as detail. Do your own test performance using fine print or a pinhole light source as subjects, comparing their appearance on-axis and in outer-zone parts of the image. Manufacturers publish modulation transfer graphs, plotting percentage modulation against position in lens field (millimetres from axis) for a particular spatial frequency (fineness of detail) in lp/mm.

● MTF curves show you how far acceptable coverage extends – therefore size of format covered. They show the changes in performance to expect when you stop down; come closer; use movements or a larger film; or accept lower standards. Plots are often made for 40 lp/mm (relevant for 35 mm format), 20 lp/mm (for large format) and 10 lp/mm. In practice, much also depends on the film used and your final viewing distance.

● A different form of MTF graph plots percentage modulation against a wide range of frequencies for one given point in the format (for example, on-axis). This is helpful when comparing lenses against each other and the known frequency range limits of your recording medium.

● When buying a lens read the manufacturer's technical information and comparative reviews in the photographic press. Focal length and maximum aperture are important, but ensure that corrections are designed for your kind of work, the lens gives sufficient coverage and weight and size are acceptable. Carefully check the physical condition and optical performance of used lenses before purchase.

● Zoom lenses use floating elements to change focal length and adjust aberration corrections without disturbing focus. Variable aperture zooms can give inaccurate exposure if you use a separate meter or flashgun. Image standards vary – the best lenses (often having more limited zoom range) are excellent.

● Mirror (catadioptric) type long focal length lenses are compact and lightweight, and very easy to handle. However, fixed aperture limits your auto-exposure modes and off-focus highlights have assertive shapes.

● Fisheyes – extreme wide-angle lenses with curvilinear distortion – give results very unlike human vision. Use them with restraint for dramatic effects, recording wide expanses of surroundings, and for their extreme depth of field. Filters and lens hood are built in.

● 'Soft focus' gives a more subtle suppression of fine detail than out of focus or general diffusion. Soft-focus lenses allow fine control of the effect by internal movement of floating elements, changing perforated discs or just stopping down. Focus, and view, at your working aperture. Soft focus spreads highlights of positive images, spreads shadows when used in enlarging negatives.

● Macro lenses are corrected to perform best at close subject distances. Most have an extended focusing movement and scale of (reciprocal) magnification numbers. For still closer technical work, use bellows and 'true' macros, each designed for a narrow band of distances. Remember to recalculate exposure, unless you measure light through the lens.

● A good teleconverter – designed for your same-brand prime lens – gives a modest-priced longer focal length option without loss of quality, but aperture is reduced. Other kinds of lens converter change normal lenses to wide-angle or fisheye, or adapt manual lenses to autofocus.

● Main factors affecting image sharpness are lens quality and condition; the camera's mechanical accuracy; movement; subject and lighting; characteristics of your light-sensitive material and its exposure and processing; enlarging and final viewing conditions.

3
Camera equipment

This chapter is mostly concerned with the hard practical considerations you must take into account when buying and using equipment. Principles of how cameras work were covered in *Basic Photography*, and your camera's instruction book will explain which particular buttons control what. Here we take an overview, comparing the good and bad features of various format cameras, and look at ways to avoid technical failures with them on what might be unrepeatable assignments. The chapter also introduces special-purpose cameras – from aerial to underwater, surveillance to stereo – plus some accessories for advanced photography.

General considerations

As a serious photographer you do not so much buy a camera as buy into *a system*. It is an important and personal decision – after all, choice of format, and even type of design, can condition the way that you work.

35 mm format

35 mm cameras probably represent best value for money because prices are highly competitive. Using equipment this size means that you can carry around a comprehensive outfit in a small case. There is an unrivalled range of lenses and accessories available, and the whole system will incorporate the very latest developments in technology. However, because 35 mm cameras sell to a huge market of amateurs you are buying into a volatile, fashionable world in which models are updated quite rapidly and bristle with every conceivable feature. This 'bells and whistles' aspect is sometimes more to upstage rival brands than to improve your photography.

Excessive control buttons or, alternatively, total automation can be counterproductive for serious work. The many mode options and viewfinder signals get in the way, even lead you into errors – perhaps through mis-selection or distraction by data displays at the key moment of some fleeting shot. Any camera for advanced amateur or professional work *must* also offer complete manual control. You need to have the assurance that you can take over and make use of your personal experience to get exactly the result required, including chosen effects.

A fully automated camera is well worth considering for fast, candid photography, including situations where you must shoot over your head in a crowd, but these cameras are only superficially intelligent. For example, they always program greatest depth of field in bright light, and they can easily be focusing on, or exposing for, the wrong part of the subject. Worse still, you may start composing your pictures in ways which ensure that the auto mechanisms work perfectly (key element centre frame, for example). So make sure that there are convenient read-then-lock facilities for autofocus and for TTL exposure measurement. If the camera autosets film speed by DX cassette code sensing (page 76) it must also have a + or − exposure compensation control. Thus you can effectively set a different speed to suit up or down rating and changes to processing. It is also essential that any SLR camera has a stop-down button to preview your actual depth of field with all pre-set aperture lenses.

Using 35 mm format means that you work with lenses having apertures wider and focal lengths shorter than equivalents for larger formats. Fast lenses are helpful for hand-held existing light work. Short focal lengths give you generous depth of field, especially useful when subjects are close. However, then you have to remember that prints blown up much beyond about 8 × 10 inches increasingly show coarser resolution and cruder tone gradation than those from larger film. You must also take that much more care in the darkroom to avoid image blemishes.

Medium format

Camera equipment using 6.2 cm wide rollfilm (giving 6 × 6, 6 × 7, 4.5 × 6 cm, etc.) is a good compromise between the slowness and immobility of large formats and the poorer final image qualities of 35 mm cameras. Equipment this size is sold mostly to experienced amateurs and to professionals – a much more restricted market. Features tend to be more conservative, and because of the small numbers manufactured you can expect to pay over twice the price of an equivalent 35 mm kit.

Medium-format cameras are small enough to use hand-held and cope with action subjects. You can use most types at waist or eye level – there is a range of direct viewfinder models (Figure 3.1) as well as reflexes. At the same time, picture size is between three and five times the area of 35 mm, so you can crop after shooting if you wish and print (or reproduce) from just part of the format without too much lost quality. An SLR this size has a large enough screen to usefully attach a drawn overlay or use an instant-picture back (Figure 3.2) for critical jobs where your composition must fit a tightly designed layout.

The majority of rollfilm SLRs have interchangeable magazine

Fig. 3.1 A range of medium-format
(rollfilm) cameras. A: 6 × 9 cm direct
viewfinder type. B and C: 4.5 × 6 cm
single-lens reflexes. D: 6 × 6 cm
twin-lens reflex. E: 6 × 6 cm
single-lens reflex. F: 6 × 7 cm direct
viewfinder camera

Fig. 3.2 An instant-picture back, accepting packs of peel-apart material, attached to a rollfilm SLR camera

backs, so you can be shooting using one back while an assistant is quickly emptying and reloading another, allowing fast, continuous photography. You can also shoot one scene on several different kinds of film stock by juggling backs. Some cameras incorporate an ISO 'telling' system in each back which you set when loading the film. Then as you swap backs it programs the camera-metering system for the correct film speed. Using rollfilm also makes it far simpler to run off an exposure-bracketed series on the same subject than when using sheet film.

On the debit side, if you are used to working with 35 mm the shallow depth of field given by the longer focal length lenses normal for medium formats can be an unwelcome surprise – especially when shooting close-up. Lenses also have maximum apertures one or two stops smaller than their 35 mm camera equivalents (typically, $f/2.8$ or $f/4$ for a standard focal length lens). The range of film stocks made in 120 rollfilm is also more limited, with the emphasis on professional rather than amateur emulsions (see *Basic Photography*).

Large-format viewcamera systems

In many ways these are a world apart. Photography with this type of equipment is more craft orientated, demands more elaborate preparation and encourages a more considered approach to your subject. There are fewer camera designs to choose from, and both cameras and lenses are expensive – especially the 8×10 inch size. However, most are monorail types unit constructed so that you can make up a camera of the right format (usually between 4×5 inches and 8×10 inches), bellows length, etc. to suit different subject situations. This same substitution of units makes it easy to remove and change any faulty part. Cameras often lack electronic aids completely, unless you add costly accessories. Therefore you must expect to use a separate hand-held exposure meter and calculate the exposure increase needed for bellows extension, etc. which is taken care of in other cameras by through-the-lens light measurement.

To get the most out of large-format photography you should understand and make full use of camera movements, which are offered in abundance (see *Basic Photography*, Chapter 6). Some will help you to improve depth of field, which is even shallower than with medium-format camera lenses. In any case, you must expect to stop down more and consequently require more light or longer exposures. Even maximum lens apertures average around $f/4.5$–$f/5.6$, some three to four stops slower than most 35 mm format lenses.

On the other hand, you can expect viewcamera lenses to have a much wider image circle than lenses intended always to be dead-centred on the film. For example, a good normal-angle 180 mm lens designed for 4×5 inches will give a circle of acceptable quality about 300 mm in diameter when focused for infinity and stopped down to $f/22$. This means that you can shift or pivot the lens until its axis is more than 70 mm off-centre if necessary for rising, cross or swing front effects before you see loss of image quality at any corner. It is a false economy to buy, say, a monorail viewcamera offering extensive movements and use it with an economy lens barely covering the format.

Fig. 3.3 Typical 4×5 inch unit-constructed monorail camera

Fig. 3.4 Catalogue data for four viewcamera wide-angle lenses. The L shape diagrams show how many millimetres you can shift the axis off-centre (for short and long sides of the film) in any one direction, yet still have good coverage. Figures apply to focusing for infinity subjects. The *f*/4.5 90 mm lens here is far more highly corrected than the *f*/6.8 design, and costs over twice as much

Lens	90 mm, *f*/4.5		90 mm, *f*/6.8		155 mm, *f*/6.8		200 mm, *f*/6.8	
At aperture	*f*/11	*f*/22	*f*/11	*f*/22	*f*/11	*f*/22	*f*/11	*f*/22
Diameter of image circle (mm)	232	236	213	.221	369	382	475	495
Negative: 4 × 5 in	51 / 46	54 / 48	40 / 35	45 / 40	126 / 118	133 / 125		
5 × 7 in	18 / 14	21 / 16	4 / 3	10 / 7	103 / 89	111 / 96		
8 × 10 in					41 / 34	50 / 42	106 / 94	118 / 105

Fig. 3.5 A rollfilm back fitted to a baseboard type 4 × 5 inch camera

A large-format camera is essentially a shot-by-shot instrument. You can insert a rollfilm holder instead and accept a smaller picture (Figure 3.5), but most of the time you bring to the camera single sheets of film which are later individually processed. Image resolution and tone qualities are better again than medium-format results when you make big enlargements. There is a restricted range of general-purpose films in sheet form, but this is boosted by some interesting special materials (line, lith and non-colour-sensitive emulsions, for example) not available as rollfilms.

Working with the relatively large focusing screen of a viewcamera is like having upside-down colour television. The equipment brings you much closer to the optical craft aspects of photography than any smaller camera, but you must understand what you are doing. Remember, too, that an 8 × 10 inch camera with a couple of good lenses can cost you over five times the price of a professional quality 35 mm outfit including three to four lenses.

Which one is best?

Clearly, no one camera will serve you well for every kind of assignment. Some give you a choice of at least two formats – a 120 rollfilm camera with a 35 mm back, for example; a 4 × 5 inch plus rollfilm back; or an 8 × 10 inch camera adapted down to 4 × 5 inches. However, the result is often an unsatisfactory compromise, with the lens too long focus and the camera unnecessarily bulky for the smaller format. Most photographers therefore opt for two camera outfits – for example, small and medium format or medium and large. Having two complementary kits means that you can exploit their advantages and minimize their individual shortcomings for the widest range of subjects. When you have made this decision go on to choose whether reflex, direct viewfinder or monorail designs (as available) will suit you best, and pick appropriate lenses.

On price, you will find that within any one category of camera the difference between cheapest and most expensive models can easily be a factor of 2 or 3 (six to eight times with 35 mm gear). Sometimes this extra cost is because the body has features utilizing the latest technology, or it is built with greater precision and finish, using much tougher components. Like hand-built cars, this lasting precision and reliability cannot really be seen unless you open up the inside.

Avoiding camera failures

Even the finest cameras are basically just machines and their users only human, so mistakes do occur from time to time. Every photographer must have occasionally lost pictures at the camera stage. The important thing is to minimize risks by setting up safety routines you follow as second nature, especially checks before and during shooting. It should be impossible for you to completely ruin any assignment through some failure of camera handling. Here are some typical hazards and suggested precautions.

Misuse of unfamiliar equipment: this is most easily done with hire cameras and lenses. Check anything complex and strange by exposing and processing a test film before using it on an important shoot.

The pre-set aperture fails to stop down within the lens of your SLR camera when you take the picture, usually due to sticky blades or a broken spring. The result is various degrees of overexposure (unless you set widest aperture). Do a quick pre-check before loading film. Set a small aperture and slow shutter speed, then notice if the diaphragm stops down by looking through the back of the open camera and pressing the release.

Your shutter fails to open, or close, or fully close. The result is no picture, or fogging and vast overexposure. Often the camera mechanism sounds abnormal, but check by looking through the back of the empty camera or make a trial exposure on instant-picture film.

Using flash, you get no image (perhaps just faint results from existing light) or, with a focal plane shutter camera, your correctly exposed flash picture only extends over about one half or one quarter of the frame. These failures are due to mis-synchronization (for example, part frames result from using fast-peaking electronic flash with a focal plane shutter at too short a shutter speed). Be wary of any camera which has an X/M (or X/FP) switch for change of synchronization. Electronic flash fired on these M or FP flashbulb settings goes off before the shutter opens – no matter what speed is selected or whether it is a lens or focal plane shutter type. This error happens easily on a camera with a hot shoe and a sync switch tucked away somewhere else on the body. Pre-check by pointing the flash and empty wide-aperture camera towards a white surface in a dimly lit area. Through the open back of the camera you should briefly see the full picture area as a white shape when the shutter fires.

A run-down battery, making the camera meter erratic or non-active: this may also cause failure of the camera's electronically timed shutter and other circuitry. Always check with the battery state button when preparing for a session. Carry a spare set of batteries too, and as further back-up include a separate hand-held exposure meter. There are clearly advantages in having a camera body which, in the event of battery failure, still allows you use of at least one (*mechanically* powered) shutter speed.

Mechanical jam-up of an SLR camera: the whole unit locks solid, often with the mirror up. Some cameras offer you a re-set lever or (medium formats) have some accessible screw you can turn with a small screwdriver to release the mechanism. The best precaution is to carry a spare body.

Shooting on already exposed film: this is most likely on 35 mm, 70 mm and sheet film, as regular rollfilm winds up onto a new spool,

Fig. 3.6 Testing flash synchronization. See text

Fig. 3.10 Front and back views of a wire-slung, electrically powered hand camera for general air-to-air or air-to-ground photography. Pictures 58 × 85 mm are shot on perforated 70 mm film, 100 ft (30 m) per magazine loading. Coloured diodes within the direct viewfinder eyepiece signal camera status

Underwater cameras

There are two approaches to underwater equipment. First, there is a bulky underwater housing for a conventional land camera, such as a 35 mm or rollfilm SLR. Here rods attached to the main camera controls pass through the metal casing to oversize knobs on the outside. A heavy-duty housing like this is expensive but safe down to depths of around 100 metres, ample for practically all professional sub-aqua assignments. The best housings allow the lens to look through a *domed* port. Otherwise, with a flat port, you introduce curvilinear distortion as well as chromatic aberration and other refractive problems.

Alternatively, you can use a compact, direct viewfinder 35 mm camera specially designed with a waterproof metal body and lens. The camera has (watersealed) enlarged controls and viewfinder. Its lens is compounded to give best performance when it is separated from the subject by water and from the film by air. Camera seals withstand pressures down to about 50 metres, which easily covers most requirements such as natural history photography in coastal waters. (Do not confuse these underwater cameras with cheaper plastic 'fun' cameras for swimming pools and safe only to 5–8 metres.)

The lens considered normal for a small-format underwater camera has a focal length of 35 mm, which in effect gives you an angle of view of 43°. (All lenses narrow their angle of view by 30% when used in

Fig. 3.11 Underwater equipment. A: heavy-duty housing for a 6 × 6 cm SLR. The domed glass port is protected by a handling ring. B and C: 35 mm camera with waterproof seals to its controls and camera back. The film plane is backed by the separate internal pressure plate

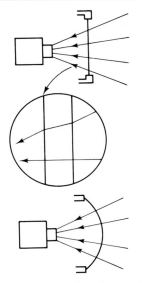

Fig. 3.12 When a flat glass port is used on an underwater housing (top and centre) oblique image light is distorted. Domed port (bottom) presents the glass at right angles to all rays

water instead of air.) Other lenses all tend to be of shorter rather than longer focal length, because you need to minimize your distance from the subject due to lack of clarity under water (see page 189). Typical maximum aperture is $f/2.8$ with shutter speeds between 1/30 and 1/1000 second. Most underwater camera lenses do not give satisfactory quality on land (the scale of focusing distances also alters). However, if the camera accepts a range of interchangeable lenses one of these is likely to be designed for use in non-underwater situations, such as surfing and other marine sports.

Surveillance cameras

A few cameras are specially designed to be extremely inconspicuous but not have a picture format too small to resolve fine detail. They are used for research observation and surveillance, ranging from the monitoring of banks to evidence-gathering by police or military authorities. A typical compact surveillance camera is the size of a small packet of cigarettes but still takes full-frame 35 mm format pictures. It is often all-electric with silent shutter and wind-on, auto exposure, and triggering by electrical or radio connections. Having a severely rectangular shape (Figure 3.13), cameras of this type are simple to house in concealed locations such as a portable cassette player, briefcase or dummy cigarette case. They can even be sewn behind the buttonhole of a coat, since the only aperture needed is a hole less than 1 cm wide for the lens to look through. Slightly larger units, wall mounted for security monitoring of rooms, take up to 800 pictures at one loading. These allow you to shoot set numbers of 35 mm frames at rates from five pictures per second to one per week. A data back imprints precise time and date alongside each exposed image. Other miniaturized 35 mm cameras with flash are used for applications such as pipeline and drainage inspection, being towed through the pipe system on a narrow-diameter sledge.

Sub-miniature cameras

This term tends to be used for cameras using film even smaller than 110 size. Most are simply novelties, along the lines of Victorian 'detective cameras', because of their poor optical quality. However, one or two cameras are made to high precision standards. The Minox

Fig. 3.13 Full-frame all-electric 35 mm surveillance camera. This can fit within the back of a radio/cassette player. There is no viewfinder. Far right: Minox sub-miniature direct viewfinder camera

Fig. 3.16 Periphery camera principle. The film is worm-driven behind a slit, keeping pace with the image of the slowly rotating subject (a piston here). 360° circumference detail is 'rolled out' into one long flat image

Fig. 3.17 A periphery camera is not normally used for portraits, but this is a shot of the equipment's inventor, Freddie Fox. Courtesy Shell Research Ltd

is like a roller, ink printing onto moving paper.) By the time the film has traversed its full width across the camera back the subject will have rotated 360°. So your processed result records details of its complete vertical circumference as one continuous flat picture (see Figure 3.17).

Periphery cameras are used for technical work such as recording wear on the external surfaces of pistons from engines; revealing the design on archaeological vases; and for forensic applications (unrolling fingerprints on cylindrical objects such as a pencil, gun barrel, etc.). The long, narrow image printed from a periphery camera shot can be joined at the ends, picture side facing outwards, to form a cylinder which closely re-creates the subject in three-dimensional form.

Stereo imaging equipment

Stereo cameras are really *pairs* of cameras with matched lenses and linked shutters and diaphragms. They exploit the fact that when you

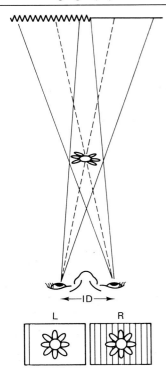

Fig. 3.18 Binocular vision. Because of the interocular distance (ID) between your two eyes, a close subject is seen in front of a different part of the far background by each eye. This gives you a visual sense of depth and distance

view a three-dimensional scene through a pair of eyes (binocular vision) parallax difference between the two viewpoints makes foreground objects appear in front of different parts of the background. To some extent you 'see around' close objects. For example, hold your thumb up about 30 cm away. Then, without moving your head, notice where the thumb coincides with some distant wall detail, just using left then right eye. This parallax difference (so much a problem with twin-lens reflex cameras) is one of the main ways in which we sense three-dimensional depth and distance. (The other clues tend to be differences in scale, tone, focus and in the greater image shift of near objects relative to distant ones when you move your head.)

The two halves of a stereo camera have their lens centres about 65 mm apart, matching the average separation or *interocular distance* between a pair of human eyes. This also leaves room for a direct viewfinder between the two. Pictures are exposed in pairs onto 35 mm film, each one being half-frame or 24 mm square format. Frames are often interleaved (see Figure 3.20) and so must be sorted and paired up after processing. Another way of working is to use a camera with a stereo attachment, or just pair up two regular cameras (35 mm SLRs, for example). Paired cameras are best used with electric releases, wired in parallel to synchronize shutters and so work with flash or shoot moving subjects. Motorwind is also a helpful feature.

A stereo attachment is a mirror box which fits over a regular camera's standard lens, like a lens hood. It splits the usual horizontal format picture into a stereo pair of upright half-format pictures. Inside, four front-silvered mirrors redirect the light (Figure 3.19C) so that your pictures are taken with viewpoints 65 mm apart. The attachment is best used on a single-lens reflex camera, where you can see the effect on the focusing screen. Results (usually on 35 mm slide film) can be seen in three dimensions, using a hand-viewer of similar design or by methods discussed below. A quite different stereo attach-

Fig. 3.19 Methods of shooting stereo pairs. A: 35 mm direct viewfinder stereocamera, having 65 mm lens separation. Few cameras like this are now made. B: lash-up using two regular SLR cameras. Both shutters are released together. C: mirror box stereo attachment. This gives two half-frames side-by-side within each normal 35 mm format; see Figure 3.20

Fig. 3.20 How stereo pairs record on 35 mm film. A beamsplitter attachment exposes half-frame pictures within the regular format. Left- and right-hand versions are correctly located when you turn pictures correct way up. But (far right) when you use a stereocamera, half-frame images record with two spaces between them. This is filled in with parts of other pairs, to save film. Your film winds on by two half-frames each time, interlinking pairs as shown below

ment takes the form of a sliding bracket fitted between tripod and regular camera. It is designed for making stereo pairs of relatively static subjects – you take one full-frame picture then slide the whole camera quickly 65 mm to one side before taking another.

Viewing results

To view each pair of photographs (*stereograms*) and make them appear as a single three-dimensional picture it is essential that left- and right-hand versions are seen by your left and right eyes, respectively. You can do this with a hand viewer for slides (Figure 3.21) or for prints. Alternatively, you can project slides using two projectors to give offset images in the same screen, then give your audience spectacles which permit each eye to see one image only. As Figure 3.22 shows, you can achieve this by fitting left or right projectors with colour filters, picking any two hues well separated in the spectrum such as deep green and red. Spectacles matching these colours allow the correct image to be seen by each eye, although the result, even from colour slides, is a kind of monochrome. Alternatively, use pairs of linear polarizing filters orientated orthogonally to each other for the projectors and have matching glasses. This arrangement allows you to show stereo colour slides in full colours, but your screen must have a metallized (silver) surface so that polarization is unaltered when image light reaches the audience.

Yet another way of showing three-dimensional results is by a special parallax stereogram print (Figure 3.23). This works without needing spectacles at all but is more suited to mass production. A lenticular screen made of clear moulded plastic must form the print's top surface. It works on the principle that beneath the screen left- and right-hand images are split into alternative strips, best achieved by photomechanical printing methods. The results are more crude than by other viewing methods.

Stereophotography is useful wherever three-dimensional information is needed – for measurement, training and education or simply for pictorial effect. It is an important aspect of aerial survey

Fig. 3.21 Hand-viewers for stereo images. Top: viewer for 35 mm half-frame slide pairs, using a mirror box system similar to the type for shooting (Figure 3.19). Bottom: simple type for viewing medium-format contact prints or transparencies

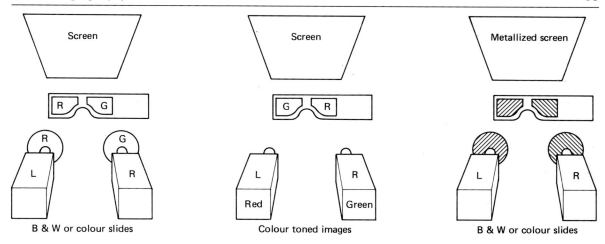

Screen · Screen · Metallized screen

B & W or colour slides · Colour toned images · B & W or colour slides

Fig. 3.22 Ways of projecting pairs of stereo images, with results encoded so that (looking through spectacles) each eye only sees its correct left- or right-hand taken picture. Left: deep colour filters over projectors; results look monochrome, even if slides are colour. Centre: black and white images colour toned; results are monochrome. Right: the best arrangement, using correctly orientated polarizing filters and metallized screen; images can appear in full colour

photography, where it allows you to observe the relative heights of buildings and the general terrain. Subject matter below a flying aircraft is almost always too far away for a pair of eyes only 65 mm apart to give you stereoscopic vision direct (the limit is about 60 metres), so stereo-pictures are taken using much greater separation. This is easy to do, by using a single camera and taking two shots one after the other, allowing time for the aircraft to fly a predetermined level distance between the exposures. Typically, separation equal to one-fiftieth of the height above ground level gives a three-dimensional effect equivalent to something just over 3 metres away viewed direct with two eyes. This expanded separation technique is known as *hyperstereoscopy*.

The opposite technique – reduced separation or *hyposterescopy* – is used with very close subjects. This time, normal 65 mm separation gives such extreme parallax difference that your eyes cannot fuse results into one three-dimensional image. For larger than life size images you work instead using a separation of 65 mm divided by magnification. If you are shooting still lifes you can use one camera and side-shift either subject or camera the required distance between pictures. (*Note:* Shifting the subject alone results in background detail appearing two-dimensional, so it is best to use a plain ground.)

Fig. 3.23 Parallax stereogram print made up from narrow alternate strips of left- and right-hand images. The embossed plastic lenticular screen over the front ensures that (at average viewing distance) each eye only sees strips making up its correct image

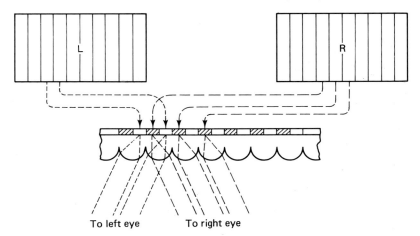

L · R

To left eye · To right eye

Fig. 3.24 Camera unit for computer graphics recording. An adapted 35 mm SLR camera images an internal flat-faced video screen

Specialized accessories

You can choose from a very large range of camera accessories. Many are unnecessary and gimmicky, but some of the more specialized add-ons allow you to interface cameras with completely different kinds of technology.

Optical adaptors

Most 35 mm SLR camera systems include different adaptor rings which allow the camera body to fit over the eyepiece end of a microscope, telescope, medical endoscope, etc. Due to reflex design you can still accurately frame-up, focus and measure exposure whatever optical device is fitted. In fact the camera becomes a film-containing back for the other device. Similarly, you can use a cowl-type adaptor (Figure 3.24) to centre camera plus macro lens over a flat-faced cathode ray tube and so record computer graphics or any other television image display. Camera, cowl and tube may be part of a video copying unit which electronically synchronizes one or more slow high-resolution frame scans with a suitable shutter hold-open period.

Camera triggers

You can buy electronic sensor units which trigger the camera in response to light, sound, radio or infra-red radiation. Normally, you wire one of these devices to a small- or medium-format camera having electric release sockets plus motor-drive so that any number of pictures can be taken remotely. The camera might be set up in some inaccessible position, such as under a jump on a racecourse, and then fired when you transmit an infra-red or radio pulse from the safety of the track-side. For natural history photography you can mount the camera in some hidden location, its shutter triggered automatically when your subject breaks the path of an infra-red beam projected out of the trigger box itself (see Figure 3.25). This works equally well at night.

With high-speed analytical work, a sudden happening – a spark or one object striking another, for instance – can trigger events via a light or sound sensor or by breaking a strategically placed beam. Here you can set up the camera in a darkened studio with the shutter locked open and using the trigger to fire an ultra-short duration flash. Most trigger units allow you to tune their level of sensitivity to suit ambient conditions, sound or light. You can also dial-in a chosen delay (milliseconds or microseconds) between sensing and firing to capture the event a little after trigger activation.

Fig. 3.25 Remote triggers. Left: breaking an invisible infra-red beam projected and reflected across the path of some event. Centre: two IR beams angled to correspond to one point in space. Only an object breaking the beams here triggers the camera. Right: ultra-high-speed flash triggered by sound detection

IR tripper   IR crossed beam   Sound trigger

Reflector

Fig. 3.26 Instant-picture back for a 35 mm SLR camera. A physical gap has to be bridged between the focal plane inside the camera and the light-sensitive surface in the pack. A 35 mm format fibre-optic block in the regular film position receives the lens image at the front, and directs light through to its back surface in contact with emulsion

Instant-picture adaptors

Instant-picture adaptors for 'self-developing' film are made to fit most regular small-, medium- and large-format cameras, 35 mm to 8 × 10 inches, provided they have detachable backs. Peel-apart instant-picture material (page 99) is necessary, otherwise your result is laterally reversed. Small- and medium-format cameras use film in pack form – two 35 mm pictures can be exposed side by side on one sheet if the back adaptor incorporates a slide-over device. Large-format cameras can use packs or individual pull-apart sheets in envelopes (see page 77). Backs for instant-picture sheets also accept some regular sheet films in envelopes. This is useful if you do not want to keep changing from an instant-picture adaptor to film holders. As discussed above, instant pictures are invaluable for quickly previewing results and confirming that all your equipment is functioning as expected, and if you use an 8 × 10 inch camera your 8 × 10 instant colour print will probably be large enough to form the final result for urgent jobs.

Programming and data backs

Most advanced 35 mm (and some medium-format) camera systems allow you to replace the regular camera back with a dedicated program or data back. The substitute back is considerably thicker and carries electronic keys and a battery compartment. It extends the camera's electronic facilities in various ways. For instance, some backs for motor-driven cameras allow you to program autobracketing – a quick series of frames each shot at a different level of exposure such as half, one or two stops' progression. The same back may also act as an 'intervalometer', so that you can trigger pictures at intervals of seconds, minutes or hours, and pre-set the total number of frames to be shot.

Usually the inside face of the back carries a printing panel of low-intensity LEDs to expose characters and figures through the base of your film, alongside or just within each frame. (The diode brightens

Fig. 3.27 Programming/data-imprinting back for 35 mm SLR. B: additional battery compartment. D: LCD panel displays your keyed-in exposure programme, number of frames, what data will be printed on film etc. K: data-setting keys or dims by varying its pulse rate to suit the slow or fast ISO speed set for the film.) This feature allows you to program in date, time, frame number, etc. or the camera can automatically imprint the aperture and shutter settings it made for each picture. A good programming/data back is expensive but invaluable for various kinds of record photography, especially time-lapse and surveillance work. It frees you from tedious logging of notes.

Special viewcamera backs

One or two specialist back accessories are made for viewcameras, principally 4 × 5 inches. They are mostly designed to make the camera quicker and more convenient to use. For example (Figure 3.28), a high-sensitivity closed-circuit television camera fits within a hood over the focusing screen. Designed primarily for one-person still-life work, it shows you exactly what appears on the ground glass, turned right way up and presented on a monitor anywhere convenient in the studio. This means that you can make small critical adjustments to elements in a still-life set without constantly returning to the camera to check the effect or relaying instructions to an assistant. It also enables you (or an art director) to mark out the television screen with the proportions of any final layout – the television image being

Fig. 3.29 Viewcamera monitoring unit. A video camera in the top end of the hood relays the focusing screen image, as you finely adjust a studio set-up

Fig. 3.29 Special viewcamera accessories. Left: time-saving sliding back arrangement. A: aperture setting indicator. L: link holds bladed shutter open when focusing screen (S) and reflex hood (H) are aligned with lens. F: film holder, with darkslide facing camera already removed. See text.

Right: TTL exposure-metering equipment. Probe (P) has a spot reading tip (S) you can move to measure any chosen area on the lens side of the focusing screen. C: control unit for setting film speed, etc. A: electronic bladed shutter which operates with all lenses

considerably larger and brighter than the upside-down image barely visible on the back of your camera.

Another device – a sliding back – reduces the delay between composing and exposing. Simple rails allow you to rapidly exchange focusing screen for film holder (Figure 3.29). Meanwhile, the shutter is closed and set en route by an electrical or mechanical link between the front and back of the camera. Working in reverse, the shutter locks open when you return the focusing screen. Other replacement viewcamera backs accept a spot meter probe. This measures image light reaching the focusing screen from the lens and can program an electronic bladed shutter to give you aperture-priority exposure control. Other forms of exposure program are unsuitable for view-camera photography because the subject itself and movements mostly determine what aperture you should set. Elaborate 'add-on' items for viewcameras are made in quite small numbers, which makes them expensive. Some more than double the cost of an outfit. So although extras make your camera quicker and more convenient to use they may not be justified unless you use large-format equipment most of the time.

Electronic imaging backs

Photography is gradually changing to include electronic as well as chemical methods of recording the image in the camera. As a part of that transition, backs normally holding 35 mm film may be changed for a bulkier and much more costly still video electronic recording back. Here the emulsion surface which normally fills the camera's image plane is replaced by a fixed, light-sensitive CCD chip. After lens and shutter have delivered an exposure in the normal way the chip outputs the image as a stream of electronic signals which are recorded on part of a 55 mm diameter magnetic disc, motor-driven at the rear of the camera back (see Figure 3.30). The disc itself is not, of course, light-sensitive and does not need processing. It can be removed at once from the camera or replayed through a video monitor or via telephone links to a distant location such as a news-paper office. You can check results immediately, erasing unsuccessful pictures and re-using their space on the 25-exposure disc.

CCD image detail does not yet compare with silver halide film results but it is steadily improving. For the moment, electronic still photography is most valid when speed of communication is vital (see

Fig. 3.30 Still video equipment. A: 35 mm SLR camera's regular camera back is changed for electronic back, which records pictures as magnetic signal on 55 mm (2 in) disc (B). Results can be played out immediately through video playout unit (C) onto TV screen, or to paper printer or' transmitter attached to car phone. See also Figure 11.29

also page 276). You can also argue that with the special aberration correction bias needed for a good video lens (page 26), and the considerably greater cost of the camera's electronic back as against its photographic front, it would be better to buy a complete video still camera in the first place.

Summary: Camera equipment

● Using 35 mm camera equipment you gain the benefit of latest technology at competitive prices. However, equipment may be either too automated or offer excessive options which get in the way. Consider manual override to be essential.

● Medium-format cameras offer a sensible compromise between equipment mobility and final image quality. They often have professional features – interchangeable magazines and instant-picture backs which produce results of a useful size. However, equipment is expensive, contains less advanced technology and has a smaller range of lenses than 35 mm. Using this format also means less depth of field and narrower choice of film stock.

● Large-format viewcameras demand a slower, more craft-knowledgeable approach. They tend to be expensive yet basic. The range of lenses is limited, with relatively small maximum apertures but most often give excellent coverage to allow you to utilize comprehensive movements for architectural, still-life and technical subject matter. You can shoot and process pictures individually, and their size means that large prints show unique detail and tonal qualities.

● It is vital to have reliable camera technique – get into the habit of routine precautionary checks before and during shooting. Look through the back of the empty camera to see that the shutter, aperture and flash work and that there are no obstructions. Take an instant-picture shot before and after a session. Carry a spare body or some back-up camera, an exposure meter, spare batteries – plus a screwdriver.

● Aerial cameras for hand-held use are rugged, have a direct-vision finder and mostly use 70 mm magazines. Lenses are corrected for distant subjects. The shutter offers no slow speeds.

● For underwater photography fit an underwater housing around a regular camera or, for shallower depths, use a waterproof 35 mm compact. The latter needs lenses designed for underwater work, shorter in focal length than lenses for land cameras.

● Inconspicuous surveillance cameras include electrically operated 35 mm units designed to be secreted into everyday articles. Remote-controlled 800-exposure capacity wall-mounted 35 mm cameras are used for security monitoring. A few sub-miniature cameras are good enough for hand-held surveillance and similar highly unobtrusive photography.

● Panoramic cameras scan a wide area of scene, using a pivoting lens and a moving slit in front of the film. Resulting dramatic perspective is unique – straight lines in the subject matter may record curved, concave shapes appear straight. Some cameras rotate 360°, giving a total horizontal record of surroundings. Uses include large groups, real estate and land-survey applications.

● A periphery camera 'rolls out' the external detail of cylindrical forms as one long, flat image. The subject rotates 360° on a turntable while film tracks sideways in the back of the camera behind a slit. It is used for forensic, archaeological and industrial research applications.

● Stereo cameras take pictures in pairs, with viewpoints normally 65 mm apart. However, by using a regular camera and shifting the camera or subject between exposures you can give greater (hyper) separation for aerial surveys or less (hypo) separation for very close subjects. Stereo attachments for normal lens cameras split each shot into half-frame stereo pairs.

● Pairs of pictures are combined by your two eyes as one three-dimensional image, using a hand viewer or twin projectors with appropriate viewing glasses. Stereo images can be mass produced as parallax stereograms, faced with a lenticular screen. Stereo photography is used for measurement, heightened realism or pictorial effect.

● Specialized accessories include adaptors to join your (35 mm) camera body to a microscope, telescope, video copying unit, medical endoscope, etc. Camera triggers work by responding to light, sound, infra-red or radio signal, with built-in control over time delay. Instant-picture backs allow most advanced cameras (from 35 mm to 8 × 10 inches) to use pack or single-sheet materials.

● Program/data backs extend 35 mm camera electronics. Use them to imprint identification, exposure and time data alongside record photographs; also take pictures at programmed intervals, shoot bracketed sequences.

● Specialist backs for viewcameras house convenience closed-circuit television; allow fast focusing screen/filmholder exchange; and contain TTL metering linked to the shutter for aperture priority exposure control.

● An electronic imaging back converts a suitable still camera from chemical photographic film to a CCD chip. Chip response to the image records as electronic signals onto a slip-in magnetic disc. Pictures can be played back immediately and unwanted shots erased and retaken. Image quality is presently still poor – the system is most valid for press work.

4
Films — types and technical data

It makes good sense to work with a limited range of well-chosen films. You get to know their performance intimately – what each can contribute to your particular style of picture, its response to different subject situations and, when necessary, just how far you can abuse the film before results become unacceptable. However, you must still pick your materials in the first place and keep an eye on interesting new products as they come onto the market. It would also be a pity not to explore some of the lesser-known films worth experimenting with for their special qualities and effects.

This chapter discusses, in an unbiased way, the practical points you should consider when choosing film. A section on reading manufacturers' data explains how products are described and compared by the graphs and tables which appear in technical information sheets. Finally, there is a review of some special-purpose films, selected for their unusual results or usefulness for solving special tasks.

Designing today's films

Early photographers were more chemists than artists. In the 1850s they had to take darkroom tents everywhere, primitively coating sheet glass with light-sensitive silver compounds just before exposure and development. However, these 'wet plates' were followed by gelatin + silver halide emulsions which could be prepared in advance, and so opened up photographic material manufacturing from about 1876. One by one, other barriers were overcome through emulsion research by chemists and manufacturers – glass was replaced by roll-up film; speed was increased over a thousandfold; response to only blue wavelengths was extended to the full spectrum. The last opened the way to practical films for colour photography (slides 1935 and negative/ positive around 1942).

Throughout this evolution there was always something of a 'knack' to emulsion making – skills not unlike cooking, passed down from one generation to the next. In more recent times the very large investment in research and development applied to light-sensitive systems plus advances in technology generally have brought much greater mastery of production. A kind of creative chemistry has evolved (typified by Dr Edwin Land's introduction of instant-picture colour materials in 1963). Emulsion chemists today are able to 'fine-tune' film performance, due to a better fundamental understanding of how an emulsion behaves when an image is focused on it in the camera. Manufacturers now have unprecedented control over crystal structuring and complex multilayer coating of film.

The end of this century approaches with *electronic* still-image recording gaining ground as a viable alternative to *chemical* photography, but film manufacturers are extremely active, targeting and upgrading every practical aspect of silver halide materials. Their main aims are to further improve light sensitivity, definition, colour rendition, convenience and stability, and minimize increases in cost. Several of these requirements are traditionally conflicting. For example, it is difficult to increase ISO speed without, at the same time, reducing ability to resolve detail and record subtleties of tone and colour. Sheer film speed has always been an attraction, and gives definitive figures which everyone understands. They also read well in sales material. However, today, unless you must have ultimate speed for some specialist application, very fast films create problems in general photography. For example, it becomes awkward to shoot pictures with shallow depth of field and/or blurred movement. Also the larger grains and thicker emulsion coating, traditionally needed for extra light-sensitivity, deprive you of fine detail.

Manufacturers now give equal, or greater, importance to improving image qualities within their existing speed range of films. One way to do this is by advanced chemical engineering, i.e. preventing silver

Fig. 4.1 Requirements for film to offer good image resolution, light sensitivity, and freedom from grain all pull in different directions. Triangles here represent four films of differing speeds. Gains in one direction inevitably result in losses in another

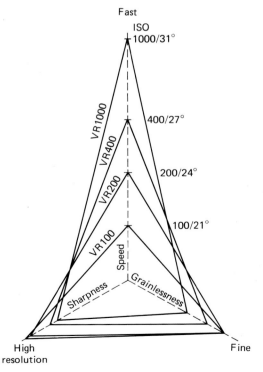

Fig. 4.2. Above: thin, tabular-shaped film emulsion silver halide grains, magnified about × 10,000. Unlike traditional flat-sided crystals these are thinner and have ruffled surfaces to increase surface area. The result is a better trade-off between speed and resolution. Courtesy Kodak Ltd

halide crystals from growing into their normal smooth symmetrical shapes so that they form flat 'tabular' crystals with a ruffled surface texture instead. Both changes greatly increase the total *surface area* presented to the image light (ruffling alone more than doubles the area of a smooth crystal). Since the new crystal shapes lie flatter in the coated film, emulsions can be thinner, improving sharpness and using less silver without loss of film speed. In other words, emulsion efficiency is improved all round.

Films now have better colour rendering and visual sharpness achieved by incorporating chemical 'inhibitors' (see DIR, page 95) which increase the colour contrast and the saturation of dominant colours without making neutral grey tones unacceptably harsh. The result is rich colour but without the sacrifice of shadow and/or highlight detail you would expect if contrast was just boosted all round. Changes of this kind aim to increase the main advantage of chemical recording over electronic recording – namely its excellent image detail, colour and tone range.

General points in choosing films

There is considerable competition between the four or five main manufacturers to capture larger shares of the world's photographic film market. At any one point in time some new (patented) development in chemistry or manufacturing technique pulls one brand ahead of another, only to be overtaken in turn by another competitor a year or so later. Whether you are choosing from existing films or assessing a newcomer, bear in mind each of the following aspects:

Accuracy; speed; exposure and colour latitude; value for money; suitability for slides and transparencies or prints; image dye stability; grain and resolution.

Accuracy

Slides (for projection) and transparencies (larger-format reversal film) on slow material remain unbeatable for resolution of detail and luminosity of colour. A projected slide in a properly blacked-out room (with no extraneous light to grey-up shadow detail) can give highlights four hundred times brighter than shadows. This is about four times the range of a print, which is severely limited by the percentage reflectance of its paper base and maximum absorption of light by its darkest dyes. The result is that often colour prints from colour negatives tend to lack the sparkle of a colour slide. For example, specular highlights merge with diffuse ones – a water droplet on a white flower petal becomes more difficult to pick out.

Publishers still prefer you to present colour work in slide or transparency form because the image has only been through a lens once. Results are closer to the original scene. However, you must also be that much more accurate with lighting, composition and exposure at the camera stage. Monochrome reproduction procedures, on the other hand, favour prints from black and white negatives, and this also gives you plenty of scope for control through cropping, choice of paper grades, shading and printing-in.

No good modern colour film can really be said to be more 'accurate' than another. The different dyes used are patented by manufacturers and used in slightly varied mixtures to reproduce image colours according to the colour response of each emulsion layer (pages 94–95). Beyond a certain point the feeling for accuracy is subjective. Some Asian manufacturers and users put a premium on brilliance of greens, while in North America consumers accept a 'cooler' bias, with greater richness of blues preferred. These differences are not easy to see in isolation, but show up clearly if you are unwise enough to shoot an assignment using a mixture of film brands.

Speed

In general, grain pattern and loss of colour saturation grow worse with increase in ISO speed. The deterioration shows up more in fast colour slide materials than when colour negatives on film of an equivalent speed are printed. Overexposure of negatives and push-processing of all films both tend to increase graininess. However, fast slide and fast black and white negative films can be push-processed most successfully for extra speed because they have lower inherent contrast. Slower films tend to respond with excessively contrasty images, and colour negative films should not be pushed at all because prints will then show different colour distortions between highlights and shadows (see *crossed curves*, page 201). Remember that manufacturers' speed figures are not sacrosanct. Use them as recommendations – they assume average subjects and lighting, standard processing and results which show maximum accuracy of tone and colour. Your own conditions and needs will sometimes be different. You must then decide from your own experience whether particular materials will perform better for you up- or downrated.

Exposure and colour-temperature latitude

Exposure latitude depends greatly on subject brightness range, being least with contrasty scenes and greatest with soft flat lighting. Having said this, slides and transparencies are least tolerant of wrong exposure, and black and white negatives offer greatest exposure latitude. Reversal colour films for slides and transparencies tolerate up to about half a stop overexposure or one stop underexposure. Colour negative films expand this latitude to one stop underexposure and two stops overexposure. However, most experienced photographers deliberately overexpose colour negatives by one stop, maintaining that they get optimum results. Latitude is considered two stops in each direction.

Colour negatives are also much more tolerant of wrong or mixed colour temperature subject lighting than reversal materials, but do not overdo it – underexposure or overexposure of one colour recording layer inevitably narrows the subject brightness range that your film can accurately reproduce (Figure 4.4). Nevertheless, colour negative films are a better choice if you are shooting under varying or mixed lighting, and they give you an extra safety margin taking available-light pictures in situations where the illumination is unknown.

With black and white material one and a half stops underexposure and two stops overexposure are about the outside limits for fast and medium-speed film. Exposure latitude is slightly less with slow films because they are more contrasty. Even this amount of overexposure is undesirable with 35 mm or smaller images because you start losing resolution through light spread, and 'solid' highlight detail in the negative demands contrasty printing paper which exaggerates grain.

Value for money

Slow-speed 35 mm reversal film still offers the lowest cost per exposure (both colour and monochrome), but the price of reversal

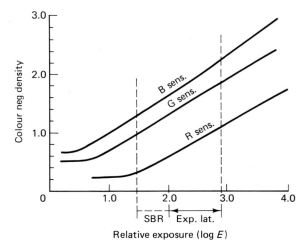

film increases significantly with size. One 8×10 inch sheet costs the equivalent of 30–40 35 mm exposures. Colour negative and black and white negative materials are now similar in price in popular sizes. Specialist films (pages 76–82) are generally more expensive. However, remember that for professional photography film stock is often a relatively small element in the total cost of a job – easily exceeded by time, travel, models, etc. In practice, choice depends on quality and suitability far more than price. It is very unwise to 'economize' by buying outdated material at a bargain price or reloading your own 35 mm cassettes.

Films for slides and display transparencies

When final results have to be projectable slides the obvious and best choice is 35 mm reversal film – if possible running off additional original exposures if more than one copy is needed. For extra copies later you can print off an original slide onto 35 mm low-contrast duplicating stock (page 82). As an alternative you could shoot on colour negative stock and print onto print film. Both routes allow some adjustments of colour filtration and lightening of density through exposure, either overall or locally by shading. Best-quality monochrome slides result from 35 mm instant-picture film or slow general-purpose film given reversal processing (see *Basic Photography*). Results almost as good are possible by shooting on regular monochrome film and printing negatives (1:1 through the enlarger) onto 35 mm film with a bromide paper type emulsion such as Kodak fine-grain release positive. You can also print on lith film developed in dilute D76 to get medium-contrast results. Large display colour transparencies for rear-illuminated advertisements, etc. are most often enlarged on special print film from colour negatives, but they can also be produced from original slides or transparencies using reversal print film (see Chapter 10).

Films for prints

Prints have obvious advantages for jobs where the photograph itself is the finished product (for example, sales albums, framed display prints, etc.). Prints also accept retouching and artwork far more easily than images on film. Often the best route to a colour print is to shoot on colour negative stock and then use neg/pos paper by the same maker. In practice, you may also get excellent results starting with a slide instead. From this you make a colour negative on internegative film (page 248) for colouring printing as above, or print the slide direct on any of a choice of reversal papers. If you choose the latter it is important that your slide is not too contrasty or overexposed in any way. Results naturally differ from one another. Prints direct from slides, for example, have a richness of colour which may suit a graphic product advertising shot but not a family portrait.

The best monochrome print quality undoubtedly comes from good monochrome negatives. Bromide prints from colour negatives (preferably on panchromatic paper) give a handy method of proofing results for facial expression, etc. but do not make finished enlargements this way, because they will lack the subtle tonal values possible from black and white film.

Image dye stability

All colour images change in the course of time. Dye stability varies with particular hue and from one brand to another. Materials which contain ready-formed rather than chemically generated dyes such as dye-bleach paper (pages 203–204) give inherently long-lasting images. However, a given dye can have good stability in dark storage but fades fairly rapidly when displayed in the light, and vice versa. Trials show, for example, that the magenta dye in most regular chromogenic colour films and papers has good dark but poorer light stability. Cyan dyes often have the opposite characteristics. So when pictures are hidden away image colours gradually become warmer, but framed on the wall (or projected) they shift towards cold hues. A colour slide left showing continuously in a typical projector starts to bleach notice-ably and colour change after about 5 minutes. In general, slides shot on fast film stock deteriorate more rapidly than slow films and black and white silver images. Much depends on how you store your final images, of course. Always file colour photographs in cool and dry conditions (below 70° F and less than 50% humidity) and avoid exposure to volatile chemicals. This includes contamination from unsuitable paper or plastic sleeves and envelopes. With properly processed and stored film you can anticipate a life of at least 20 years without perceptible colour change.

Understanding technical descriptions

The technical information departments of film manufacturers, and most technical photographic magazines, publish comparative data on products in the form of graphs, tables, etc. Some parts of this material are more useful than others, but provided you can read and under-stand it there is more information to be found here about practical film performance than in purely advertising literature. Topics covered include granularity; acutance; MTF performance; characteristic curves; spectral sensitivity; reciprocity failure; and DX coding.

Grain

The grain pattern seen in a processed photographic film is like 'noise' in an audio or video electronic signal – an overlaid mealy pattern breaking up image tones and fine detail. You are always most conscious of grain in mid-tone parts of the image, especially flat, even areas such as the sky or a plain grey studio background.

Grain is coarser in fast films than in slow materials, partly because larger silver halides are more sensitive to light and partly because fast films tend to have thicker emulsion layers. Thinner coatings of tabular-shaped silver halide crystals (page 62) help to minimize this relationship, but it is still inherent. In most colour films each colour-developed silver halide produces a slightly larger, roughly spherical patch of dye. Only these dye clouds remain after all silver is removed towards the end of processing, so although the dye coupling has effectively enlarged original grain size its *character* is softer, more globular and diffuse.

The grain qualities of a film are sometimes expressed by the terms 'granularity' and sometimes 'graininess'. They are not quite the same

Fig. 4.5 Granularity measurement. A micro-densitometer trace across an apparently 'uniform' density

thing. *Granularity* is an objective figure. It is measured under laboratory conditions by a micro-densitometer which tracks across the processed image of an even mid-grey tone. The instrument's readout (Figure 4.5) can be converted into a number based on the average fluctuations of density above and below the mean density level. Manufacturers therefore publish figures called 'diffuse RMS granularity ×1000' for their regular film range, usually measured from an area with a density of 1.0. (RMS means Root Mean Square – an average you get by adding up the squares of the variations from mean density and taking the square root of this total.)

A very fine-grained, ISO 25/15° thin-grained emulsion might rate 4 or 5 on this scale, whereas a black and white film of ISO 400/27° typically has a granularity figure of about 12. When you look at granularity figures for increasing densities black and white film continues to rise but colour tends to decrease slightly (Figure 4.6). One reason for this is that dye clouds tend to merge together more readily than silver grains. You should over- rather than under-expose colour negative film. Granularity figures are useful in comparing one film stock against another (they help to explain differences in film MTF graphs, for example, pages 69–70). However, in practice many other factors influence the way grain looks in your final image.

Unlike granularity, *graininess* is a subjective, generalized term, taking into account the overall visual impression of your enlarged result under practical viewing conditions. It has to be based on 'average' observers reporting on just acceptable levels of grain pattern. The main factors influencing graininess are:

1. The granularity of the film you use.
2. Type of image and sharpness, proportion of even midtones, whether your subject has a lot of fine detail, and the optical sharpness of its image. A soft-focus or movement-blurred camera image is more likely to display its grainy structure, as this emulsion pattern may be the only sharp detail you can see. However, a sharp negative printed through a diffused or mis-focused enlarging lens will lose its grain pattern along with image detail (Figure 4.7).
3. Exposure and contrast. A black and white negative wholly under- or overexposed shows lower contrast and needs more contrasty printing, which emphasizes its grain pattern. Overexposure additionally scatters light, further reducing contrast so the prints made on high-contrast paper end up with more graininess. Low-contrast subject and lighting conditions result in flat images which again need contrasty paper, emphasizing graininess.
4. Degree of development – normal, held-back or pushed. Also (monochrome silver emulsions) your choice of developer type. Overdevelopment and the use of speed-enhancing developers both increase graininess.
5. Chemical aftertreatment of the film image. Most solutions which reduce or intensify image density also increase graininess.
6. Enlarging. Obviously, degree of enlargement is important, but so is type of enlarger (diffuser or condenser light source). Printing paper contrast and surface texture – glossy or textured – is a major factor, but not paper emulsion structure because this is very slow and fine grained and not itself enlarged.

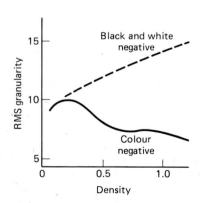

Fig. 4.6 A major difference between colour negatives and black and white negatives is that as density increases image granularity pattern becomes less (colour), and greater (black and white). On this basis colour negative film survives overexposure better than black and white film

Fig. 4.7 Left: normal photography on grainy reversal colour film. Centre: shot with a diffuser over the camera lens. Grain is still apparent, being inherent in the film. Right: reversal print from the left-hand transparency, with the enlarger lens diffused. Grain is lost along with image detail

7. Your viewing distance and the brightness of lighting on the final result. Also the conditions of viewing – a transparency surrounded by strong light on a viewing box shows less graininess than when masked off with dark surround.

Graininess is not always a thing to avoid, of course. As long as it can be controlled you can use it creatively. Grain simplifies images by destroying unimportant small detail, evokes atmosphere and breaks up large monotonous areas of tone and colour. To maximize grain, shoot with a small-format camera and high-resolution lens on fast film. Keep the image small (for extra enlargement later) and use flat subject lighting so that you can step up development to increase graininess without creating excessive image contrast. Silver image negatives can be slightly overexposed, then overdeveloped and reduced in Farmer's Reducer (page 158). You next enlarge with a condenser type enlarger (preferably a point source) onto contrasty glossy paper. As a less subtle but easier-to-handle alternative, print through a grained screen sandwiched with your film in the enlarger. Screens can be bought or made yourself by exposing coarse-grain film to an image of an evenly lit plain surface.

Fig. 4.8 Grain can usefully contribute to the atmosphere of a picture. This promotional advertising shot for a brewery works through what it suggests in terms of a Sunday morning at the 'local'. (By Dick Swayne)

Fig. 4.9 Adjacency effect. When a subject boundary between dark and light (top left) is imaged onto film the density change in the processed negative does not show the expected profile (solid line). Instead, chemical changes across the boundary give an exaggerated edge effect. This improves visual sharpness. Right: the effect as recorded by micro-density trace across an actual film image

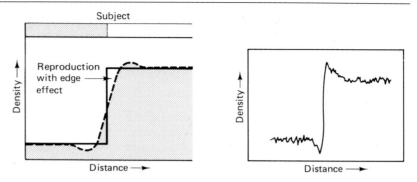

Acutance

Boundaries between contrasting areas of the image – light and dark – tend to be exaggerated when silver halides are developed. Figure 4.9 shows how the higher density becomes greater and the lower one less along the edge of light and dark. This so-called adjacency or 'edge effect' is due to chemical changes during development. Active developer diffuses from the low-density area where it is underused, boosting development along the adjacent high-density one. Meanwhile the oxidation by-products – bromide and iodide – released in largest quantities from the high-density side slow development on the low-density edge of the boundary.

All this is of practical importance, since exaggerated edges give a stronger impression of image sharpness. A graph like Figure 4.9 can be mathematically expressed as a number which gives an *acutance* value to the particular film. All emulsions are designed to give highest possible acutance (maximum edge effect). The same applies to high-acutance black and white developers formulated to exaggerate these results. However, do not confuse acutance with fineness of grain. Acutance developers may even increase graininess by sharpening up edge contrast.

Film	Resolving power (lp/mm)
Pan X (ISO 32/16°)	200
High contrast process film	160
Slow pan (ISO 125/22°)	125
Tri-X or HP5 (ISO 400/27°)	100
B & W infra-red	80
RX pan (ISO 1250/32°)	63

Fig. 4.10 Maximum resolving power figures for a range of films, each given its recommended form of processing. Response steadily improves as new types of silver halide crystal are introduced. However, these figures offer very limited information on their own

Film MTF curves

In Chapter 2 we saw how the quality of *lens* performance can be shown by a graph which plots accuracy of response (in percentage modulation or contrast) to images ranging from coarse to fine detail (low to high frequency). This kind of modulation transfer function is also published for films (see Figure 4.11). Notice how the graph runs to over 100% modulation with coarse to medium detail because edge effects have greatest influence here and boost contrast. At the finest detail, highest frequency end of the scale grain size and light-scatter within the emulsion take their toll, so that response dips. The point on the frequency axis where the graph line drops to 10% response is sometimes quoted as the maximum resolving power of the film. Typical limits are about 200 lp/mm for slow black and white film and 100 lp/mm for a medium-speed colour negative material.

Most manufacturers' technical data sheets on films include an MTF graph for comparative purposes. These prove, for example, how a fine-grain thinly coated (i.e. slow) film gives a generally higher plot

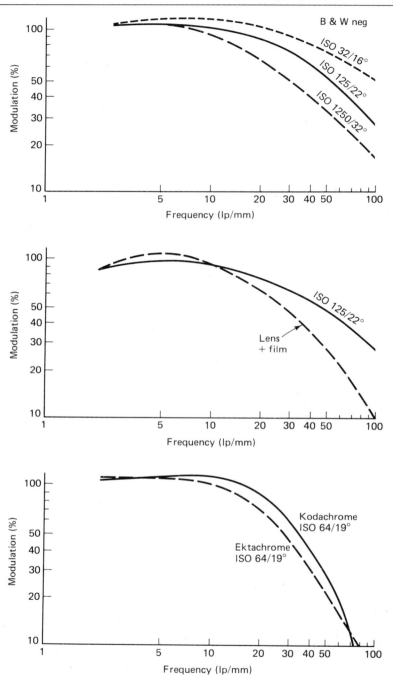

Fig. 4.11 MTF curves. Top: slow, medium and fast black and white films. Centre: another ISO 125/22° film, and the combined effect of this film and the MTF of a camera lens. Bottom: two slide films. When judged down to 40 lp/mm Kodachrome gives better modulation than Ektachrome of equivalent speed. See also Figure 2.19.

than a fast one. You can also add to the graph the MTF curve for the lens you are using, 'cascading' the two together by multiplying their percentage values at each frequency. The result shows the combined performance of your lens + film. Clearly, a low-resolution film can demolish the effective practical performance of an expensive lens, just as a poor lens nullifies a high-resolution film. MTF can be taken

Fig. 4.12 Typical modulation transfer function of the human eye, viewing a print from normal reading distance. (Multiply figures on the frequency scale by seven to relate them to a 35 mm film which will be enlarged to 8 × 10 in)

even further by adding the performance of enlarging lens and printing paper. As discussed on page 24, you can also apply a cut-off frequency beyond which performance is unimportant (say, 40 lp/mm). The exact figure will depend on camera format and degree of enlargement and the distance expected for viewing final pictures.

Characteristic curves

Curves like Figure 4.13 are the oldest type performance graphs for light-sensitive emulsions, pioneered by scientists Hurter and Driffield working in Britain in 1890. Traditionally known as 'characteristic curves', they are also called H & D curves, density curves, or D log E curves. The drawing plots a wide range of 'light dosages' (log exposure) given to the film and scaled on the base of the graph against the resulting image densities measured after processing and scaled on the upright axis. Both axes are scaled in logarithmic units.

As shown in *Basic Photography*, a quick comparison of characteristic curves for different films shows you many of their vital differences. Relative contrast can be seen from the general slope of the curve; speeds can be compared broadly from how far to the left

Fig. 4.13 Characteristic curves for (near right) normal-contrast films differing in speed. Far right: two much slower and higher-contrast films. Lith film in particular can reach maximum density level above 5 before 'shouldering off'

the curve rises from horizontal (see Figure 4.13). Exposure latitude can also be gauged. This is done by seeing how far the range of exposure units representing your subject from the shadows to highlights (1:100 brightness range = 1.0 log E) can be moved in either direction along the log E axis before they fall on the unacceptably tone-flattening toe or shoulder of the curve. Characteristic curves published in sets like Figure 4.14 also show the effect of different degrees of development on density and contrast.

Reversal materials have characteristic curves which slope *downwards* as light dosage increases. See Figure 4.15. After reversal processing, parts of the image that contained most light reproduce as having least density – a directly positive result. The slide or transparency must be more contrasty to be acceptable as your final picture, unlike a negative, which is an intermediate for contrast-boosting printing later. It also needs good clear highlights. These features are shown by (1) a steeply angled curve and (2) low density at the bottom of the curve (0.2 is mainly the density of the plastic film base itself).

Fig. 4.14 Sets of characteristic curves show you the effects of development time. This is Tri-X developed in D76 at 20°C (68°F). Highlights build up most, therefore contrast rises. CI means contrast index; see page 293

Characteristic curves of colour film images are most often prepared by exposing the material to a transparent scale of grey tones, the light, of course, matching the colour temperature for which the film is balanced. The great majority of colour materials recreate all the colours of the picture through superimposed images in yellow, magenta and cyan dyes. So after film processing every tone on the

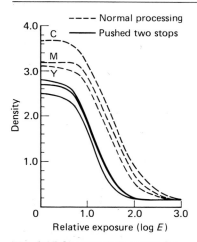

Fig. 4.15 Characteristic curves for Ektachrome P800/1600 film, given normal and (two stops) pushed processing. Unlike negatives, extra development lessens the final density of shadows

grey-scale image is checked out three times with a densitometer, reading through a blue filter to measure yellow dye density, then a green filter for magenta and a red one for the cyan layer density. All three plots must coincide in shape along most of their length, as in Figure 4.4.

It is vital that the same filters and densitometer colour response be adopted worldwide when making comparative measurements of this kind. Certified conditions known as *Status A* are used for positive colour film images. Three slightly different filter values are needed for evaluating colour negatives because the dye images here are geared to best suit the colour sensitivity of colour printing paper, not your eyes. Conditions are then called *Status M*.

Looking at Figure 4.4, you can see that characteristic curves for a typical colour negative film, read through correct blue, green and red filters, are similar in contrast to regular monochrome negatives. They are also offset vertically. This displacement is due to masking built into the dye layers, designed to compensate deficiencies in negative and print dyes (see page 94). Provided there is no displacement horizontally, and all curves match in shape, colour printing will cancel out this apparent discrepancy. Programs for quality control of colour processing make similar readings of test strips which are put through the system at regular intervals to check any variations in solution chemical content, temperature, etc. (see page 215).

Spectral sensitivity

A film's response to different colours of the spectrum is shown by a graph in which wavelength is shown against sensitivity (usually 'log sensitivity', being one divided by the exposure needed to give a density of 1.0 above fog and film base). The main points to look for in spectral sensitivity curves for black and white films are:

1. The highest wavelength cut-off point (Figure 4.16), showing whether a film is panchromatic, orthochromatic or only blue-sensitive. Ortho films finally reproduce red lips, red lettering, etc. as black or very dark, but films can be handled under deep-red safelighting. Blue-sensitive materials extend dark reproduction to greens but they are safe under bright amber bromide paper lights.
2. The uniformity of response of panchromatic film. Most films are panchromatic, but some fast materials have extended red light response which helps to boost speed and records more detail in deep-red subjects but also tends to bleach lips and other pale reds.

Fig. 4.16 Colour sensitivity curves for four types of black and white material. Extending panchromatic sensitivity to 720 nm boosts speed, especially in tungsten lighting. But for general work reproduction of reds may be too bleached to be acceptable

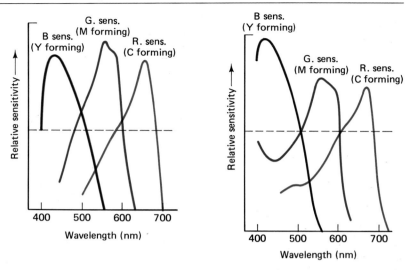

Fig. 4.17 Colour sensitivity curves for (right) daylight balanced, and (far right) tungsten light balanced slide film. Only response above the broken line is significant. Notice the extra blue sensitivity of tungsten light film. If exposed in daylight it needs an orange filter to avoid excessive blue

Colour film sensitivity curves are in sets of three for the blue-, green- and red-sensitive layers. Each curve should just overlap so that every colour in the spectrum is recorded by some response in one or more layers.

Colour balance

Colour films balanced for tungsten-lit subjects have blue-sensitive layers slightly faster in speed than red ones (Figure 4.17). This compensates for the fact that tungsten lamp illumination is deficient in blue wavelengths relative to daylight. It has a lower 'colour temperature' (page 111). Therefore by adjusting emulsion sensitivities the manufacturers can make different films balanced for practically any light source which gives out a continuous spectrum, i.e. contains a mixture of all visible wavelengths. In practice, only a few colour balances are on offer because, apart from daylight type, the market is quite small.

Fig. 4.18 The three main colour film types and their (unfiltered) compatability with various white light sources

Film type	Colour temperature	Light source
'Tungsten' or type B	3200 K	Studio tungsten lamps
Tungsten movie stock or type A	3400 K	Photolamps
'Daylight'	5500 K	Sunlight + skylight and most studio flash

You may often have to pick the nearest film type and then make good any mismatch with a suitable colour-compensating filter over the lens. Even with colour negative film it is still best to match up lighting and colour balance as closely as possible at the camera stage rather than rely too much on filtering back during colour printing. See also Chapter 10.

Reciprocity failure

The reduction in film speed which occurs when you give a very long exposure to a very dim image is usually presented as some form of

Fig. 4.19 Reciprocity failure varies with brand and film type. With colour reversal film the CC filter shown is needed to compensate for colour balance shift too

Indicated exposure time ▶	1	10	1000 seconds
Most B & W neg films	+1 stop −10% dev	+2 stops −25% dev	+3 stops −35% dev†
Fujicolor 400	+1 stop	+2 stops	+3 stops
Kodacolor 400	+½ stop	+1 stop	+2 stops
Agfacolor 400	+½ stop	+2 stops	+3 stops
Ektachrome 400	+½ stop	+1½ stops CC10C	+2½ stops CC10C
Fujichrome 400	None	+½ stop	+1 stop CC5Y
Agfachrome 200	+½ stop	+1 stop CC5G	

† Reduced development retains normal contrast.

table (Figure 4.19). Short-duration reciprocity failure is less important. Most modern films are designed to respond normally for very brief (up to 1/10,000 second) bright images because this is needed for regular forms of flash. However, long-duration reciprocity failure means that you must extend exposures of 1 second or beyond. Remember this when using an AE camera in aperture preferred mode which rarely takes reciprocity failure into account. Make corrections with the camera's exposure compensation dial.

With colour materials some form of pale correction filter may also be specified. Filter colour varies with different brands and types of film. Reciprocity correction is most critical on professional colour films, where sometimes separate types are made for different exposure

Fig. 4.20 Type L professional colour films are formulated to be exposed at 1/30 second or longer. Use Type S films for exposures of 1/15 second or shorter. Type L films are also balanced for tungsten light 3200 K colour temperature, and Type S for daylight

times (see Figure 4.20). Try to work strictly to manufacturers' recommendations for critical record work, studio portraits, etc. Fortunately, in a great deal of existing light photography – taken at dusk or night, for example – slight colour variations are accepted as natural. Provided that you remember to bracket your exposures towards longer times, complicated filtration and multiplication calculations (leading to still more reciprocity failure) can usually be avoided.

Product coding

Manufacturers mark up their products in various ways to identify type and batch. Most sheet films have coded notches (Figure 4.22) to show type, and may have a batch number impressed into the rebate of each sheet as well as printed on the outside of the box. Notches have the advantage that in the dark you can 'feel' the type of film you are loading. Rollfilm type information appears on the start and end of the backing paper and is printed by light along the film rebate for you to read after processing. Most 35 mm cassette-loaded film is DX coded to program the camera automatically for the film's characteristics.

Fig. 4.21 Facing page: part of the manufacturer's data sheet for a slow black and white film. It quantifies practical performance and allows comparisons with other film types, provided you know how to read the information. Courtesy Agfa

AGFAPAN 25 PROFESSIONAL

Speed

ISO 25/15°

Density curve

Exposure: daylight 1/100 s
Development: REFINAL, 4 min at 20 °C
Densitometry: Status M

Sharpness

Modulation transfer function (MTF)

Densitometry: visual filter
Exposure: daylight

— 35 mm film
----- sheet film

Resolving power

185 lines/mm (contrast 1:1000)

Granularity

Diffuse RMS granularity (x1000) = 8

Measured at diffuse density of 1.0 and with visual filter (Vλ) with a 48 μm aperture. This value is equivalent to a 12-fold enlargement.

Spectral sensitivity
(related to equal-energy spectrum)

Panchromatic.
The curve shown is of a density of 1.0 above fog level. The sensitivity is the reciprocal of exposure (in mWs/m²) necessary to produce the density given.

Emulsion structure

Single layer with supercoat.
Thickness: 7 μm.

Base

Safety film (acetyl cellulose) to DIN 15551.

Thickness: 35 mm film   130 μm
rollfilm   95 μm
sheet film (on polyester)   175 μm

Anti-halation layer

35 mm film:
Grey tinted base with AHU layer which turns transparent in the developer.

Roll and sheet film:
Dark green gelatine backing which turns transparent in the developer.

Reciprocity effect

Measured exposure time (s)	$\frac{1}{10000}$ − ½	1	10	100
Exposure correction (stops)	–	+1	+2	+3
Development correction (%)	–	−10	−25	−35

To obtain the same contrast range the developing time must be shortened.

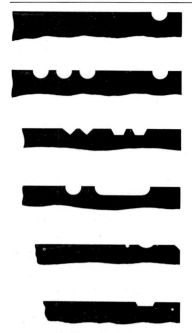

Fig. 4.22 Some notch codings from the top right corner of sheet films. From top to bottom: Agfapan 25; Agfapan 400; Kodak Tri-X; Kodak Vericolor type S; Fujichrome 50; Fujicolor 160

DX information is communicated through a panel of twelve squares on the outside of the cassette, making up a chequerboard mixture of bright metal and insulated (painted) patches. As shown in Figure 4.23, shiny patches 1 and 7 are always unpainted electrical contacts. Probes in the camera film chamber use this common area as an earth. Battery power applied through probes in other positions 'read' information according to whether they touch bare metal and complete the circuit or are insulated by paint. Five patches communicate the film's ISO speed. Three more tell the camera film length – to program its LCD 'frames left' counter and film rewind, for example. A further two patches encode whether the film has narrow exposure latitude (colour slide material) or wider latitude (colour negative), information used to modify camera auto-exposure programs. These data are also useful if the camera's light-reading system works by comparing several highlight and shadow 'spot' measurements (see page 148).

The simplest 35 mm cameras have just sufficient circuitry to sense broad ISO speed groups, for which only three to four contacts are needed. More advanced models have 10 probes in two rows to fully utilize all the DX-coded information. What happens when you load the camera with an uncoded cassette depends upon the camera design. Most cameras set ISO 100/21° in default; some memorize and reset for the last film you loaded, then flash a warning in the viewfinder and top display panel. So take care if you refill old cassettes from bulk film of a different kind.

35 mm cassettes also carry an external bar code which equipment at the processing laboratory reads immediately on arrival to sort films into batches for different processes. Finally, a code pattern, light-printed along the entire film rebate, can be read after processing by an automatic printing machine, which then adjusts its filtration and exposure to suit the parameters of your particular type of film. The machine's database will already be programmed to recall the colour

Machine readable bar code

Camera sensing code

Latent image bar code

Fig. 4.23 DX coding. The cassette's chequer-board pattern (numbered here) completes circuits through probes in the camera's film compartment. Centre: basic cameras use only three or four contacts. Right: advanced types have six more contacts, four covering squares 7–10 (film length, latitude etc.)

balance and typical image density range of your film (along with the characteristics of dozens of other film types).

Special materials

Instant pictures

A good range of instant-picture materials are made for different kinds of applied photography as well as for the general professional

Fig. 4.24 Using 8 × 10 inch peel-apart instant-picture material. 1: a special holder hinges open to receive one sheet of material in a flat envelope. You reclose it, then remove envelope through bottom of holder. 2: film holder is used as normal for camera exposure. 3: holder, plus receiving paper and chemical pod, is faced up to processor unit. 4: motor draws exposed material out of holder, passes it with the paper through pod-breaking rollers. Later you pull the two sheets apart

photographer and the amateur snapshotter. In black and white these include high-contrast peel-apart types for line copying, and high-speed (ISO 3200/36°) material for instrument recording under difficult conditions. Most peel-apart and integral-type materials come in packs which fit instant-picture cameras and special backs which attach to regular large-, medium- or small-format cameras. Some are made as 4 × 5 inch sheets in individual envelopes (page 98) and a few are still available in rollfilm form for the older Polaroid rollfilm cameras and backs. Peel-apart 8 × 10 inch colour material, in special envelopes, fits large-format viewcameras. These materials are 'processed' by feeding through a separate pod-crushing unit with 8-inch wide motorized rollers.

Both integral and peel-apart instant pictures are important aids for the photographer or scientist needing to confirm results immediately. However, unless you repeat shots of the original subject or use a reclaimable black and white negative type (page 102) it is difficult to run off duplicates or make enlargements without loss of quality. The complex chemistry in instant pictures is also temperature-sensitive. It is difficult to get results at all when photographing outdoors in near-freezing conditions unless you can warm the material while it processes. Instant pictures are more expensive than regular films, even including savings on processing costs. The colour materials are balanced for daylight and flash illumination. You can fit camera lens correction filters for other light sources, but these filters may differ slightly in density and hue from types needed for conventional colour films.

Lith film

This black and white film gets its name from lithographic photo-mechanical reproduction, and is used extensively in the printing industry for line originals, lettering, etc. The material comes in 35 mm (bulk cans), sheet and wide-width roll forms. When processed as recommended it gives extreme contrast and very high maximum density (see Figure 4.13). Lith film is very slow, and most types have ortho sensitivity so you can handle and process them working conveniently under deep-red safelighting. It is designed to be developed in lith developer which works in an unusual way. By-products of development increase the activity of the solution, so development starts slowly and accelerates as the image forms. This so-called 'infectious' development gives lith film its extremely rich blacks combined with clear white and no midtones in between. It also creates edge effects (page 69) which help to improve sharpness.

Accurate exposure and processing times are very critical if you want repeatable results – both overexposure and overdevelopment begin to veil and spread the image, losing fine detail. The high contrast also exaggerates any uneven subject lighting. As with most materials of this kind processed to extreme contrast, you get a rash of clear 'pinholes' in the image from time to time, and these have to be spotted with opaque. The hydroquinone developing agent used in lith developer loses much of its activity below 10°C, so maintaining the correct temperature is important.

Lith film is good for any subject consisting of pure black and pure white. It turns diagrams, charts and lettering into bold (negative) slides. It can also be used to make highlight masks (see page 163) and frame masks for audiovisual purposes (Chapter 11). You can make monochrome slides by exposing 35 mm lith film to regular continuous-tone negatives, under the enlarger or through a copy camera set-up. Three kinds of result are then possible: by processing in a D76 type developer the film gives normal-contrast continuous-tone monochrome slides. If you overexpose and then process by inspection in lith developer diluted to about one quarter correct strength, results are normal in contrast but extremely warm in tone. (This is like lith paper treated the same way, see *Basic Photography*.) Alternatively, by careful exposure and standard lith development you can turn your continuous-tone pictures into stark black and white.

Autoscreen lith film

Kodak make a lith film which is lightly pre-fogged behind a finely cross-ruled screen during manufacture. The result is that when you accurately expose it to a continuous-tone image through the (copy) camera or under the enlarger, and then give regular lith processing, the resulting image consists of tiny half-tone dots. This is intended for photomechanical reproduction of photographs (page 269), but you can also use it for effects – results range in appearance from fine to coarse newspaper-type reproduction. Autoscreen has a screen ruling of 133 lines per inch and comes as large sheet film only. For coarser effects you can cut off and expose onto a piece, say, 35 mm wide and then process and enlarge up this image.

Process/line films

These come in sheet film sizes and are also high contrast, although they cannot reach the intensely opaque black of lith film. However, you can process them in any high-contrast developer (D11 type or even print developer) which has better keeping properties than lith developer and needs less critical timing because infectious development is not involved. Resolution is about 160 lp/mm, higher than lith. Process materials are used extensively for photomechanical reproduction (page 268). They are also a convenient way of turning general line originals into line negatives you intend to print on bromide paper as pure black and white.

Black and white infra-red film

You can buy normal-contrast 35 mm or sheet negative film which is sensitized to respond to near infra-red wavelengths (see Figure 4.25). This means it will react to the infra-red in sunlight which is reflected off living green vegetation, for example, giving a strange 'snow-

Fig. 4.25 Colour sensitivity curve for black and white infra-red film. Although sensitivity extends well beyond the (700 nm) limits of visible light the film is also sensitive to red, blue and ultra-violet. This has to be controlled by using a deep red or IR-only passing filter

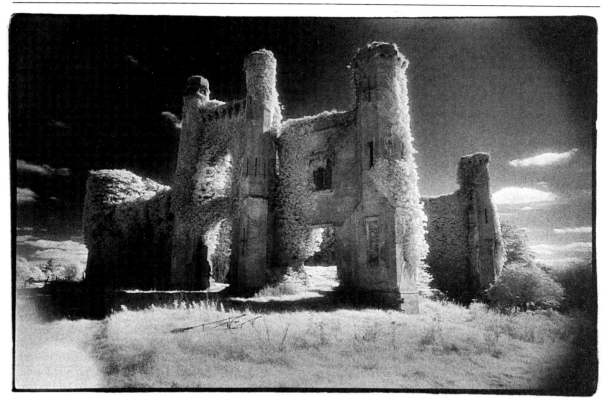

Fig. 4.26 Simon Marsden took this shot of Moydrum Castle, Ireland, on infra-red black and white film, using a deep red filter. IR film helps to give a romantic, ghostly effect. Chlorophyll in living green vegetation strongly reflects infra-red from sunlight, and appears luminescent. The filter darkens the blue sky, making clouds stand out starkly

Fig. 4.27 A portrait taken using the same IR film and filter, by Jon Barnes. Dark eyes stare out at you from bleached facial tones. The material also picks out features just below the skin surface, such as veins across the man's chest

Fig. 4.34 The false colour response of infra-red Ektachrome varies according to the IR content of the lighting. In direct sunlight the chlorophyll in living vegetation reflects IR along with green wavelengths from its surface pigment. The leaf image therefore reproduces as magenta (see text). Red paint reflects red and infra-red, which this film reproduces as yellow. On an overcast day, or when in shadow, little IR radiation reaches the leaf. It then reflects green only, which reproduces as blue. See also Figure 4.30.

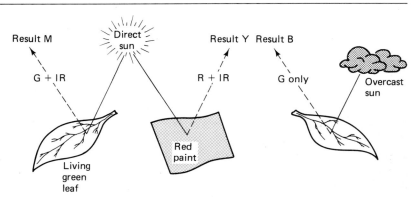

like a fisheye lens – with great restraint. You will produce most striking results by shooting landscapes in direct sunlight during spring (fresh growth contains most abundant chlorophyll, which reflects infra-red). For different false colour effects try changing the deep-yellow filter for other strong filters; see Figure 4.33. Focus the camera lens normally, because despite its infra-red response the film still uses predominantly visible wavelengths. Infra-red Ektachrome at present must be given E-4 processing – once used for all Ektachrome. This is offered by a few laboratories only.

Colour duplicating film

There are several kinds of duplicating colour film made in bulk 35 mm and sheet film sizes, both reversal and colour negative types. All of them are slightly low contrast and have characteristic curves (Figure 4.35) which are predominantly long and straight with very little 'toe'. The reason for this is that when you are copying a colour photograph, duplicating a slide or turning either into a colour negative for subsequent colour printing you have to avoid two hazards. One is building up excessive contrast. The other is having correct midtone values but compressed tone and colour values in shadows or highlights, so that your result *looks* like a copy from its degraded darker tones or veiled highlights. You will meet both problems if you try duplicating on regular camera films.

Duplicating colour materials are normally balanced for tungsten light, as it is assumed that you will be working with studio floodlights or a light-box. Films are designed for either normal E-6 (reversal) or C-41 (negative) processing.

Photomicrography reversal colour film

Film designed for photography through microscopes has to overcome the low contrast many specimens give when imaged by this kind of optical system. So photomicrography slide films have characteristics of slightly higher-than-normal contrast and strong colour saturation. These same features make the film useful for turning coloured or black and white drawings, line artwork, etc. into bold slides for projection. Exposure is very critical, and it is best to bracket exposures at no more than half-stop differences.

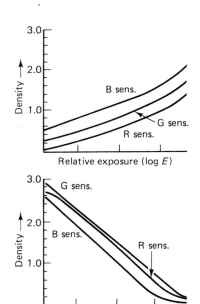

Fig. 4.35 Characteristic curves of colour films designed for duplicating existing photographic images. Top: internegative neg/pos colour film. Bottom: Ektachrome Slide Duplicating film

Summary: Films – types and technical data

● Early silver halide emulsions were blue-sensitive only, and crudely hand-coated onto glass. Today the industry has unprecedented control over crystal formation, thin multi-layer coatings and the use of additives. The result is new standards of light-sensitivity, colour-fidelity, sharpness and freedom from graininess – but in growing competition from more convenient electronic methods of still-image recording.

● For resolution, tone range and richness of colour, slides and transparencies are hard to beat. They are still preferred for printed reproduction. However, expect differences in colour bias between brands.

● Speed ratings are subjective in many ways. With most materials much depends on the degree of processing you choose to give (least flexibility with colour negatives). Processing, in turn, depends on subject and lighting contrast.

● Slides and transparencies are least tolerant of errors in exposure and lighting colour. Shoot colour (or black and white) negatives under the most difficult conditions – then you can make improvements at the printing stage.

● Other things being equal, the most direct route from camera to final result is usually best. Repeat exposures of the subject when runs of slides are required (colour or black and white); shoot colour negatives for colour prints or large display transparencies and monochrome negatives for monochrome prints.

● All colour dyes change with time. 'Dark' and 'light' storage stability varies with different dye types and colours. Avoid humidity, heat, fumes and prolonged bright light (including slide projection).

● Grain ('noise') linked to fast, thick emulsions shows most in image midtones and can be measured objectively in terms of *granularity*. More subjective *graininess* combines visual effects of grain size, image detail and contrast, exposure and processing, aftertreatment, enlarging and final display conditions.

● Chemical effects at tone boundaries improve the visual appearance of detail. Edge effect is encouraged in emulsions and developers formulated to give high *acutance*.

● MTF graphs plot an emulsion's modulation against cycles per millimetre frequency. This can be combined ('cascaded') with the MTF performance of the camera lens.

● Characteristic curves plot image densities against exposure to light. They help you to compare contrast, speed, palest and deepest tones, and the effect of degree of processing. Densities of colour film materials are measured through appropriate A or M 'status' tricolour filters.

● Spectral sensitivity curves plot emulsion response (log sensitivity) against wavelength. Plots show you uniformity of response and cutoff frequency. The relative spectral response of the three primary emulsion layers in colour film are designed to be balanced to record subject colours accurately under lighting of a particular colour temperature.

● Reciprocity-failure loss of film speed differs in severity according to film type and brand. Published data show how to correct it through additional exposure, preferably by widening the aperture. Black and white materials can be given altered development to compensate for reciprocity-failure changes to contrast. Colour films may need a correction filter. Type S and L colour films are designed for shutter speeds and lighting colour balance appropriate to short or long exposure times, respectively.

● Codings on packaging and on the film itself (notches, numbers and code light-printed on rebate) give identifying information. 35 mm DX cassette code communicates film speed, length and exposure latitude to the camera, provided that there are sufficient sensing probes in the film compartment. Lack of DX information may set ISO 100/21° automatically.

● Instant-picture materials come as peel-apart types (fit backs for regular cameras) and integral types for cameras having a mirror in the optical path. Advantages of almost immediate results must be balanced against cost; only camera-size pictures (unless reclaimable negatives are enlarged); and failure to work at low temperatures.

● Lith film gives extreme black and white density and contrast in lith developer (infectious development). Exposure is critical; pinholes common; remember to maintain developer temperature. Uses include line subjects, highlight masking, frame masks for audiovisuals, etc. Processed in low-activity developer, lith film will give continuous-tone projection positives from normal-contrast negatives.

● Autoscreen film converts continuous-tone photographs into half-tone dot screen images, 133 lines per inch. High-contrast process or line film gives less maximum density than lith, is simpler to process, has better resolution and still gives bold black and white line results.

● Infra-red monochrome film has sensitivity extended to about 900 nm. Used with a deep red or infra-red-only passing filter it records sunlit living foliage, lips, etc. as white and blue sky as black. Highlights have a diffused appearance. Landscapes and portraits take on a strange, grainy, 'other-world' look. Reset your focusing scale or stop down well.

● Infra-red colour reversal film (yellow filter) gives a mixture of false colours. Infra-red reflecting vegetation records as magenta, lips and red paint yellow, giving bizarre, dreamlike results. The material is important for aerial surveys of vegetation and some medical applications.

● Colour negative (or reversal) duplicating films are intermediate materials – they offer low contrast and long straight-line characteristic curves needed for turning existing prints or slides into copy colour negatives or duplicate slides.

● Photomicrography reversal films have higher-than-normal contrast, useful for making slides from low-contrast microscope images (also for colour diagram copying).

5

How camera materials work

This chapter discusses how our light-sensitive camera materials work, especially colour films. It traces the way that ingenious principles have been put into practice and compares how films *record* relative to the way our eyes *see* subjects directly. So the chapter begins by describing how eyes and brain receive and interpret the sensation of colours and comparing this with the far more fixed chemical response of colour films. Differences between seeing and photographing are important to grasp in order to control results.

The basic principle of chemical photography – the changes which happen when a silver halide crystal is struck by photons of light – was outlined in *Basic Photography*. Briefly, there are millions of silver halide crystals in every square centimetre of film emulsion. Silver atoms accumulate at specially structured faults or 'sensitivity specks' in every crystal, according to the light received and the crystal's sensitivity (for example, surface area). Later these specks form catalysts for liquid developer chemicals to darken exposed crystals, turning the invisible or 'latent' image into a black silver negative.

You will see how exploiting this principle over the years has allowed today's different kinds of colour films and instant-picture materials to evolve. The end of the chapter inevitably brings us to the *electronic* recording of still images. Here it looks to the future, where silver halides and processing solutions are increasingly challenged by CCD chips and still-video floppy discs.

Colour as seen and photographed

Many ingenious inventions are based on 'observations of nature'. The way colour films work owes much to scientists' basic study of just what colour *is,* and how human eyes and brains respond to coloured surroundings. In the seventeenth century Sir Isaac Newton showed that white light is really made up of all the spectral colours. In 1801 Thomas Young suggested that the retina of the human eye does not contain receptors for each discernable hue. Instead it has a mixture of three different kinds of receptor – sensitive to blue, green and red, which Young called the *primary colours* of light (not the same as *pigment* primary colours, familiar to the artist as blue, yellow and red). This 'three-colour vision' gives your brain the sensation of any spectral colour from the combination of signals it receives. James Clark Maxwell proved this in the 1850s by demonstrating with light from blue-, green- and red-filtered lanterns overlapped on one screen. Dimming or brightening individual lanterns re-created all the colours of the spectrum, while an equal mixture of the three primary colours formed a patch of white.

Today it is well established that our retinas contain many millions of rod- and cone-shaped cells. The rods are more sensitive to light but have no colour discrimination. The less-sensitive cones react to colour with their three types of reception determined by chemical content. Some aspects of colour vision are not fully explained by the tricolour theory, but the discoveries of these nineteenth-century scientists remain highly relevant for understanding colour photography. At the same time, remember that your eyes are virtually an extension of your brain, connected to it by over 750 000 fibres in each optic nerve. In dealing with colour *vision* the brain's ability to interpret is as relevant as the actual stimuli received from eye response.

The aim of colour photography seems to be to re-create accurately subject colours as they looked at the time. However, here problems begin, because of three factors which do not quite match up:

1. Colours are measurable and can be objectively defined, using terms such as hue, saturation etc. However,
2. Colours as seen by the eye and experienced by the human brain are not fixed at all and are subjective. Colour appearance changes under different surroundings and viewing conditions, and is influenced by psychological reactions such as colour experience and association.
3. Only three dyes are used in colour films to make up all the final image colours. Since these dyes are far from perfect it is impossible to always match (1). At the same time, a film's response is relatively consistent and determined by its chemical structure – it can never be as flexible and accommodating as human colour vision (2).

1. Colour in factual terms

Instead of vaguely describing colours met in life as 'pink', 'yellowish', etc., physicists use the terms *hue, saturation* and *luminance*. Hue is the name of the colour itself, the dominant wavelength expressed as a colour title such as green, yellow and so on. Saturation (or chroma) means the purity of a colour. The more white, grey or black mixed in with a colour, the less its saturation. Pastel colours are desaturated and strong vivid colours are highly saturated. Luminance (or value) is a measure of the brightness or brilliance – how much incident light it reflects.

There are two main systems which can pinpoint a colour and label it with a numerical code. One devised by the American artist A. M. Munsell classifies colours through a collection of over 40 charts of patches. (The charts themselves make up a three-dimensional sphere, see Figure 5.2.) The Munsell system gives every colour a reference number which identifies its chart (Hue), and then its vertical

(Value) and horizontal (Chroma) location, like a street atlas. Munsell numbers are used as matching standards for artists' paints, printing inks and any pigmented colour products. It is limited by the actual pigments available for printing the charts.

The other system is the chromaticity diagram, introduced in the 1930s by the Commission Internationale d'Eclairage. The CIE system identifies colours by matching them to mixed quantities of blue, green and red light. The exact mixture can be given a position on a graph which maps the relative strengths of the three sources (see Figure 5.3). Most colours – whether in the form of pigment or light – have a matching position somewhere within the CIE diagram, so you can describe any one by quoting graph coordinates.

Colours, of course, originate from all kinds of sources. This is what makes them difficult to reproduce exactly with any dyes or pigments, let alone mixtures of the three dyes in colour film. Any or all of the following forms of colour may be in front of your camera:

(a) Pigments and dyes which selectively reflect, transmit or absorb incident light. Colours here are greatly influenced by the colour of the light and the subject surface. (At certain angles a smooth surface will reflect a high proportion of incident light unchanged off its top surface, mixing with and desaturating the colour selectively reflected from underneath.)

(b) Colours derived from white light by diffusion and scatter. For example, the blueness of clear sky caused by scatter of the shorter wavelengths in sunlight by water and dust molecules in the atmosphere.

(c) Colours formed by interference – as seen on soap bubbles or reflected from oil on a wet road. These changing hues are caused by two reflections from inner and outer surfaces of a thin transparent film. Displacement by half a wavelength interferes and cancels out this wavelength colour, forming other colours from remaining white light.

(d) Colours produced by diffraction – for example, reflected from a compact disc or the sheen of a rayon-type fabric. These are caused by the change in direction of some wavelengths in white light when reflected from a surface covered in a fine pattern of lines.

(e) Fluorescent colours. Special inks or coatings, as on 'dayglow' poster papers, etc. which generate visible coloured light under sunlight or any other source containing ultra-violet radiation.

(f) Phosphorescent colours. The 'glow' from substances able to store energy from light and release it in a coloured form later (for example, the luminous coating on the hands of a clock).

2. Colour as seen

Normal human eyesight is quite good at comparing two coloured objects and judging if they match, provided they are seen together under identical illumination. However, colour seen in isolation is another matter. Judgement here varies from person to person and from one set of circumstances to another. Colours become personalized and you cannot even trust your own eyes. Look at the way people adjust the television to get 'realistic' colour – some have it bright and garish, others muted and restrained.

Fig. 5.1 A wide range of colours can be formed by adding different amounts of blue, green and red light. Yellow is formed when green light is added to red. White forms where equal amounts of all three primary coloured lights overlap

Fig. 5.2 Munsell system of colour classification (below). The Munsell 'solid' represents the three dimensions of the system. The central axis (neutral) runs from white at the top to black at the bottom. Saturation increases away from this central axis. In practice this sphere takes the form of dozens of charts, hinged along the vertical axis and each one dealing with a different hue. (The lopsided shape here is because printing inks have to be used rather than theoretical colours. Inks still have severe colour limitations.) Shown below are just two strips out of one chart for a red hue, saturation increasing to the right and luminescence increasing vertically. Any colour patch can be referenced by quoting hue, value, and chroma co-ordinates. The table gives four examples

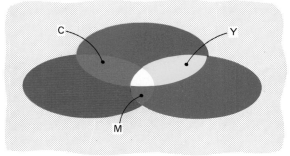

Fig. 5.3 CIE colour classification (below). In basic terms imagine this as a white screen with lights — blue, green and red — shining inwards from three positions (see broken lettering). The middle of the triangle formed by the lights is neutral white. Light from any one corner is at zero in the centre of the opposite side. Spectrum colours from blue through to red are located along the dome-shaped locus (bold line). Quoting x and y co-ordinates pinpoints any colour for matching purposes. The table gives examples for some subjects shown on chart

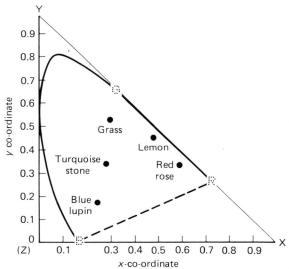

	Hue	Value (luminance)	Chroma (saturation)
Titanium white	White	9.6	0.1
Cadmium red	6.6R	4.3	13
Emerald green	4.6G	4.0	8.8
Ivory black	Black	1.5	0.9

Subject	Chromaticity co-ordinates		Reflection factor
	x	y	
Red rose	0.586	0.330	12.2%
Lemon	0.473	0.467	51.3%
Grass	0.290	0.518	29.7%
Polished turquoise	0.253	0.325	22.4%
Blue lupin	0.228	0.182	8.3%

There are all kinds of eyesight inconsistencies and differences that exist between individuals:

(a) *Colour adaptation.* The dimmer the light, the wider the iris of your eye becomes (its range is about five stops). After this the retina itself slowly adapts to increase sensitivity, relying less on the cones and more on highly responsive but colour-insensitive rods. Eye peak sensitivity shifts (the *Purkinje shift*) further towards the blue–green, then even this colour response fades to zero. After about 20 minutes' adaptation in extremely dim light you may just make out things in monochrome, with very poor resolution and a degree of visual 'noise' which destroys almost all detail. In a garden in dim moonlight you can only see the dark-grey shapes of flowers – but flash a lamp and their sudden colour brilliance emphasizes what our eyes have lost. To a lesser extent, the same thing occurs in a scene with contrasty lighting – your eyes see fewer colours in shaded areas than in midtones and highlights. (A point to remember in colour printing – colour inaccuracies are least noticeable if restricted to dark areas of the print.)

Adaptation also makes visual judgement of 'white' light suspect. Walk from one area lit by daylight-type fluorescent tubes into another lit with incandescent tungsten lamps and you are first conscious of the 'yellowness' of the lighting, but within a minute or so you accept this as neutral white. When you return to the tube-lit area it first strikes you as 'blue'. . . .

Eye adaptation is useful in life but a handicap in colour photography. Colour films cannot respond in the same way. Long exposure in dim light (despite reciprocity effects) will record a range of subject colours which just could not be seen by eye. Film is also balanced for white-light illumination containing a known mixture of colour wavelengths (quoted as 'colour temperature', see page 111). Under lighting of a different colour temperature, which your eyes soon ignore, film will not reproduce colours or neutral tones accurately. You will have to use correction filters.

(b) *Colour fatigue.* You eye's assessment of a coloured object is greatly influenced by the colour surrounding it as well as what you looked at previously. For example, if you stare at a bright blue shape for about 15 seconds and then immediately look at a blank white sheet the shape is re-seen on the sheet in pale yellow.

Fig. 5.4 Both centre grey patches here are identical. But they seem to differ visually because of the influence on the eye of strongly coloured surrounds

Blue receptors in the retina have become 'fatigued', but green and red receptors in the same area are unchanged and so temporarily respond more actively and produce the yellow after-image. Similarly, a pastel colour seems to change hue when taken away from one brightly coloured backdrop and set in front of another totally different in colour. Changes in eye sensitivity also sometimes make it difficult to judge colour prints – the longer you compare any two test prints with different colour casts, the more you think correct colour is midway in-between.

(c) *Individual colour vision.* Everyone differs slightly in their response to colour. Can you be sure you see what someone else sees? Around 10% of the male population and 0.5% of women have some form of defective colour vision. Their trichromate response may simply be uneven or, more severely, they cannot distinguish between red and green. Add to this the fact that the optics of your eyes grow yellower with age and it seems that we must all see colour differently. In jobs involving critical assessments – such as colour printing – good colour vision is essential. You can test yourself using charts in S. Ishihara's book, *Tests for Colour Blindness* (H. K. Lewis, London).

(d) *Psychological influences.* We are also all influenced in our judgement of 'correct' colours by experience and memory. I may not see quite the same green as you but to me the grass in that photograph is the same colour it appeared on the lawn. Similarly, you *know* that certain favourite flowers are yellow, city buses are another familiar colour and so on. Familiarity can even make you accept and overlook a colour which is somewhat distorted – you unconsciously 'read into' it what the colour should be. On the other hand, certain subject colours such as flesh tones and common foods are read quite critically. Your eyes tend to detect small deviations. Colour photographs of totally unfamiliar things are almost impossible to judge unless some reference (such as a grey scale) has been included alongside.

It is an interesting point that colour can really only be remembered by comparison. Can you imagine a colour you have never actually *seen*? Colours have broad emotional connotations too, also based on experience. Red suggests warmth; blue cold. These are old clichés but they are still used effectively in advertising. Therefore you have an orange bias in a sales picture of hot soup and an emphasis on green–blue for 'tingling fresh' toothpaste.

3. Colour as photographed

As you will soon see in more detail, manufacturers have to work within the limitations of having only three dyes present in colour films. From different mixtures of these dyes all image colours from all kinds of subjects have to be reformed. Some, such as fluorescent and phosphorescent colours, are therefore impossible to reproduce accurately. Even subjects with regular colours will only reproduce acceptably if illuminated by light for which the tricolour-sensitive halide emulsions have been balanced. 'Adaptation' by using filters is only possible to a limited extent. In choosing their three image-forming dyes film manufacturers have to compromise between high accuracy in only a few colours and the acceptable reproduction of many. Different brands solve the problem in different ways, so final colour images vary slightly in appearance according to the film you choose, even though each one was used correctly.

With all these variables and provisos it is incredible that colour photography is so realistic. 'Correct' rendering of colours seems so unlikely it is barely worth striving for. On the contrary, you must tightly control all the technical aspects of colour reproduction so that results are consistent and reliable, leaving human vision as the *only* variable. Fortunately, too, you rarely examine final results right alongside the original subject – here, at least, the way that your brain interprets what your eyes see is a plus factor.

How colour films work

The principles on which most of today's colour films are based were established long before anyone could actually put them into practice. The French scientist Louis Ducos du Hauron published a book, *Les Couleurs en Photographie*, in 1868, forecasting several of the colour-reproduction systems we now use. However, it was not until the 1880s that Dr Hermann Vogel's research in Germany into sensitizing additives made possible orthochromatic and panchromatic emulsions to add to the blue-sensitive materials used exclusively up until this time. Panchromatic response to all colours, and ability to control colour sensitivity, unlocked the door to practical colour photography.

'Subtractive' methods

To see how today's materials have evolved, imagine that you were working in the 1930s, photographing something to get colour prints. You would have to take every picture as a series of three black and white negatives on panchromatic material – through deep blue, green and red filters. Subjects were therefore mostly still lifes, although a few expensive one-shot colour cameras (Figure 5.5) let you expose all three 'separation negatives' simultaneously.

When developed, the blue filter negative recorded subject whites and blues as dark silver, blacks and the colours from the remainder of the spectrum (predominantly greens and reds) as pale density. The negative taken through the green filter showed whites and greens as dark and blacks and colours such as blues or reds as pale. On the red filter negative whites and reds were dark, blues and greens pale. Other colours and neutral grey recorded as midtone values on either two or all three negatives.

The next step was to print these colour separation negatives, each one in a different coloured dye. Then by sandwiching the three positive images together in exact register you formed one multi-coloured print. Follow this through more closely. The blue filter negative naturally printed subject whites and blues as white but blacks and all colours complementary to blue as dark. This black and white image had to be printed in *yellow* dye which is complementary to blue (Figure 5.6), logical when you remember that all the dark parts here are 'non-blue' areas. The print from the green filter separation negative was printed in magenta (whites and greens appear

Fig. 5.5 A 'one-shot' colour camera as used in the 1930s to expose three colour separation negatives simultaneously. Inside it had semi-reflective mirrors and blue, green or red filters just in front of three plate holders. The long-focus lens used a bladed shutter

Fig. 5.6 Primary and complementary colours of light. The white light spectrum can be broadly divided into three primary bands: blue, green and red. If any one of these bands is removed the remaining two form a combined colour which is said to be complementary (or secondary) to the missing band. So when red is missing the remaining light appears cyan — its complementary colour. Similarly yellow is complementary to blue, and magenta to green

white, all non-greens are magenta), and the red separation was printed in cyan dye. When all three prints were transferred onto one sheet of white paper (or clear film for a transparency) the stacked dyes made up all the original subject colours.

As Figure 5.7 shows, a *red* flower appears colourless on the cyan print from the red filter negative but is represented by dye in the

Fig. 5.7 Principles of subtractive colour reproduction. Top: subject exposed on panchromatic film through blue, green and red filters (or more commonly on three stacked layers of emulsion sensitive to blue, green and red). Each image records one-third of the spectrum. Bottom: final transparency or print consists of three positive images, each in a dye complementary to the colour response of its 'taking' layer. Each of these complementary colours transmits (T) two-thirds of the spectrum, subtracts one-third from white viewing light. Most colour films work on this basis

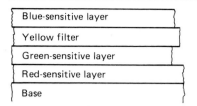

| Blue-sensitive layer |
| Yellow filter |
| Green-sensitive layer |
| Red-sensitive layer |
| Base |

Fig. 5.8 Layout (simplified) of a multi-layer emulsion colour film

yellow and magenta prints. In the red flower area white light illuminating the final result has blue subtracted from it by the yellow (leaving its green and red content intact), then green is subtracted by the magenta. All that is left (red) is reflected back to you from the white paper base as a red flower. Other subject colours reform the same way – trace them through on the diagram. Paler and other colours not shown here are made up by mixtures of lesser amounts of the three-colour image, but always just using three dyes. Think of each dye as 'subtracting' the colour of its taking filter from different areas, so that what finally remains from white light forms the colour picture. It is important to see why each dye layer cannot *match* the original filter colour as you might at first expect but must be complementary (negative) to it.

The actual mechanics for doing all this 60 years ago were diabolically labour-intensive. Negatives had to exactly match in image dimensions and contrast, and so had the three enlargements. Earlier image-colouring processes such as carbon, bromoil or wash-off relief were used for the printing stage, the results being transferred in exact register onto a final support. Today we still use the same subtractive principle, but this kind of *physically assembled* result only remains in regular use for systems like photomechanical printing, as used for the colour pictures in this book. Here original colour artwork or photographs are basically copied into three blue–green–red separations and printed in turn onto the page in yellow, magenta and cyan inks. (A fourth unfiltered separation printed in black ink is added to improve tone range and contrast: see Chapter 11.)

As a photographer today you do not have to handle mechanical aspects of subtractive colour reproduction any longer. Emulsion chemists have built all these stages into modern multi-layered colour films. In most colour reversal (slide and transparency) films the stack of emulsions has at the top a blue-only sensitive layer. Below this comes green- and then red-sensitive emulsions. (Usually these emulsions have some sensitivity to blue as well, nullified by a yellow filter located directly below the blue-sensitive emulsion which lets green and red pass freely. The filter becomes colourless later during processing.) So today one exposure effectively records three colour separations, in any camera.

With the exception of a few materials (such as Kodachrome, page 200), all reversal films use silver halides with 'colour couplers' attached – in the blue-sensitive emulsion these chemicals will later

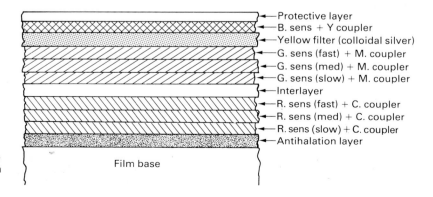

Fig. 5.9 In practice a colour film contains additional emulsion layers to improve image tone range. Antihalation dye absorbs back-scatter of light, and a top coating helps to protect from abrasion damage. Collectively these layers may only be 0.005 mm thick in the dry state

Protective layer
B. sens + Y coupler
Yellow filter (colloidal silver)
G. sens (fast) + M. coupler
G. sens (med) + M. coupler
G. sens (slow) + M. coupler
Interlayer
R. sens (fast) + C. coupler
R. sens (med) + C. coupler
R. sens (slow) + C. coupler
Antihalation layer

Film base

form yellow dye when triggered during processing. Similarly, there are other couplers to form magenta dye in the green-sensitive layers and cyan-forming couplers in the red-sensitive ones. After exposure in the camera the first stage of reversal processing is black and white development, which forms monochrome separation negatives in the emulsion layers. Then remaining halides are fogged (chemically) and the film goes into a colour developer. This developer acts on the fogged halides, which in fact form a positive image in each layer. However, as halides are turned into black silver, particular developer by-products are produced which turn the couplers in each layer into their designated dyes. Note that dye only forms where fogged halides are developed, so yellow, magenta and cyan dye-positive images are created in their layers.

At this stage you cannot yet see image colours because of the presence of so much black silver – the negative images from first development, plus the positive black image formed in colour development as a means of 'colour coupling' the dyes. However, the last stages of processing bleach and remove all black metallic silver, leaving dye images only. So your result is just like the old hard-to-work assembly routine, but done for you internally by multilayer film and 'chromogenic' (dye-forming) development.

Colour negative films use the same principle of having blue-, green- and red-sensitive layers with yellow-, magenta- and cyan-forming couplers, respectively. Processing here is similar to the latter half of reversal processing. The film goes first into colour developer which turns image-exposed areas into black silver and, via by-products, coupled dyes. Then all remaining silver halides and black silver are bleached away. As Figure 5.10 shows, the result is an image which has negative tones and complementary colours – red flowers are cyan, blue sky yellow. The density and contrast given by negative films and their processing, together with the spectral characteristics of dyes formed, are all geared to suit the same maker's colour printing paper. Neg/pos colour paper works on the same general principle as colour negative film, forming a colour negative of a colour negative – in other words, an image which is positive and correct colour.

Masking

Negatives are not judged as ends in themselves but are intermediaries. This fact allows manufacturers to do some tinkering with the negative production stage to improve final prints. For example, chemically formed dyes do not perform as well as they should in practice. Magenta dyes tend to subtract (absorb) some blue light as well as the intended green light. Cyan is worse and absorbs a little blue and green, as well as red. By the time colours have been generated twice – once in the negative, once in the print – these deficiencies accumulate. The practical effect tends to be that blues and greens look too dark relative to yellows and reds. Reds also appear orangey, while greens shift towards blue.

To overcome these dye deficiencies, negatives are 'colour masked'. Take, for example, the magenta coupler in a green sensitive layer which goes to form a dye wrongly absorbing 10% of blue light. Manufacturers make all the original coupler here not colourless but *yellowish* (absorbing 10% blue). So although during processing this

coupler changes from yellowish to magenta where colour development takes place, everywhere else it remains as a faint yellow
(positive) mask. As far as blue light is concerned, then the whole
layer – yellowish mask or magenta dye – subtracts an even 10%.
Image-wise it now controls only green light as intended, and has no
more effect on blue light than a grey filter. See Figure 5.11.

In the same way, cyan couplers are made pale pink to absorb the
same amount of blue and green as the deficient cyan dye. The
presence of these built-in masks is the reason colour negatives appear
with an apparently overall warm tint (a feature which makes it
difficult to judge images by eye for correct colour and density).

Recent chemistry takes improvements beyond this integral colour
masking by adding small quantities of DIR (development inhibitor
releasing) couplers. These use the amount of dye formed in any one
layer of film to affect the amount of colours produced adjacent to it
in other layers. This is done by releasing a colour developer inhibitor
which splits off from its own couplers and diffuses upwards and
downwards without also affecting the 'host' layer. The result is
improved richness of dominant colours in an image and more colour
contrast, without unduly altering neutral tones which would otherwise
give a harsh, contrasty result. Also, with inhibitors at work the centre
parts of coloured areas get slightly less colour development than the
edges. This gives an extra boost to density difference around the
edges of detail and improves the appearance of sharpness (see edge
effect, page 69). Inhibitors are used for reversal films as well as colour
negative types.

'Additive' methods

A quite different approach to reproducing colours was also
pioneered at the turn of the century and is used in a few modern
forms today. It relates back even more directly to Clark Maxwell's
demonstrations using light from primary filtered lanterns and
nineteenth-century recognition of the human eye's blue, green
and red receptors. Remember, too, that during the 1870s and
1880s French Impressionist painters such as Monet, Pissarro and
Seurat were making use of *pointillism* – the technique of juxta-
positioning tiny brush strokes in paints of strong luminous colours
and subtle tones. It is a significant fact that the very first colour
photography materials to go on sale were manufactured in France
(Lumière's 'Autochrome', 1907) and worked on what is known as
the *additive* principle.

Additive-type colour film has a mixture of thousands of primary
coloured blue, green and red filters permanently built into the
film base, like a microscopic patchwork or mosaic. There has to
be equal numbers of the different colours (Figure 5.13) so that
from normal viewing distance the eye just sees the film as neutral
pale grey. Panchromatic emulsion is coated on one side of this
base and the film is exposed in the camera with the base facing
towards the lens. Light from red parts of the subject can therefore
only reach the emulsion through the tiny red filters. It is absorbed by
green and blue filters, just as red light would be if shining through
green and blue parts of a stained-glass window. Light from green
parts only affects the emulsion behind green filters, yellow light

Fig. 5.10 Colour negative film. Exploded view of the basic layers before processing; after colour development (centre); and after processing is completed (right). Layer 1 has blue-sensitive emulsion plus colourless yellow-forming couplers. Layer 2 is a yellow filter which becomes colourless during processing. Layer 3 has green-sensitive emulsion plus pale yellow magenta-forming couplers. Layer 4 has red-sensitive emulsion plus pinkish cyan-forming couplers. The negative's warm cast is due to the yellow-plus-pink mask remaining in layers 3 and 4 in places where magenta or cyan dye is not formed. Colour printing paper is balanced to suit this colour-masked image

Before processing   During processing   After processing

Fig. 5.11 Why dye-deficiency colour negative masking is needed. An ideal magenta (left) should transmit as much blue light as clear film, but in practice (centre) it absorbs 10%. But if dye absorbing 10% blue is incorporated into clear areas of the magenta image layer (right) the whole layer acts as even density to blue light and no longer influences image blues. Similarly deficient cyan dye which absorbs 20% blue and green light is improved if unused cyan couplers remain pink

Fig. 5.12 Development inhibitor-releasing (DIR) couplers. The amount of dye formed during colour development in the magenta coupled layer here is designed to retard the formation of yellow in the layer directly above. This way unwanted blue absorption of magenta dye is offset by having less yellow dye formed. Colours are richer and edge sharpness visually improves

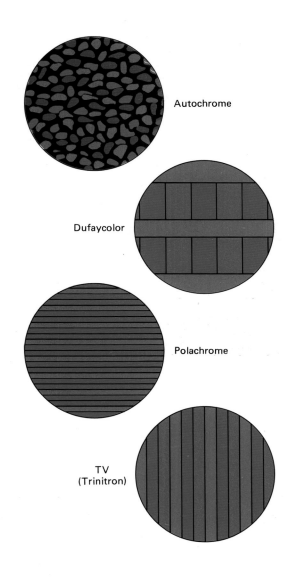

Fig. 5.13 Additive colour reproduction, using a filter mosaic. 1: cross-section of film. The pattern of tiny filters faces the image in the camera, backed by panchromatic emulsion. Image colours pass through the filters that do not absorb their particular colour. Film is then given reversal black and white processing. 2: appearance after first development. 3: negative image removed by bleaching (Polachrome by later physical stripping). 4: remaining halides blackened to form positive. 5: viewed or projected by white light, each area of the film transmits light matching original image colours. Provided filters in mosaic are small enough, the coloured areas appear continuous. Right: detail of various methods for producing the filter mosaic. Earliest Autochrome used dyed starch grains, randomly distributed. Dufaycolor used a grid, printed in dyes (greatly enlarged here). Present Polachrome has colour bands 0.02 mm wide. Colour mosaics or bands are similarly used on TV screens to reproduce colour images

(which is a mixture of two primaries) passes through both green and red filters, and so on.

To see results, you give the film black and white reversal processing (see *Basic Photography*). During this processing a tiny patch of black silver develops behind each filter which has let through light. Then this silver is removed and the remaining silver halides blackened to give a positive result. So when you finally hold the film up to white light, wherever there are red parts of the image only red filters are 'unlocked', in green parts you see green light and in yellow areas a mixture of red and green specks of filtered light add up to yellow. The whole system relies on the human eye's inability to resolve individual filters but to fuse together different *additions* of red, green and blue light to reform a complete range of subject colours.

An additive colour photography system of this kind is relatively simple to process because no colour development is needed. However, results are limited to slides and transparencies, and these cannot be much enlarged because you then start to see the mosaic pattern. Images also look much dimmer than on subtractive materials. Even in white areas only one third of possible illumination is really being transmitted, two thirds being absorbed by each filter. The same loss of light makes additive materials very slow in speed, typically about ISO 50/18°. However, as a system it has been revived for instant-picture slides (page 102). The additive principle is also exploited for colour television monitors and receivers. You can see the filter pattern on your television set by closely checking the lit screen.

Instant-picture materials

Instant-picture materials date from 1948, when the American scientist Dr Edwin Land's Polaroid Corporation (originally set up in the 1930s to produce polarizing filter material) launched the first 'Polaroid Land' one-minute camera and (roll) film. Land's process was based on diffusion transfer chemistry – the fact that while an exposed monochrome image is developing a *negative* on one material coated with suitable silver halide emulsion, by-products from its unexposed areas can be made to migrate (diffuse) over to a receiving material and appear there as a *positive* image.

Film packs and single-shot 4 × 5 inch film (in envelopes) largely replaced rollfilm from the 1960s onward. These materials were all 'pull-apart', meaning that you remove a sandwich of exposed and receiving material from the camera, wait long enough for transfer to take place, then pull negative and positive apart. By 1972 original research into chemical engineering added packs of 'integral' type instant material – the kind that are ejected from the camera as a single white sheet that you can watch as the colour image forms.

Evolution of instant-picture materials has always been closely aligned with the design of suitable cameras. This is because, with the exception of reclaimable negatives (page 102), the picture formed in the camera is the same size as the final print. Manufacturers

Fig. 5.14 How peel-apart black and white instant-print material works. Top: the light-sensitive material exposed in the camera, and (far right) print material afterwards sandwiched face-to-face with it. Rollers break the reagent pod and spread its contents between the two.

1: The first, negative-forming phase of processing. 2: by-products transfer and form positive image. 3: peeling the two materials apart. (Moisture-proof paper mask M prevents silver transfer, giving your print white borders, instead of black) 4: retained final print

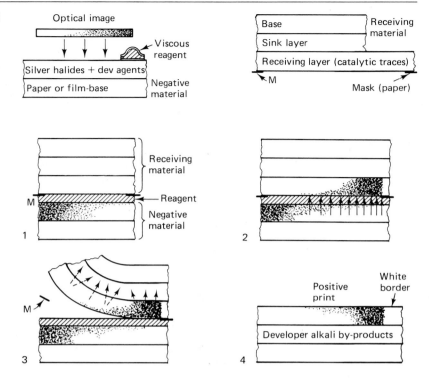

have to trade-off camera bulk against a usefully large picture. Also the integral materials only give a right-way-round result if your camera system reflects the image off a mirror fixed behind or in front of the lens. For this reason, instant-picture backs for conventional cameras (page 55) still use peel-apart materials.

How peel-apart materials work

The basic reactions within typical peel-apart black and white instant-picture material are shown in Figure 5.14. There are three units:

1. Light-sensitive emulsion containing silver halides and inert developing agents, coated on a film or paper base.
2. Receiving material, usually paper or permeable plastic or, in some instances, film. This is non-light-sensitive but contains invisible trace elements, i.e. a few atoms of silver to form *catalytic* sites (explained later).
3. A pod of reagent, containing a powerful alkali plus silver halide solvent, in jellified 'viscous' form.

In practice, (1) is exposed to the camera lens image, then brought into face contact with (2) with the reagent from the pod spread evenly between them. The actual mechanics of doing this, using pack or envelope backs, is shown in Figures 5.16 and 5.17. Inside the sandwich alkali rapidly activates developing agents in the emulsion which develop up a negative black metallic silver image within seconds. The solvent contents of the reagent, overcoming an induction period, next

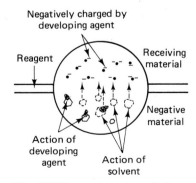

Fig. 5.15 Internal reactions during black and white peel-apart processing. Activated developing agent, plus solvent from the reagent, first work on the exposed negative material. Then they encourage formation of a black silver positive in the receiving material. See text

Fig. 5.16 Instant-picture peel-apart film pack. (Only arrangement for one picture shown here.) Rollers are a permanent part of the camera or pack-holding back. Above left: after fitting pack, cover sheet is removed. Light-sensitive negative material (N)

now faces lens. Positive sheet (P) is held in rear compartment of pack.

1: after exposure you pull tab 1, bringing the end of tab 2 out between the rollers.

2: pulling tab 2 allows you to remove

the whole sandwich from the camera, breaking the pod and spreading reagent at the same time. Negative and positive bases are opaque to light, allowing processing outside camera without fogging until time to peel apart.

Fig. 5.17 Instant-picture enveloped material. A: special sheet-film unit inserts into 4 × 5 inch view camera like a regular film holder. It contains rollers (R) which may be opened or shut, and locking lip (L). B: one envelope loads into holder at a time. Inside, light-sensitive sheet (N) is face up and attached to metal cap (M). Print receiving paper (P) is face

down and tab-attached to enclosing envelope E.

1: the back, fitted in camera, accepts envelope, which you then partly withdraw leaving sensitive material locked in focal plane by lip.

2: after exposure you re-insert envelope fully.

3: turn catch to spring the rollers together and also release lip. Now the complete envelope can be pulled clear of back, spreading reagent between exposed and receiving sheet. After the required processing period you tear envelope open, peel sheets apart

act on the remaining silver halides. These change to soluble silver ions which, if they were in a conventional fixing bath, would diffuse out into solution as by-products. Here, however, they diffuse out from the emulsion directly into the receiving layer of the print material in contact with it. See Figure 5.15.

Meanwhile, the viscous alkali has also penetrated into the positive material, followed by active developing agents, mostly from shadow areas of the exposed emulsion where there has been little to blacken. The developing agents donate electrons to the catalytic sites they meet in the receiving layer, making them negatively charged. So when soluble silver ions diffuse over from the other material a few seconds later they are attracted to the charged atoms – combining with them to form black silver. Most silver diffuses over from image shadows and least from highlights, so a positive black and white picture forms in the receiving material.

After a suitable period for all this to happen (10–90 seconds, according to the product), you peel the two apart. Your print needs no fixing – the underlying sink layer on the receiving material accumulates and neutralizes the alkali and other chemicals. The negative is thrown away unless it is a reclaimable type (on a film base) which is then soaked in 15% sodium carbonate solution, swabbed clean and dried. From reclaimable negatives you can make enlargements on regular printing paper. Results are excellent, provided your

Camera image

Transparent plastic support
Positive image receiving layer
Clearing coat
Antiabrasion top coating
Blue sensitive silver halide emulsion
Primary developer
Yellow dye release layer
Yellow filter dye
Spacer layer containing silver ion scavenger
Green sensitive silver halide emulsion
Spacer layer
Magenta dye developer and releasable anti-foggant
Interlayer
Red sensitive silver halide emulsion
Spacer layer
Cyan dye developer and releasable anti-foggant
Timing layer
Spacer layer
Acid polymer layer
Opaque base

Here reagent enters from pod.

P

N

Print

Reagent

Fig. 5.18 Integral type instant picture colour material: (top) during exposure in the camera, and (bottom) after ejection and the spreading of reagent to trigger processing. See text original camera exposure is chosen to give best quality in the negative rather than the instant print.

Peel-apart slides

Polachrome instant colour slide films combine an ingenious variation of peel-apart black and white chemistry with an additive system for recording colours. The 35 mm film base with its mosaic of filters (Figure 5.13) has three main layers – a transparent image-receiving layer next to the base, then a 'release' layer and a top layer of silver halides. You expose the film through the base, then place it inside a small processing unit with a processing pack. Here alkaline processing fluid feeds onto a 35 mm wide plastic applicator band which is wound up in tight contact with the film on a drum. Exposed silver halides are immediately turned into a weak negative while unexposed ones migrate down to the receiving underlayer, where a much denser positive image is formed.

You leave film and band rolled up together for a set period (typically, 60 seconds) then rewind them back into cassette and processing pack, respectively. As they separate, the applicator band cleanly strips off the film's top negative-carrying layer along with any remaining liquid, and these end up inside the processing pack, which you throw away. The film itself is left with an effectively dry positive silver image, blacking out some of the colour filters in different coloured areas, so when the slides are held up to white light you see all the original subject colours.

Other instant-slide materials work on the same basis and give high-contrast colour (for line artwork) or have no filter mosaic and give normal or high-contrast black and white slides. Since each film comes with its own processing pack the type of developer is always correctly matched to film type.

How integral materials work

Integral instant pictures work on subtractive principles, using a single sheet which is exposed in the camera, is expelled, and then forms a finished colour picture while you watch. The chemical arrangements are highly original. Each sheet comprises a stack of 19 extremely thin layers, which looks highly complex at first sight (Figure 5.18). However, to see the principle by which they work, follow through this structure step by step.

Before and during exposure the viscous alkali-processing reagent is stored out of the way in an internal pod at one end of the sheet. The top four layers are completely transparent before processing, so that your image in the camera can reach the blue-, green- and red-sensitive layers lower in the pack. After exposure, motor-driven rollers expel the sheet from the camera, spreading the reagent between layers 3 and 4. Its contents include opaque white chemicals which instantly shut off the lower still-sensitive layers from light during processing. This also forms the white background to the final picture, which will gradually diffuse up from below.

The reagent's alkali content travels down through the pack, activating the three developer layers, 6, 12 and 16. Exposed silver halides are quickly changed to black silver negative images above. However, where areas of silver are formed the dye developer directly below it is immobilized, while the rest releases yellow-, magenta- or cyan-coloured dye, which then rises vertically until it reaches the positive image-receiving layer. An image of a red flower, for example, exposes parts of the red-sensitive emulsion. Here it develops into silver, and in so doing immobilizes the cyan below it, so that only magenta and yellow rise to the receiving layer here – appearing as red.

In 60 seconds or so the image-forming dyes have built up a full-bodied colour picture you can view against its white titanium dioxide background through the clear plastic top of the sheet. By this time, too, the alkali and the acid polymer (layer 19) have reached and neutralized each other. The instant colour print is therefore left in a chemically stable, permanent form.

Electronic image recording

How it works

Recording the image in the camera by electronic means is gradually challenging chemical recording on silver halide emulsions which photographers have used for over a hundred years. Instead of film, a charge-coupled device (CCD) in the form of a single flat 'chip' of silicon fills the image plane (see Figure 5.19). When a photon of light strikes this surface, its energy liberates an electron. (In a sense this is like releasing an electron within a silver halide crystal, but from here onwards the CCD makes purely electronic, not chemical, changes.)

For a working 35 mm CCD the chip is divided into a million or so picture elements (*pixels*). Unlike silver halides, pixels are formally arranged in parallel columns, separated from each other by a microscopic line of insulation. After the camera shutter has exposed the picture the different numbers of electrons which have accumulated in each pixel within every column are 'read out'. This is done by passing their charge to the next pixel down the column and so on, to an external circuit – like emptying columns of coins in a change-giving machine. (Transfer of charge in this way gives the device its name.)

Your picture has now become a stream of electronic signals which are amplified and fed to a standard 47 mm diameter magnetic 'still-video floppy', spinning in another compartment of the camera back. Typically, each disc will record 25 pictures 'frame' mode (complete video pictures containing two interlaced fields each), or 50 pictures 'field' mode (only odd or even lines recorded, giving half the vertical resolution). The effective light-sensitivity of the CCD also alters. A chip equivalent to ISO 80/20° in frame mode, for example, becomes ISO 160/23° in field mode, and by using a gain switch this speed can be raised to ISO 320/26° at the cost of poorer contrast and greater noise.

Significance

Provided that image quality is acceptable, electronic recording allows the same kind of freedom that a video camera gives to someone used to a movie film camera. You can check results on the spot, like instant pictures but at much less materials cost. Each picture can be replayed through the camera viewfinder, if this is electronic, or via a attached to the halides in each emulsion. These react to by-products wherever colour developer forms black silver.

● In colour negatives it is practical to incorporate integral masking to help to overcome image dye colour deficiencies. Magenta dye-forming couplers and cyan couplers are made yellowish and pink, respectively. They stay that way in areas where their dyes are not actually formed to compensate for unwanted absorption of blue and greeny–blue. Negative and slide films also contain developer inhibitors to step up the brilliance of colours without making neutrals harsh.

● Additive colour reproduction – used for the earliest colour materials, present-day instant slides and colour television – works on the principle of a permanent mosaic of primary coloured filters. On films, panchromatic black and white emulsion is exposed through the filters and then reversal processed to 'block up' unwanted colours. The colour mixes which are left reproduce all subject hues when seen against white light. Additive-type film materials are slow, results are denser than subtractive types and resolution is limited by fineness of filter pattern.

● Instant-picture materials are founded on diffusion transfer chemistry. They use migration from unexposed parts of the light-sensitive surface to form a positive image in a receiving layer.

● Peel-apart materials comprise a surface coated with light-sensitive emulsion and developing agents; receiving material and a pod of reagent containing jellied alkali plus solvent. Sandwiched together with the reagent spread in-between, a black silver negative develops in the emulsion, then the solvent releases salts which transfer and blacken to give a positive print.

● Peel-apart colour slides are exposed through an additive filter mosaic in the film base. Reagent forms a top surface negative and underlying silver positive. Negative (and chemical remnants) are physically stripped off, leaving semi-dry colour transparencies.

● Integral (one-piece) instant-picture materials contain a pod which, after exposure, spreads reagent and opaque white chemicals between the top few receiving layers and the rest of the 19-layer stack. Yellow, magenta and cyan dye is released from areas that are not developed to black and white negative status. Dyes rise into the white layer and are viewed as a positive colour image through the material's clear plastic top.

● Electronic image recording uses a CCD in the camera image plane. After exposure, the response of large numbers of pixels read out as a stream of electronic signals, magnetically recorded onto a still-video floppy within the camera back. Images can be video replayed, transmitted, enhanced, titled, superimposed or erased. Capital cost is still high, and the image quality is limited by pixels per unit area and present methods for printing out on paper.

6
Lighting control

This chapter gathers together technical aspects of lighting, from principles and aims in illuminating the subject to setting up a studio and choosing tungsten or flash equipment. It looks at practical ways of controlling contrast and colour balance, and out of this shows the roles played by lighting ratios, colour temperature and mired filter values. You also need to control *mixtures* of lighting – natural and artificial or existing light augmented by a photographic source such as flash. In fact, flash has become perhaps the most useful of all light sources for still photography, in or out of the studio. Being able to confidently handle lighting is one important way of controlling the tone values of your final picture. This is discussed further in all its aspects in Chapter 7.

Principles and aims

Lighting challenges you in two ways at once. First, you need to illuminate the subject in such a way that its own important qualities are stressed and it has the right mood to suit your style and purpose. In other words, it must *look* right. Second – equally important and often more difficult – you need the technique to make it appear this way in the final picture. Here the challenge is to understand how the appearances of scenes alter when they are imaged and reproduced on film. Often you have to marginally alter the way the subject looks at the shooting stage, anticipating and allowing for this *photographic translation*, so that the finished result appears just as originally planned.

Lighting control is easier to practise in the studio or at least where subjects and light sources are fairly close to hand. If you are shooting great landscapes or architectural vistas on location, control of lighting is more a question of picking the best time of day, weather and viewpoint.

Aim to avoid these four most common lighting problems:

1. *Excessive contrast.* It is very easy to light something so that it looks bold and dramatic, only to find that it photographs with ugly

Fig. 6.3 Changes in lighting ratio. By increasing the amount of fill-light from the camera, lighting ratios were (A) 1:64, (B) 1:20, (C) 1:8, (D) 1:4, and (F) 1:1.5. Reproduction here on the printed page has altered some tone values – they only approximate results on photographic bromide paper

A   B

Practical control of contrast

The brightness range or contrast in a scene is mostly made up from (1) the inherent reflectance range of the subject itself, multiplied by (2) the lighting ratio (or lighting contrast). Subject reflectance range means the difference between light readings from the palest and darkest areas of significant detail when your scene is flatly lit. With a subject like Figure 6.3, for example, the difference between the plaster shapes and the background might be 1:4. Lighting contrast means the difference between readings of one element in the picture, where it is in deepest shadow and where most strongly lit. In the case of Figure 6.3C, lighting contrast might be 1:8. Put the two together and the total contrast here is 1:32 (the difference between extremes of the background in shadow and the plaster where it receives most light).

As a general guide (Figure 6.4), reversal films will record a maximum brightness range of about 1:32 with full detail throughout. Monochrome negatives, however, can handle about 1:128, or more if you hold back development (page 152). For the record, harsh direct sunlight on a subject in the open under clear blue sky gives lighting contrast of about 1:10. Related to this, a so-called average subject with a reflectance range of 1:13 gives 1:130 or seven stops total brightness range. Kodak suggest that very few situations give a range greater than nine stops (1:500).

Colour negative film can record a 1:128 range in terms of *detail*, but *colour* begins to distort towards the extremes of this range. When you include the still more limited range colour paper will accept off the negative it is safer to work within a brightness range of four stops (1:16) or even three (1:8) for critical subjects where both final colours and tone values must reproduce as accurately as possible. Most pictures do not need recording with this degree of colour precision, and you can usually regard five stops (1:32) range as acceptable when shooting general subjects.

When controlling your lighting contrast:

1. Remember broadly the capabilities of the film you are using. Reduce your lighting ratio for colour materials, especially reversal types.

	Maximum subject brightness range	No. of stops
Human eye	1:800	
Continuous tone B & W neg only	1:200	7.5
Through to print	1:128	7
Reversal colour slide	1:32	5
Through to colour print	1:16	4
Colour neg only	1:128	7
Through to print	1:32	5

Fig. 6.4 The subject brightness range (subject reflectance range × lighting range) within which detail can just be seen, or recorded at one exposure setting. Often film records more than printing paper will accommodate; you must then select your range of tones on the print through choice of exposure, and improve local areas by shading or burning-in

C   D   E

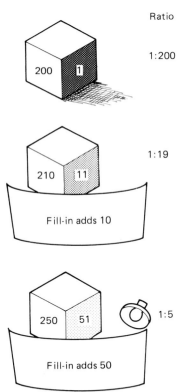

Ratio

1:200

Fill-in adds 10

1:19

Fill-in adds 50

1:5

Fig. 6.5 How 'filling-in' shadows reduces lighting contrast. Top: no fill-in. Shadow part of subject receives only one two-hundredth of the illumination in lit part. Centre: adding reflector which redirects 10 units to lit and shadowed parts drops ratio to 1:19. Bottom: boosting light from the reflector directs 50 units towards subject. Ratio is now down to approximately 1:5

2. Look at the subject reflectance range. A black cat in front of a white wall, for example, cannot take as much lighting contrast as a grey cat against a green hedge.
3. Think whether the shot really *needs* detail from brightest highlights right through to deepest shadows. If you can accept darkest parts as featureless black then increase lighting contrast and expose mostly for highlights and midtones.

To reduce lighting contrast, position a white reflector surface to add general diffused illumination into the shadow side of the subject. Outdoors, you can wait until parts of the sky away from the sun contain more cloud, change viewpoint or move your subject so that a nearby white surface acts as reflector. For more contrast reduction, illuminate this reflector with flash or some other suitable form of artificial light. Alternatively, change to a main light source which is physically larger and which gives softer quality illumination.

In the studio this may mean fitting a 'soft box' (page 118) or tracing paper over your light source or bouncing its illumination off an umbrella, reflector board or white wall. When working outside, wait until the sun is diffused, or shoot totally in an area shaded from the sun and illuminated only by light from the sky (but beware of colour-temperature changes, see below). Remember, however, that, unlike shadow-filling, anything you do to soften the quality of your main light also makes shadow edges less clear-cut throughout the subject.

With experience you can judge the combined effects of subject and lighting contrast by eye with reasonable accuracy, but it is far better to play safe and actually measure ratios. Here you appreciate the value of a camera or hand meter which gives spot readings, or at least allows close-up brightness range readings from highlight and shadow areas (see also page 147).

Colour temperature

For accurate colour photography it is essential to know and (if possible) control the colour of your lighting so that it relates to the colour balance of your film. This means having a working knowledge of colour temperature and its measurement.

Fig. 6.10 Colour temperatures for some typical light sources. CRI stands for Colour Rendering Index, quoted by fluorescent tube manufacturers

12 000 K	Light from clear blue sky only
– 27 000 K	
6 500	Fluorescent lamps (CRI 90)
6 000	Daylight (sun & clear sky)
5 800	Elec. flash (small guns)
5 600	Elec. flash (studio units)
5 400	Mean noon sunlight, and blue dyed flashbulbs
4 200	Clear flashbulbs (zirconium)
4 000	Fluorescent lamps (CRI 83)
3 800	Clear flashbulbs (aluminium foil)
3 400	Movie/TV tungsten-halogen lamps
3 200	Photographic studio lamps, and slide projectors
2 800	Typical 75 W domestic lamps
2 600	Typical 40 W domestic lamps
2 200	Sunlight at sunset, and bottled kerosene lamps
1 900	Wax candle

Bluer — Redder

3. Atmospheric conditions filter sunlight (see Figure 6.7).
4. Other types of light source with different colour temperatures are present, strong enough to influence results.

Colour-temperature meters

If you always shoot colour in your own studio, with your own lighting and other known conditions, most of the difficulties above can be avoided. However, where the lighting is uncertain – especially with indoor assignments on location – it is very helpful to check out colour temperature with a special meter. A typical colour temperature meter has three silicon photocells filtered to detect blue, green and red under an integrating diffuser (see Figure 6.11). The meter circuits compare the *relative* responses of the three colours to obtain a profile of the spectral content of your lighting. For example, tungsten lamps make the red cell give a stronger response than the blue one, whereas daylight produces an opposite effect.

Colour-temperature meters are always designed to make incident light readings from your subject position because, if pointed directly, they would measure the colour of the subject instead of the colour of light reaching it. Note, too, that within the meter's operating limits the *intensity* of your lighting is unimportant. The instrument's cells can still make their comparisons whether the illumination is a 60 W lamp or brilliant sunlight. Good professional meters can also read the colour of brief-duration sources such as flash. You point the meter with its white diffuser facing towards the camera, preferably from the subject position or at least where it receives the same lighting. Pressing a button gives a direct readout in kelvins. Alternatively, you pre-program some meters with the colour balance of the film you are using, whereupon the readout gives the value of any correction filter needed.

Fig. 6.11 Colour-temperature meter. Light is measured through the flat white diffusing disc near the top. Meter is presently programmed for daylight type film, and reads out reference for the colour compensation filter needed over camera lens or light source. Programming buttons allow you to select readout in kelvins, and to make settings for other types of film

'Warm up' filters (positive mired values)		'Cool down' filters (negative mired values)	
85B	+127	80A	−125
85	+112	80B	−110
85C	+86	80C	−81
81EF	+53	80D	−55
81C	+35	82C	−45
81B	+27	82B	−32
81A	+18	82A	−18
81	+10	82	−10
CC20M	+8	CC30G	−10
CC10M	+4	CC10G	−4

Fig. 6.12 The mired shift values of some Kodak filters

Colour-temperature meters are expensive but, together with a good range of filters, they offer insurance to any photographer aiming for lighting colour accuracy on location. They are also helpful to check for faults and changes in the studio. Remember that the meter is designed to read continuous spectrum light sources. It will give rogue readings of sources such as lasers or most sodium or mercury vapour lamps because they all emit lines or bands of wavelengths with gaps in between (Figure 6.8). This confuses the meter's sensors.

Mireds

Colour temperature meters may read out any correction filter you need in terms of a 'mired value' instead of a manufacturer's reference number. For example, instead of Kodak 81 the meter may display +10M. In fact, all filters for colour-correction work, whatever the brand, tend to have a mired rating as well as a number (see Figure 6.12). You would think it would be more straightforward to simply have filters marked as having, say, 50 K or 100 K colour-temperature effect upwards or downwards. The trouble is that the actual colour content of light sources does not change pro rata with colour temperature. So a filter which raises colour temperature by 100 K at 2800 K has a 130 K effect at 3200 K and a 300 K effect at 5000 K (see Figure 6.13). (This is because the colour-temperature scale is based on physical temperature rather than proportional colour content.)

To solve the filter calibration problem you convert kelvins into MIcro REciprocal Degrees by dividing the colour temperature into one million.

Mired value = 1 000 000 divided by colour temperature in K.

For example, the mired value of 2800 K household lamps is 357M, whereas type B colour film is designed for 3200 K (312M). A filter to balance the film to the lamp needs a mired shift value of −45, or as near this as possible. Used with photolamp lighting of 3400 K (294M) the same filter would change the colour content to 249M, which is 4000 K. Notice how the first change of 400 K has become a change of 600 K, in terms of the colour-temperature scale. A filter can therefore be given a mired shift value (+ or −) which holds good, irrespective of the colour temperature of the light source. Notice also that the higher the mired value, the lower the colour temperature. So 'warm-up' yellowish-orange filters have positive mired values and 'cool-down' bluish filters have negative ones.

Fig. 6.13 Why mireds are used. Left: the relative blue content of an (incandescent) light source does not increase proportionally with colour temperature. Therefore a bluish filter, which has a fixed upward influence on blue content, causes more change of kelvins when illumination is 5000 K than when 2800 K. It cannot be given a 'kelvin shift value'. Right: by converting kelvins into mireds you have a regular scale directly relating to blue content. A filter has the same 'mired shift value' at high and low positions on the scale

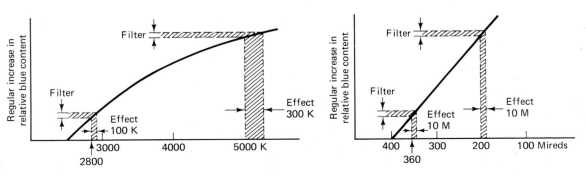

Colour temperature (K)	Mired value
6500	154
6300	159
6000	167
5800	172
5600	179
5400	185
4200	238
4000	250
3800	263
3400	294
3200	312
3000	333
2800	357
2600	385
2400	417
2200	454
1900	526

Fig. 6.14 Kelvin/mired conversion table

Another useful feature is that the effect of filters can easily be added together. If your meter, or simple calculation, shows that a +127M filter is needed to colour balance the light source to your film you can either use a Kodak 85B (+127M) or combine an 85 (+112) with an 81A (+18). If mireds are not already shown on your filter containers, calculate and mark them up. If you have a colour-temperature meter you can finally check any proposed filter by holding it over the sensing head and re-measuring your light source. The meter should show correct colour. Sometimes filters and colour-temperature meters quote 'decamireds' instead of mireds. One decamired equals 10 mireds.

Practical control of colour

Using filtration

Even if you do not have a colour-temperature meter, keep a selection of colour-balancing and (paler) colour-correcting filters in the camera case to cope with lighting or environments you know will give colour-cast results on your film. Have straight conversion filters like an 85B and 80A, plus some weak yellow or red colour correctors such as CC 05Y, 10Y, 20Y, etc. Stronger values can be made up by combining two of these gelatin filters.

Some colour-correcting filters will be needed to comply with batch variation instructions you find in boxes of colour sheet film. You will also want them to improve results when a job allows test shots to be exposed and processed first. Remember, when you are viewing reversal film test results with a cast you should look through colour-correcting filters of the complementary colour until image *midtones* look accurate. Then reshoot using a filter half this strength over the lens. For example, if a bluish slide appears corrected seen through a 10Y filter, use a 05Y over the lens. Make your assessment over a light-box containing colour-matching tubes. Do not use this technique on instant pictures when you intend to shoot finally on regular colour film. Instant-picture materials differ slightly in their response to filtration.

Another useful filter is an 81A or 81B to warm up the somewhat cold light delivered by some flashtubes, and for outdoors a pale-pink or CC 05R helps to compensate the bluish result that films such as Ektachrome give under sun-plus-blue-sky conditions. When shooting film from which prints will be made do not assume that negatives (or slides) can be fully colour corrected by filtration at the enlarging stage. Optimum quality comes from having correctly colour-balanced film originals in the first place.

The amount by which colour temperature can be in error before results show a noticeable colour cast varies with film type and subject. Latitude is as critical at about 10 mireds either way on tungsten-type slide film when the picture contains mostly pastel tints and the subject is easy to assess (for example, Caucasian skin tones). Daylight film and bold colours tend to be less noticeably affected by a slight cast. Greater errors of colour temperature in kelvins can be tolerated at the high (daylight) end of the scale than at lower (studio lamp) levels.

Avoid mixed lighting (light sources of two or more different colour temperatures illuminating the same scene) whenever you want

Fig. 6.15 Mixed colour temperature lighting. White plasterwork within this room is lit by a 3200 K tungsten lamp, while details beyond the bars are in daylight. It was shot on daylight type slide film (left), and on tungsten light film (right)

accurate subject colours. This is where filtering the camera lens is of little help. Instead, you can:

1. Filter one of the light sources to match the other. Some acetate sheeting is made for this purpose, so if, for example, you are shooting interiors mostly lit by tungsten lamps you can cover the outside of windows with orange 85B acetate to make the sunlit view match internal details. (Acetate is tougher and cheaper than gelatin filter, although optically too poor for lens use.) Alternatively, place blue 80A acetate filters over the tungsten lamps only, and then shoot on daylight film.
2. If no subject movement is involved and you are using a tripod, split the exposure into two halves. In the example above you can put black material outside the windows and shoot on tungsten light type film. Then remove the blackout, switch off the interior lights and give the second half of the exposure with an 85B orange filter over the lens.

Even on colour negative film it is extremely difficult, if not impossible, to correct a mixed lighting colour shot during colour printing. You may end up having to have an important job expensively airbrush-retouched.

Do not become obsessive about colour temperature/film balance matching. The whole point is to have *control* so that you can make *choices*. What exactly is it you are trying to show in your picture? The classic case here is the photographer who ruined a romantic evening landscape by shooting it through a blue filter because the setting sun was a lower colour temperature than regular daylight. A portrait with an orange cast may look a disaster in close-up or against a plain background giving no indication of environment. However, the same orangey face becomes acceptably natural when the picture also shows a fire in the hearth, a red shaded lamp and generally warm surroundings. Do not destroy the very atmosphere which attracted you in the first place.

Mixed lighting also allows one or two attention-grabbing special effects. For example, you might photograph a figure out of doors in daylight surroundings but in shadow, lit up locally by 3200 K tungsten lamps. When exposed onto tungsten light film this figure detail records correct colour but the surrounding landscape has a dream-like, strongly blue-biased appearance.

Working environment

It is essential that unwanted tinted light should not find its way to your subjects in the studio. Any windows should have shutters or

Fig. 6.16 Some lighting equipment and accessories. 1: studio flash head with a soft box fabric diffuser. 2: window light — fabric or opalized plastic over several flash tubes. 3: tungsten floodlight (internal bounce reflector). 4: portable diffuser hoop filled with white fabric, twists into figure of eight for packing into camera bag. 5: flash head or tungsten head fitted with metal snoot to limit light spread. 6: flash head bounced from white-lined umbrella to soften light. 7: 'flag' useful to shade backlighting from lens, or to shadow a part of subject. 8: ceiling-track slung tungsten spotlight, fitted with light-restricting barndoors

blinds so that when you are using unfiltered tungsten lighting there is no risk of mixing in any daylight. Internal finishes must be colourless – preferably neutral-grey floor and matt-white walls and ceiling. Even white paint yellows with age, and since you will often bounce light from these interior surfaces they will need regular redecoration. Beware of coloured background papers left hanging on the wall which easily create a cast on a nearby set through reflected spill light.

Other factors which upset the colour balance of your lighting are discoloured diffusing materials used over the front of soft boxes and window lights (Figure 6.16) as well as lamp reflectors and bounce boards. If necessary, hire a colour-temperature meter for the day to check out your environment and equipment from time to time. Remember, even your own clothes can create a local colourcast (for example, if you wear a highly coloured shirt when working with the camera close to your subject). Do not mix flash units from different manufacturers and avoid shooting with studio flash on low power but with its tungsten modelling lamp at full power (it may just add an orange cast). Where you have to work in an improvised studio, use barndoors, snoots and honeycombs to restrict your lighting to where it is really needed, instead of spread over possibly coloured surroundings.

When outdoors, remember the influence of surrounding greenery, coloured walls, posters, etc. on the colour balance of your lighting.

This is where folding white reflectors are so useful to 'clean up' the light as much as to reduce contrast. Electronic flash and daylight have the same colour temperature in theory, but in practice the flash maintains a steady colour temperature while daylight varies according to time and weather conditions. So although using fill-in flash may produce matched colour around noon in direct sunlight, at other times the flash may look colder than the ambient lighting. A warm-up filter over the flash head is the answer. Some photographers position a small square of orange filter over the centre part of the flash head just to warm the colour slightly. It is best to use a colour-temperature meter to forecast what filtration to use when your subject matter is critical.

Guidelines for lighting

Aim to be able to create any chosen lighting effect, no matter whether the light source be tungsten studio lighting, flash, daylight or some form of existing artificial light. With *all* these sources the following six guidelines apply:

1. *Lighting quality* (hard or soft) is controlled by the size of the light source relative to its distance from your subject. A large, relatively close-diffused source always gives softest shadow shapes; a compact, distant direct source gives the most hard-edged shadows.
2. *Direction* of shadows and position of highlights in the picture is controlled by the height and direction of your light source relative to the subject and the viewpoint chosen for the camera.
3. *Contrast* or brightness range of the picture you present to the lens is the combined result of your highlights-to-shadows lighting ratio and the subject's own reflectance range, discussed on page 110. Brightness range is best controlled by the amount of 'fill' light you can introduce into the shadows.
4. *Evenness* depends on the relative distances of the nearest and the furthest parts of your subject from the light source. Evenness improves with a more distant and softer light.
5. *Colour content* is controlled by your type of light source and any colouring influences (filters, reflector surfaces, etc.) it meets on its path to the subject. With incandescent lights colour also alters with change of voltage.
6. *Intensity* depends on the light output and distance of your source, plus any light-absorbing material it may pass through or be reflected from before reaching your subject.

Unless you are after theatrical effects, the aim of most artificial lighting is to create a general sense of naturalness. After this, it should emphasize the form, shape and texture of your subject, wherever you decide these features are important and relevant. Third, it may contribute to the 'atmosphere' of the shot through colour, softness/harshness, etc. When aiming for naturalness in the studio, remember the features of typical daylight conditions – light coming predominantly from one light source, directed from above rather than below your line of sight. There is always *some* light present in shadows.

All this means that if you switch on a spotlight in a darkened studio you will not simulate direct sunlight. Your lighting is more like moonlight on a clear night or the light astronauts experience in space, because nothing reaches your subject from the rest of the 'sky'. Any subject under a single hard light will need some shadow fill from reflectors (large and distant or smaller but close) to begin to look like natural sunlight. You can help the situation by simulating hazy daylight, enlarging the source itself perhaps by changing from spotlight to a soft box or window light, or just bouncing your spotlights off a large area of white wall or ceiling. Softened light has many advantages. It gives more gentle, subtle modelling of shapes; it avoids conflicting shadows in pictures containing a complex mixture of objects; and it reduces contrast and unevenness.

Of course, there are many situations where one light (even a soft source) cannot adequately model subjects with complex multi-plane forms or illuminate and separate foreground, mid-distance and background. For example, the subject, as lit by one source, may seem to disappear into a black abyss. Here your second light source

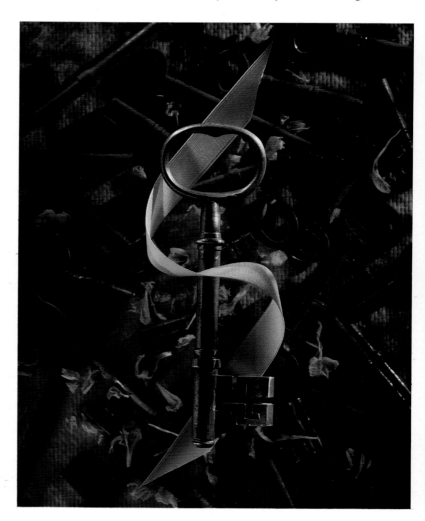

Fig. 6.17 A multilayer studio subject (the key and ribbon are on glass) which needs several light sources. Tim Imrie used three tungsten spotlights. One was tightly directed on the top key from the top right. Another side lit the keys below, and the third was diffused and amber filtered to fill in the shadow side from bottom right

can be put to work to brighten or accent the background from a position to one side or below. Another separation technique is to backlight the main subject from above and behind, to give some mild rim-lighting. Here you need a barndoor or flag between light and camera (Figure 6.16) to shade the lens from flare. Try to avoid this effect looking unnaturally like a second sun.

Complex subjects such as furniture or machinery, with many planes or facets to be shown, often need a second light. Do not have both sources at equal heights, equal angles to the camera or equally bright. Symmetry in lighting is seldom a virtue unless you are copying. Try to make one (or both) of the units a soft source. Pick height and direction to make every subject surface and plane in the picture a different intensity, and remember that it often helps to create depth and distance if front surfaces are darker than top or sides. You may need your second light source simply to fill shadows to a level not possible with reflectors just bouncing back some main light. In this case, the extra light needs to be soft and shadowless, perhaps diffused or wholly bounced. The skill is in deciding just how much fill is appropriate to the subject and the mood you want to create as well as fulfilling the film's technical requirements.

Third or fourth lights may be necessary to tackle some of these functions in difficult situations, but, all the time, try to make *one* source predominate (the one which gives the main shadows). Every additional source must have a clear role or it will only complicate matters. Good, professional lighting often has an incredibly simple look.

Combining flash and continuous light

Various kinds of interesting lighting possibilities occur when you combine flash with existing light. Be sure that the flash and the other light source match in colour temperature unless you want special

Fig. 6.18 Never overdo fill-in flash. For natural effects it pays to underexpose the flash by at least two stops, diffusing it or bouncing it to give soft light directed mostly from the camera. The camera settings here remained 1/30 second at *f*/16. In the far right version flash diffused with tracing paper was used at one-quarter correct power for this aperture.

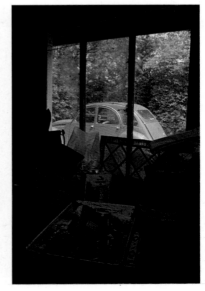

Fig. 6.19 In this series different intensities of fill-in flash were combined with different camera settings to maintain the same flash exposure. Unlike Figure 6.18, this makes a sunlit environment change appearance from natural daylight through to a night scene.
A: one-eighth full flash output, 1/60 second *f*/8. B: half full output, 1/125 second *f*/11. C: full flash output, 1/250 second *f*/11. D: flash distance halved, 1/500 second, *f*/16. (Camera had a bladed front shutter suitable for flash at all speed settings)

effects. For example, you can orange filter the flash to match tungsten. It is best to work with a camera which has a shutter offering a wide range of speeds for use with flash. Some cameras with dedicated flashguns have automatic facilities you can select for techniques such as fill-in flash. However, there is more scope if you have your flashgun set to manual, and, when using a camera offering a range of exposure modes, set this to manual as well. Then experiment with the following routines.

Fill-in flash

The function of fill-in flash is to reduce the lighting ratio by adding illumination to the shadows formed by existing light, so you need the flashgun mounted on the camera, and preferably diffused. Work as follows:

1. Measure exposure from midtone parts of the subject lit directly by existing light (use a grey card if possible). Take the reading for a

A
◄
B
►

C
◄
D
►

shutter speed at or longer than the flash-synchronization speed. This might, for example, work out at 1/60 second at $f/11$.

2. On the flashgun set an ISO number (arithmetic) four times your film's true ISO rating. Read off the flash-to-subject distance for $f/11$ or calculate it from the gun's Guide Number.
3. Shoot at this distance to get a flash:existing light ratio of 1:4.

If the distance is too far to be practical, turn down the flash to half power *or* fit a flash neutral-density filter or diffuser which halves the illumination. Then come about one third closer to your subject. If, on the other hand, the distance is impractically close, change to 1/125 second at $f/8$ (provided 1/125 is within synchronization range). Then you can move back until about one and a half times as far from the subject, keeping the flash at its original power.

Use similar manoeuvres to work at a smaller or larger aperture when depth of field is important. A powerful flashgun with output control giving 1, 1/2, 1/4, 1/8 and 1/16 of full power is ideal for fill-in flash technique. Whenever possible, bracket your results with variations of flash power, and if in doubt always *under-* rather than *over*fill.

Overlaid mixture of sharpness and blur

This is a combination of a relatively long exposure time, while you move the camera, and movement-freezing flash. Results (Figure 6.20, for example) show near parts of the scene sharpest, with background highlights streaked, giving an impression of action. The existing light should not be too bright, especially on the foreground. If necessary, work in an area of shade. Have your flashgun on the camera.

1. Load slow film.
2. Set a slow shutter speed, somewhere between 1/15 and 1/2 second.
3. Take a general existing light reading and set the aperture indicated.
4. Set your flash power so that it gives correct exposure at this aperture for the distance between flashgun and the nearest part of the main subject.
5. When you shoot, purposely pan, rotate or jog. Sometimes you have to fit a neutral-density lens filter to avoid overexposing in day-light and use a more powerful flashgun to keep flash exposure correct.

Most cameras fire the flash when the shutter first opens, so if you are panning the scene blur lines may extend into the 'leading edge' of the flash-frozen detail. In some instances your subject seems to be hurtling backwards. If your camera shutter offers 'second blind sync', opt for this mode, and the flash will fire just before the end of exposure, which avoids the problem.

Do not overlook the value of flash just to help 'sharpen up' a fairly long exposure you are forced to hand-hold. For example, in dim lighting conditions you may have to set a 1/15 or 1/8 second shutter speed to record surroundings by ambient light and preserve a naturalistic effect. This makes sharpness a gamble, however steady your hands may be, but by the addition of some (underexposed) flash from the camera you ensure that nearest objects at least are exposed at 1/1000 second or less. At worst, they will record as a mixture of sharpness and blur which is often visually acceptable.

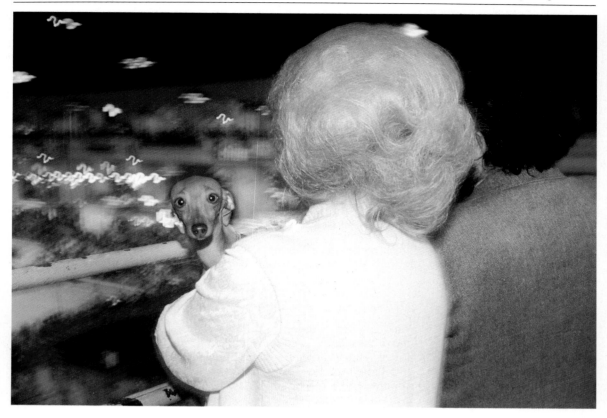

Fig. 6.20 A mixture of (camera) movement blur and sharp foreground detail frozen by flash adds an unreal element to this picture by Andrew Heaps. For results like this use about ½ second shutter speed. See page 123

Foreground objects 'shadow' scene detail behind

This surreal effect images all detail sharply, but moving objects in the foreground seem to cast a shadow on the background (landscape, for example). The result is like a three-dimensional object in front of a two-dimensional billboard or stage scenery. Pick a scene in which the general level of illumination is again low – preferably with the ambient light making the background area brighter than the main (foreground) subject, even to the extent of semi-silhouette.

1. Load slow film.
2. Set the shutter for around 1/8, 1/15 or 1/30 second, depending on subject speed. The more the subject's image shifts during exposure, the larger (but less dark) the shadow formed.
3. Take a general existing light-reading of the background area only and set an aperture which will underexpose this by one stop.
4. Set your flash output, or filter or diffuse the head, to give correct flash exposure for your main subject distance at this aperture.
5. Shoot with the camera static while the subject moves. The 'shadow' forms where the underlit moving subject blocks out background detail while the shutter remains open. As before, the shadow tends to appear *ahead* of the subject's direction unless you use second blind sync or arrange for the action to take place backwards.

Fig. 6.21 Left: shot in existing, overcast daylight, 1/60 second at *f*/8. Right: same daylight but shot with a flashgun held two metres to the right of urn; 1/60 second at *f*/16, the correct aperture for this flash outdoors

Flash as 'sunlight'

Flash here is used to add the appearance of hard, directional sunlight when your actual ambient subject lighting is excessively flat and dull. You need a powerful flashgun connected to the camera by a long lead.

1. Set the shutter to a speed suitable for flash.
2. Take a general exposure reading of the subject, then stop down two settings beyond the *f*-number shown for your shutter speed.
3. Position your undiffused flashgun high and about 45° to your subject, at the correct distance from it for the *f*-number in use. Think carefully about where to place the flashgun (have it held by an assistant or set up on a tripod), because having it too low gives an impression of light at sunset. Do not attempt to 'sunlight' large areas either – this technique suits portraits, architectural detail, carvings, etc. Also, avoid having the flash so close to your subject that its light is uneven and no longer looks natural. If necessary, increase the distance and turn up the power.

With all these flash-plus-other-lighting routines remember that when your flashgun is used outdoors its effective Guide Number (subject distance × *f*-number) becomes less than the figure printed on the gun. This is because published guide numbers assume that you are working in an average domestic interior surrounded by 'average' reflective ceiling, walls, etc. Outdoors, the light that these surfaces would return to the subject is lost. Try working with a Guide Number about two thirds normal as a basis for your own tests.

Invisible (infra-red) flash

If you filter your light source so that only infra-red wavelengths reach the subject you can record the image on infra-red-sensitive film, but no one around at the time will see any illumination or imagine that pictures are being taken. Electronic flash units, like tungsten lamps, deliver a good proportion of infra-red radiation along with visible light. The easiest way to work is with flash on the camera. Tape a visually opaque, infra-red-passing filter such as a Kodak 87 tightly over the window of the flashgun so that no visible light can escape. Use black and white infra-red film (see page 78). As for exposure, try using a Guide Number *half* what it would be if you had no filter and used regular ISO 100/21° film.

If you want to work in complete darkness, position and clamp the camera and pre-focus the lens in normal lighting first. Alternatively,

IR-only passing filter

IR autofocus pulse

Fig. 6.22 Fitting a black-looking, IR-passing filter over the flash window allows you to take pictures without the flash seeming to fire. The flash unit may also have an IR pre-pulse unit for autofocusing

Fig. 6.23 Camera shot from the hip, using infra-red filtered flash on IR film. The flash could not be seen going off, and the subject had no idea she had been photographed. An exposure time of 1/15 second also picked up brightest ambient lighting in the background

use an autofocus camera and flashgun which sends out a weak pulse of infra-red from a separate window just prior to the flash, allowing the autofocus mechanism to focus whatever is currently centre frame. In practice, you can often shoot under dim half-light which is sufficient to focus and frame up (but too dark for people to realize that you are actually taking pictures). If there is a lot of ambient light around you could also fit an 87 filter over the lens. This will then absorb most of the ambient lighting but pass the flash (already filtered and invisible). However, since you can no longer see through the lens of a SLR camera it is easier to work with a direct viewfinder camera instead. Infra-red flash results have the same 'unearthly' appearance – pallid face, dark eyes – of infra-red portraits in daylight (see page 80).

Fluorescent (ultra-violet) photography

Certain materials fluoresce and 'glow' in the dark with white or coloured visible light when they are radiated with (invisible) ultra-violet wavelengths. Plastic jewellery, dayglow inks or poster paper, shirts of manmade fabrics, even washing-up liquid and teeth all glow to a greater or lesser extent. Most blue-rich light sources emit ultra-violet, including sunlight, mercury vapour ultra-violet health lamps and purple-dyed window display spotlamps. As Figure 6.24 shows, the light source should include a filter which allows ultra-violet but very little visible light to reach your subject. All films are sensitive to

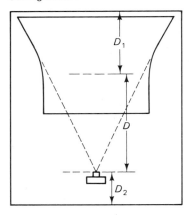

Fig. 6.24 Some materials glow with visible light when illuminated by (invisible) ultra-violet radiation. But to record what you see you must filter out the reflected UV which would otherwise record on colour film too. See Figure 6.34

Fig. 6.25 Planning a studio space. For useful workspace D_1 plus D_2 should equal D, which is lens-to-subject distance. Plan as drawn is for 46° angle of view lens

Fig. 6.26 An office divided from the studio by large folding doors (left) allows you to use the whole area for large sets (right)

nearest ultra-violet wavelengths, so you must stop the ultra-violet itself reaching the film while letting through the visible light from the fluorescing subject. This means filtering your lens with a (clear-looking) ultra-violet absorbing filter such as a Kodak 1A.

It is best to shoot fluorescing colours on daylight-type colour film, working in a blacked-out studio with your subject lit by one or more ultra-violet health lamps or spots. These units are so heavily filtered that they only give out a dim blue glow plus a great deal of ultra-violet you cannot see. Fluorescent parts of your subject now glow brightly, and, provided that there is an ultra-violet absorber over the lens, the film will record exactly what you see. (Without the filter the subject records as if doused with blue light, blotting out most colours.) Often you need to add a little general visible light, or the fluorescent parts float in a sea of black. So introduce a low level of daylight from the side or rear, perhaps by partly opening a window blind and diffusing incoming light. Judge correct balance by eye. Measure exposure from the fluorescing parts using regular reading techniques with your camera or hand meter. Avoid staring directly at any UV lamp unless your eyes are protected with UV-absorbing goggles.

Planning a studio

The studio itself

You may not need your own studio if you work in a large town or city. The chances are that you can hire a fully equipped photographic studio by the hour or day as required for jobs, passing on the cost to the client. Again, your kind of photography may be so location based – travel, architecture, photojournalism, sport, etc. – that you can just work out of a darkroom and office. For most photographers, however, a studio forms a base in which to experiment, accumulate props, have time to build sets you can photograph and check before dismantling, and generally work on into the night if necessary. Your studio represents privacy and technical convenience, and although at other times it might have to revert to barn, garage or even sleeping quarters, no professional photographer should really be without one.

Studios are hardly ever too big, and it is probably true that sets expand to fill, or exceed, whatever space is available. Shape and height are as important as size, and a simple squareish/rectangular floor plan is much more flexible than a room with additional corners and alcoves (see Figure 6.25). To decide size, think of the largest subject you are likely to tackle and the longest camera lens focal length you would want to use on it. Then the distance you will need

Fig. 6.27 In a studio with a tall ceiling some flash-heads and power packs can be suspended from track. The lower beams here supporting lamps can be pulled along the cross-beams above. Suspension gear is spring counterbalanced, making lamp-heads effectively weightless. Packs and monoheads are triggered by IR pulse from camera

between subject and lens will be the height of the subject divided by the negative height, multiplied by focal length. For example, a full-length figure with ample space top and bottom might be 2.5 metres high. Shooting with a 6 × 7 cm camera and 90 mm lens you need to be 3.2 metres away, or with a 165 mm lens the distance is 5.9 metres. On top of this, you must add space to work behind the camera, plus sufficient room behind the subject for a separately lit backdrop, back-lighting, etc.

The area you can light from different distances can be worked out from polar curves published for lamps or lighting units fitted with a reflector. A polar diagram such as Figure 6.28 plots the spread of light from the source, so you can relate this to a plan or scale model of your proposed studio.

Fig. 6.28 Polar curves for two lighting units maps intensity and distribution. Solid line shows illumination from a floodlight; broken line from a typical spotlight. (The symmetrical form of most lamps and reflectors means that often only the left or right half of a polar diagram need be shown)

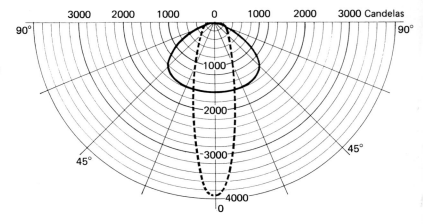

Most still-photography lighting units are supported and moved around on rolling floor stands, but if the ceiling is high enough (over 3 metres) you have the option of fitting ceiling track to carry tungsten or flash units, see Figure 6.27. Rigging some of the lighting overhead gives you more floor space and fewer cables to walk over, but make sure that units track easily between a wide range of positions, or your lighting may start to become stereotyped.

A good studio should have at least one window of generous height and width to allow you to work in daylight. Organize shutters or a blind to reduce window size and so produce harder lighting quality at will. You must also be able to black-out the studio completely to avoid mixed lighting. Consider access too, especially if you expect to move large objects, lighting booms, backgrounds, etc. in and out of the studio. Floor-to-ceiling double or folding doors are best here, ideally leading directly outside or into a corridor free of awkward corners or stairs.

Make sure that studio electricity supplies are ample to power all the lighting you can plug in at one time. Have plenty of sockets distributed around the studio, mostly in corners and alcoves, where they are out of the way of sets and backgrounds. Surface finishes must be matt-white or black, with the floor perhaps neutral grey. Floors should be flat, even and solid enough not to vibrate if someone is moving about during a time exposure.

Fig. 6.29 Floor-standing tungsten lighting units. A: boom with fabric soft-light head. B: tungsten halogen hard light (lamp can be wide or narrow beam focused in reflector). C: tungsten flood using folding umbrella. D: fold-open twin lamp unit with own reflector board. E: small flood designed to clip onto other units, tops of doors etc. B–E are lightweight and highly portable. All fabrics are suitably heat-resistant. See also Figure 6.16

Fig. 6.30 The effects of decreasing or increasing the voltage applied to a tungsten lamp. Reducing the supply greatly extends life but reduces colour temperature; also fewer lumens of light are produced per watt consumed, and illumination dims

Fig. 6.31 Basic schematic layout of an electronic flash fitted with modelling lamp. Electricity from normal household supply builds up a charge in capacitors (C). A second circuit powers modelling light M close to the flash tube. A third circuit runs through step-down transformer (T) and contacts in your camera shutter or other triggering device to a wire passed around the outside of the flash tube (F). When this 10–12 V circuit is closed it lowers the resistance of gas in the tube, allowing the capacitors to discharge through it with a brilliant flash. At no time does high voltage pass through the triggering circuit

Tungsten lighting

Most tungsten lighting units used in the studio contain tungsten halogen lamps, which are more efficient, compact and consistent than conventional filament types. Where the unit is designed to give soft-quality lighting the illumination is spread into a larger area source by being directed into a reflector or through a diffuser (Figure 6.29). Lamps vary in size and shape, cap type, working voltage, wattage and the colour temperature they give out at correct voltage. You can buy most photographic types in a choice of either 3200 K or 3400 K (the latter colour temperature is standard for movie film). Avoid mixing up these two. The visual difference is slight, but 3400 K gives a cold cast on still-photography tungsten-light colour films. You can also buy lower-output lamps blue tinted to give daylight matching colour temperature, useful for daylight fill-in. Photographic lamps are quite expensive, and for black and white work you can greatly extend their life by reducing voltage by, say, 10% through a resistor or transformer. However, do not try doing this for colour photography – underrun lamps also drop in colour temperature (Figure 6.30).

The main advantage of tungsten lighting over flash is that it is easy to see exactly what effects you are going to get. The precise position and quality of a shadow or highlight and the balance of brightness between one source and another are easily checked by eye. Having continuous light makes it easier to take subject-brightness range exposure readings, and you have the option to show movement through a controlled degree of blur. You can even move a light unit during exposure to spread and soften its lighting effect (see *Basic Photography*).

Studio flash

Flash illumination, on the other hand, creates little heat or continuous glare (big advantages for portraiture). The colour temperature of the flash is consistent, even when the unit is turned down to fractional power or where there are minor supply voltage fluctuations. This is because the tube is powered by a pulse from storage capacitors and only indirectly from the supply. Flash, of course, freezes camera shake or subject movement, giving you much greater freedom to move around the studio. Also, provided that each flash head has a tungsten modelling lamp matching the flash tube in size and position you can preview the direction and evenness of your lighting. Accuracy is greatest with soft light heads.

Most popular studio units give a flash of 5500 K or 5600 K colour temperature. This is less blue than small hand-flash units, but tests may show that it is still advisable to use a very weak warm-up filter for some brands of daylight slide film. Like any other lighting unit, colour temperature may also differ according to the reflector, diffuser or other accessories you may use with the head. A colour-temperature meter (page 114) will check this out for you. Do not mix different brands of flash in the same studio.

The duration of studio flash is typically 1/500–1/1000 second, but this changes according to the proportion of power you select to be discharged and whether this is split up between a number of heads. The same studio unit may deliver a 1/400 second flash at full power using one head or 1/3000 second at fractional power with three heads

Fig. 6.32 Electronic flash heads with separate or integral powerpacks. Left: large window light powered by 5000 W s powerpack. Several other types of heads can be plugged into same unit. Centre: 500 W s monobloc unit. The powerpack is directly behind the reflector. Right: 2000 W s separate powerpack flash. All flash heads contain modelling lamps

plugged in. Remember this when shooting fast-moving subjects (pouring liquids, dance, moving mechanisms, etc.). The more your flash unit is turned down, the more 'frozen' the subject will record. Self-quenching portable flashguns give you an even wider range of flash durations, as short as 1/40 000 second at close range.

In general, studio flash is designed in two forms, an all-in-one monobloc unit or a powerpack with separate plug-in heads (Figure 6.32). Monoblocs are cheaper and lighter but less powerful. By combining powerpack and flash head you have a compact single unit you can mount onto a floor stand or track and plug into the electricity supply just like a tungsten lamp. Separate powerpack units accept a variety of heads which can include ring flash, strip tubes or even a front-projection unit (Figure 6.33). These give a wider range of lighting than is possible by simply adapting a monobloc via clip-on reflectors and diffuser units. The power unit rests on the floor forming a weighty base to one of the flash heads or it hangs from track for you to adjust controls, the heads being located freely on the track like the tentacles of an octopus.

The output of a flash unit is usually quoted in watt seconds (or the older equivalent 'joules'), but this refers to the maximum energy the power unit gives out through the tube, ignoring what type of head and reflector are fitted. So it is more practical to know exactly what exposure Guide Number the equipment provides. International practice here is for the Guide Number quoted in sales literature to mean use of ISO 100/21° film and the head fitted with a reflector giving about 65° spread (light measured at 2 metres). Modelling lights are often quite high intensity – helpful to see the effect when lighting

Fig. 6.33 Front-projection flash unit. Flash unit (F) illuminates transparency (T) which is imaged by a projector lens and reflected off 45° one-way mirror towards special screen (S). Beaded screen material is highly directional, reflects light back along same path through mirror to camera lens. The less reflective figure appears in silhouette in front of brilliant image of background detail. You illuminate the figure separately, from an angle. Any light reaching the screen from this flash is reflected back to source, so does not wash out background

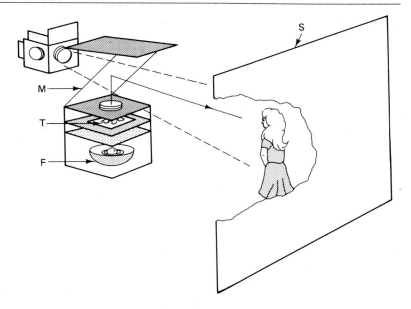

is bounced or heavily diffused. This means that you often have a blower built into the head to prevent overheating. Powerful modelling lamps can be dimmed (manually or automatically) pro rata to flash output. You can also photograph just using the modelling lamps alone as continuous light sources. However, if you shoot colour in this way all lamps must be running at the same colour temperature, matching the colour balance of your film.

If you do not have a flash meter a studio flash with modelling light can be read with an ordinary (non-flash) exposure meter or camera TTL system. First, discover the illumination relationship between lamp and flash, as follows:

1. Light a subject in the normal way using, say, two flash heads set to equal power and having matching modelling lights.
2. Take a meter reading, and note down the shutter speed/aperture combination it gives.
3. Take a series of flash exposures bracketed at different-guessed *f*-numbers and check results to see which one was correct. Now check back to see what shutter speed your meter gave for this *f*-number. Forget that it refers to the shutter – just remember it as your 'datum mark' for flash readings. Next time you shoot with this flash equipment, repeat stage (2) but read off your aperture for flash as the *f*-number shown opposite the (shutter speed) datum mark.

Even with a fairly low power unit, remember that you can shoot still lifes, room interiors and other non-moving subjects with a *series* of flashes, provided the camera is on a stand. A second flash (after pausing for recharge) doubles the light, and so allows an extra stop depth of field. A total of four flashes allows you to close the aperture two stops, and so on. Another reason for repeat flashing is to give the effect of several light sources by moving the unit between flashes. This way you can light a long room from various hidden flash positions. However, if you are now illuminating different areas with

Fig. 6.34 Fluorescent product label lit up by a UV lamp from front left. Weak tungsten light from the rear picks out shapes, gives a warm cast on daylight film. See pages 126–127

Fig. 6.35 Microflash shot of rifle bullet passing through a balloon at about Mach 1.4 (450 m/s). Taken in a darkened studio with the camera shutter locked open and flashes triggered by microphone and delay system. (Dr Gary S. Settles and Stephen S. McIntyre/ Science Photo Library)

each flash the exposure must be based on the average distance between flash unit and subject for any *one* flash.

Microflash

Occasionally you need to produce 'frozen' pictures of very fast-moving images. Flying insects in close-up, sprays of water droplets, breakages, collisions, even small explosions are all likely to be beyond the capabilities of normal flash. You can then hire or buy a microsecond flash unit, as used for scientific recording work. A microflash will give a flash lasting one millionth of a second. At this duration its photographic effect is much weaker than normal studio flash, especially when you add the influence of (short-duration) reciprocity failure on the film. So expect to have the flash quite close, and use fast film if you must also stop well down. For critically timed action such as breakages, work in a darkened studio with the shutter open – then use a sound or infra-red beam-breaking trigger (page 54) to make your subject fire the flash. Unfortunately, microflash shots of some rapid actions give you all the detail but results look too unnatural. So you can add in longer-duration regular studio flash to contribute some blur. Fire both units together either by subject trigger or shutter.

Studio lighting accessories

Each manufacturer of tungsten or flash lighting units provides a supporting cast of interchangeable accessories. These include lighting supports (wheeled or folding stands, clamps, booms) and all kinds of beam shapers and diffusers which you attach over the front of the head. Beam shapers mean wide- or narrow-angled conical reflectors, snoots, honeycomb grids, barndoors and flags, all of which help you to restrict light to where it is needed. Clipover diffusers, soft boxes and umbrellas are all devices for turning compact, hard light sources into large soft ones, albeit with loss of intensity.

Fig. 6.36 Fibre-optic attachment fits over front of studio flash head, piping heatless flash or tungsten light to any small delicate subject (S)

You can buy accessory spotlight optics to fit over the front of a flash head and its modelling light. This hardens up the light and gives a controlled beam like any tungsten-focusing spotlight. Another accessory, useful for still lifes, is a fibre-optic attachment (Figure 6.36) which 'pipes' light from a flash tube or low-power tungsten lamp into some difficult location (to pick out some key area, for example). This way you can duct light into an architect's scale model building or introduce it as a light source into a tank of water. The flexible, stranded glass fibres duct the light without heat, very helpful for delicate subjects such as flowers and some foods. However, fibre optics must be designed for photographic lighting purposes. Some fibre systems green-tint the light they are ducting.

Choosing lighting equipment

Really, you need both tungsten and flash equipment, for each of their particular lighting advantages. Opinions vary, but still photographers equip their studios primarily with flash, keeping some modest power tungsten units for special situations (where movement must be shown, for example). (Tungsten light is also essential for video movie work in the studio.) You should find lamps of 500–1000 W amply bright for still photography, unless you are lighting cars or huge room sets. Overpowered lights create problems of both heat and space. Remember, too, that it is easier to soften a compact, hard-quality light unit (by bouncing or fitting diffusing attachments) than to harden up a broad, soft-quality lighting source.

If you are equipping with flash make sure that the system you are buying into is sufficiently versatile to give a wide range of lighting. Check the range of accessories. Consider an infra-red or photocell slave triggering unit as essential, as well as an umbrella or soft box. Be certain that spares such as modelling lamps are easily available, especially if equipment is foreign. Flash units of monobloc design are handiest to use on location as well as in the studio, but separate powerpack systems are more powerful and often more convenient when several heads are wanted. They also accept a wider range of flash head types and accessories.

As for power, a pair of 500 W second monoblocs may be sufficient for 35 mm work at wide apertures, but if you are shooting large format the extra stopping-down needed may justify a system giving 5000 W second or more, at about ten times the price. Flash output reduction in percentage steps is a worthwhile feature, especially for exposure bracketing and to allow some choice of flash duration. Carefully compare flash recycling time (the period power storage capacitors need to fully recharge for the next shot). Studio flash recycles faster than most battery flashguns, but a 5000 W second unit can still take 5 seconds at maximum power. This is insignificant for a still life, but a long delay for action subjects. Some lower output units are designed to recycle in 0.3 second, which means you can work them with a motor-drive camera or create strobe-type multi-image effects.

Also think about the general styling and visual design of your chosen system if it is to be used in public – after all, it is a part of your professional image. Studio electronic flash is an expensive investment and you need to thoroughly assess what you intend to buy. The best way to do this is to hire a set of the proposed equipment and try it out on typical subjects under your own working conditions.

Location lighting equipment

Here your choice naturally depends on whether a household type electricity supply is available. Even if it is not, you may be able to carry in the back of the car a small trolley-mounted generator. This can deliver a steady 1 kW or so of power – not much use for tungsten lighting units but enough to power a pair of regular monobloc 500 W second studio flashes with modelling lamps. Some flash units are specially designed as portable kits, and will operate through appropriate power converters from household/generator supply, your car battery (see Figure 6.37) or NiCad batteries. Using studio type flash on location in this way allows you to light subjects even in the middle of a field or on the beach.

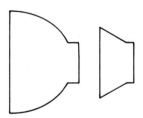

Fig. 6.37 Compact location flash kit. Main 250 W/s flash unit (F) contains circular flash tube, modelling lamp, and power level controls. Power converter (P) is used with regular household electricity supply. Alternatively unit B allows supply from car battery, via cigar lighter socket or through battery clips

There is a wide range of lightweight, open-fronted quartz-iodine tungsten lamp units. Typically, output ranges from 500 to 1500 W. Most are designed for video-movie work and produce hard light and much heat. They are best used bounced. By adding a heat-resistant blue filter you can convert colour temperature to 5500 K – useful when you are supplementing daylight.

Battery-powered units

One or two battery-powered tungsten lamp 'sun guns' are made primarily for video news gathering. They give hard light, which can be somewhat softened with a small clip-on diffuser. Each gun is powered from a battery belt or hip-slung accumulator and typically operates for about 20 minutes per charge. Recharging them takes 6–8 hours. Sun guns are not very practical for still photography when there is such a range of sophisticated flashguns available instead.

Battery-powered hand flash differs from studio flash in several important practical features – it is self-contained, offers no modelling

Summary: Lighting control

● Lighting must have the right visual effect on your subject, but at the same time anticipate changes that will occur when the picture is recorded onto film. Main points to avoid are: excess contrast; unnatural overlighting; unwanted colour casts; lighting which is technically correct but atmospherically wrong for your theme.

● Subject contrast = subject reflectance range × lighting ratio. The less the reflectance range, the higher your lighting ratio can be. Guide total subject contrast limits for detail in both shadows and highlights is about 1:128 (black and white); 1:32 (reversal films); also 1:32 for colour negatives, but 1:8 where colour is critical throughout. The best way to control lighting contrast is through different strengths of fill-light.

● The higher the colour temperature (degrees Absolute, in kelvins), the greater the blue wavelengths, the less red wavelengths. However, non-incandescent sources may not give out a continuous spectrum and, at best, have only a colour temperature equivalent. Films are mostly balanced for 3200 K or 5500 K. Lighting colour changes occur with wrong lamp supply voltage; non-neutral reflectors/diffusers, or coloured surroundings; atmospheric conditions/time of day; and when different colour temperature sources are mixed.

● A colour-temperature meter measures your light source for the *proportions* of red, green or blue wavelengths present, reads out in kelvins or mireds (micro reciprocal degrees). M = one million divided by K. Filter mired shift values (+ or −) remain constant whatever colour-temperature source they are used with. The effect of combining filters is shown by adding their mired values. A decamired is 10 mireds.

● Have conversion filters and colour-correction filters, and preferably a colour-temperature meter. When slide results show a cast, reshoot using a filter half the strength needed to correct slide midtones visually. Errors of 10 mireds can give noticeable casts. Aim to match lighting to film colour balance, even with neg/pos colour. If mixed lighting cannot be avoided, filter one source to match the other, or split your exposure and use a lens filter for one part as necessary. Have neutral surroundings and matched light sources in the studio; on location, white reflectors help to 'clean up' coloured environments, but do not be obsessive and destroy atmosphere.

● Basic principles of quality, direction, contrast, evenness and colour apply to your lighting, no matter what the source. Most lighting schemes should be simple and naturalistic.

● For combined uses of flash plus existing light set your camera and flash to manual. Control fill-in flash by exposing for existing light, then adding flash (on camera) at quarter correct power. Using flash with slow shutter speeds produces mixtures of sharpness and blur, depending whether camera or subject moves. For synthetic sunshine use correctly exposed flash from well-off camera and underexposed soft existing light. Remember, flash GN is reduced when working outdoors.

● Flash filtered to give out only infra-red forms an 'invisible' source to use with black and white infra-red film. Fluorescent materials which glow under ultra-violet light record on daylight colour film as they appear to the eye, provided you use a UV-absorbing filter.

● In planning a studio, consider shape, size, removable blackout, decoration, ventilation, electrics (placing of sockets and total loading), access from outside. Consider tungsten or flash units, either on floorstands or hung from track. Match up the colour temperature of all your tungsten sources – usually to 3200 K. In black and white work lamps can be underrun for economy.

● Studio flash, mostly monoblocs or power units with plug-in heads, works at 5500–5600 K. Typical flash duration is 1/500–1/1000 second at full power. Output is stated in W second, typically 500–6000. Unless otherwise stated, the Guide Number quoted is for ISO 100/21° film when using a standard reflector. Each flash (and modelling lamp) can be stepped through a range of power output ratios. Exposure is best read by flash meter, but you can measure the modelling light with an ordinary meter and calculate flash exposure from this. For freezing ultra-fast subjects hire a microflash.

● Aim to have both tungsten and flash studio equipment, with a range of accessories for beam shaping, diffusing and bouncing light. Fibre optics allow flash or tungsten light to be ducted into difficult areas and pick out local detail. Powerful flash outfits are far more costly than tungsten systems.

● Working on location, use lightweight QI lamps or portable studio units. If necessary, run them off a generator. When choosing a flashgun pick something having a Guide Number over 30, with manual mode and fractional power ratios and facility to slave at least one other head. Long-peak flash allows you free use of all focal plane shutter speeds but gives progressively less exposure at fast settings.

● Be safety-minded when handling lighting. Prevent tall units toppling, do not overload or damage cables or add items to lampheads which then overheat. Keep lighting and water apart, and resist the temptation to service your own studio flash – it may finish you off instead.

respectively. Remember that film manufacturers design most monochrome negative materials to be exposed on the lower part of the characteristic curve. If you can do this consistently the negative density range will 'fit' printing paper performance like two pieces of a jigsaw and give a full tone range print (see page 145).

6. *Developer and development.* In black and white neg/pos work your choice of film developer and amount of development can often be geared to suit imaging conditions. Increasing the development expands the tonal separation (contrast) of the negative, useful for compensating for low-contrast images. Extending development serves the opposite function for contrasty situations (see Zone System, page 149). Colour film processing is less pliable. Pushing or holding back slide film is acceptable for some compensation of under- or overexposure (altering ISO speed) but not good practice purely for contrast control, because of side effects on image colour balance. Also make sure that your processing solutions are in good condition, at the correct temperature and are properly agitated. Any safelights you are using must really be safe, and there must be no light leaks in your darkroom to give the slightest tone-degrading fog.

7. *Image manipulations after processing.* This includes chemical reduction or intensification of your film to improve a poor tone range. Less drastically, you can 'mask' an image by sandwiching it with a weak negative or positive version which reduces or increases the tone range before printing or (slide) duplicating (see page 160).

8. *Enlarger and enlarging technique.* The film illumination system in your enlarger influences final print tone range – from a harsh point-source through condenser systems to a fully diffused lamp-head for least contrasty results. Lens flare is an influence again here. When enlarging negatives it smudges shadows and spreads them into highlights. Minimize flare by keeping your enlarger lens and the inside surfaces of the enlarger clean, and do not allow light to spill through the rebate of the negative you are printing. On the other hand, you can purposely reduce the tone range of prints from excessively contrasty negatives by 'flashing' the paper to light (see page 166).

9. *Printing material and its development.* Surface finish mostly determines your print material's maximum black – poorest with matt, richest with glossy. Working in black and white, you have a choice of grade and also base tint (affects brightest attainable highlight). Black and white and some dye-bleach colour print materials also allow you choice of developer and the amount of development you give. It is vital to be accurate with print exposure and the developer timing and temperature. Using poor-quality or badly stored materials and chemicals gives prints with degraded tone values, and again there must be no sign of fogging from safelights or light leaks.

10. *Final viewing conditions.* Prints behind glass softly lit from the front will have blacks which look only grey and all dark tones degraded. For maximum richness of tones display a print free of glass on a wall lit obliquely by a spotlight, masked down tightly to illuminate the picture area only. Project slides in a 100% blacked-out room.

Fig. 7.3 The effect of printing paper on final tone range. The Record Rapid here has a glossy surface — all grades give richer blacks and therefore a wider overall density range than matt surface Portriga Rapid. If papers had tinted bases the bottom of these curves would flatten out at about 0.4 or greater, limiting range still further. Notice how contrast (slope of curve) varies. Grade 1 on Record Rapid is equivalent to between Grades 2 and 3 on Portriga

Fig. 7.4 The importance of fully developing printing paper. RC and fibre base materials react differently. RC papers develop quickly — most tones have built up after 20 seconds and maximum density is reached at about 60 seconds. Fibre paper images build up more slowly and progressively. Full density takes a further 30 seconds in this developer

If your pictures lack tonal quality it will almost certainly be due to lack of care at one or more of these stages. A combination of slight neglect at several points – perhaps erratic temperatures and a dirty enlarger lens – will insidiously undermine the excellence of all your results. Sometimes it is only when you compare your work against actual prints by masters in exhibitions that these deficiencies show up. Not every picture works best with a full, rich tone range, of course, but most do, and you must be able to achieve this when required.

Tone control theory

Some of the links in the chain just discussed are shown diagrammatically in Figure 7.5. This illustrates the contraction and expansion of tone values you can expect when a subject is imaged in the camera, turned into a black and white negative and then enlarged onto black and white bromide paper. Subject brightness range chosen here is 1 : 160 or just over seven stops – marginally in excess of the maximum recommended range for black and white when it is important to preserve all shadow-to-highlight detail. Dense blacks and tiny specular highlights are even further apart in value.

The light from the subject is put through a lens with a flare factor (subject range divided by brightness range of its image) of 2. This might be for a long focal length lens used outdoors, especially if fitted with a filter. A modern, multilayer coated normal lens in low-flare

Stops difference	= Ratio =	Difference on $\log_{10}$ scale
1	1:2	0.3
2	1:4	0.6
3	1:8	0.9
	1:10	1.0
4	1:16	1.2
5	1:32	1.5
6	1:64	1.8
	1:100	2.0
7	1:128	2.1
8	1:256	2.4
9	1:512	2.7

Fig. 7.7 Three alternative ways of expressing ranges (lighting, subject brightness, image density etc.). The log scale is most often used when exposure and density ranges are plotted as a characteristic curve performance graph

subject tones will be so compressed and slight that appearance is unnaturally grey and flat, even on hardest grade paper.

3. Gear your exposure and development technique to suit the characteristics of your enlarger and preferred surface printing paper. The penalty of having a negative with a density range way beyond what the paper will accept is bleached-out delicate highlight tones and lack of detail and tone separation in shadows. Both are bad news if your result is due to be reproduced on the printed page. It helps to have interchangeable heads for your enlarger, to allow both hard and soft forms of illumination. Using a condenser head, you can enlarge an 0.8 density range negative onto the same grade of paper as would be needed for a 1.05 range negative enlarged with diffuser head equipment. Remember that warm tone (chlorobromide) papers give better separated dark tones than regular bromide ones.

4. Over- and underexposed negatives will not fit any paper exactly. The 'damaged' end of the tone scale will need a different (usually harder) contrast grade than the other tones in your picture. However, it may be physically possible to use variable-contrast paper, shading and then printing back these areas with a higher-contrast filter.

5. Under laboratory conditions, computer programs based on data such as Figure 7.6 can be used to control image reproduction. The optimum level of film exposure, development, print material exposure and processing may all be calculated in advance. This is useful for jobs such as bulk printing of aero films and movies, mass printing of copy negatives and so on. As a practising photographer, you can seldom work in such an analytical way, but it is important to remember these links in the chain as warnings of where you must always take care if final pictures are to have the right tonal qualities.

Precision measurement of exposure

Accurate subject exposure reading is vital for tone control. As shown in *Basic Photography*, one centre-weighted measurement through the camera or a general reading made with a hand meter are adequate for average situations. However, readings of carefully chosen parts of the subject give you far greater information, although they take more time and knowledge to do. The main point to remember is that any one light measurement will give you camera settings which record the area read by the meter as a *mid-grey tone*.

A general reading mixes the light from dark, medium and bright items in the picture, taking greater account of large areas than small ones. The whole lot is scrambled on the theory that this integrates all subject values to grey. A centre-weighted system does the same thing but takes less account of corners and edges of the picture because important elements are assumed not to be composed there. A similar single-reading approach is to measure a mid-grey card held where it received the same light intensity as the subject. Kodak make 18% reflectance cards for this purpose (on the basis that 18% of incident light is reflected from an 'average' scene). Again, you can fit an incident-light diffuser attachment over a hand meter and make a

Fig. 7.8 Sensitivity patterns of different through-the-lens metering modes. Centre-weighted: concentrates about 60% of light-reading sensitivity over a large area, centre screen. Pattern is also designed to play down sky in landscapes. Partial, and spot: these give a smaller reading area that you must align with key element, then use exposure lock if this element is re-composed off-centre. Some SLR systems 'matrix' multi segments which read four or five parts of the screen at once, allowing contrast measurement with one reading. Bottom: spot-reading a large-format image using a probe that you can move to measure any part of the picture

SLR centre-weighted

SLR spot

SLR partial

Large-format spot

reading from the subject towards the camera. Results should work out the same as for the grey card technique.

For selective area readings, bring your general-reading camera or hand meter close to chosen parts of the subject. If this is impossible, measure nearer substitutes your eye judges an exact match. Best of

Fig. 7.9 Add-on exposure reading system for monorail viewcamera. You set ISO film rating and required aperture using dials on control box. Then align probe with chosen part of image (sensor facing lens) and insert darkslide to prevent light entering through back of focusing screen. Pressing button on external end of probe takes reading, and sets shutter speed on bladed shutter at front end of camera. Exposure here is 1/30 second at f/22

all, use a spot hand meter or a camera offering spot reading mode – both allow you to measure quite small parts of the subject, even from a shooting position some way back. Some large-format cameras have add-on meters which also make spot readings from any small selected part of the subject imaged on the focusing screen (see Figure 7.9).

Selective area reading means that you can pick the part of a scene which you want mid-grey in the final picture and base exposure purely on this. Alternatively, you can discover your subject's brightness range by measuring a diffuse highlight area such as clouds in a landscape, then measure the darkest part where you want detail to just record. Read off the difference in stops (for the same shutter speed). If this warns you the scene is beyond the range of your film (page 110) you can either:

1. Add some fill-in illumination to reduce the range, if practical;
2. Increase exposure and curtail development to avoid a negative with excessive contrast; or
3. Decide to sacrifice one end of the tone range (top or bottom) for the sake of recording all the rest. In this case, it is usually best to expose reversal materials to preserve highlights, even though you lose shadow detail. With neg/pos materials expose to just preserve shadow detail.

Having identified the top and bottom of the subject range you want to record, average their two readings and set exposure accordingly. Some of the small-format cameras that provide spot metering automatically average readings for you. As soon as the second measurement is taken, camera settings for midway between the two appear in the viewfinder display. Some cameras have so-called 'Highlight' and 'Shadow' modes of spot reading. Lining up important pale detail and pressing 'Highlight' makes whatever the spot is reading set an exposure typically one and a half stops more than a normal reading, so that in the final picture this area is sure to be paler than midtone. The 'Shadow' button has the opposite effect. Using one or the other you can 'peg' elements in your picture to particular tone values (although, with care, you can achieve the same result manually by using the exposure override control, for example).

Just how much over- or underexposure Highlight and Shadow controls give really needs to depend on the exposure latitude and type of film you have loaded. This information can be programmed by the checkerboard pattern printed on the cassette (see DX coding, page 76). Where it is not communicated in this way bear in mind that most 35 mm camera meter systems assume that you are shooting on negative material. (The great majority of films sold to amateurs are neg/pos colour.) This means that the circuit is 'tuned' to set sufficient exposure to preserve shadow detail. When you use reversal films such a setting can lose much-needed highlight detail, overexposing by perhaps half a stop. You may find that it helps to adjust for this on the camera's exposure override control every time you shoot slides.

Flash exposure can be measured with the same brightness range technique provided your equipment allows you to spot-read a trial flash. Flash is still often measured and controlled by an in-flashgun sensor which takes a general reading or, when you use a dedicated gun, by a centre-weighted TTL reading from inside the camera.

Fig. 7.10 Exposure override controls. Top: mechanical dial, set to make meter underexpose by half a stop. Bottom: electronic re-set button and camera top display showing same half-stop underexposure, here for frame 10

Separate flash meters tend to give only incident light measurement, but you can use them to check lighting ratios. Take a reading from the subject pointing towards the main light, then towards any light illuminating shadows.

Remember, when using a separate flash meter, to take into account any filter or extra lens-to-film extension which will call for additional exposure. It is easy to forget to increase exposure when using a close-focusing macro lens, extension tubes or bellows for close-ups. Working with small- or medium-format cameras, you become used to relying on an in-camera meter which takes all such influences into account *when measuring continuous lighting*. However, unless it also measures your studio flash results may be underexposed. One practical way to check the correction needed is:

1. Place a white or grey card over your (focused-up) subject.
2. Take an exposure reading through the camera of the card, under modelling light illumination.
3. Take a hand meter reflected-light reading off the card, same illumination.

The difference between (2) and (3) in *f*-stops is the exposure increase needed when using and measuring flash with a separate meter.

The zone system

The famous American landscape photographer Ansel Adams devised what he called the 'zone system' to put tone theory into everyday practice. The system is helpful in two ways:

1. It shows you how to work out a personal routine to get the best quality out of film, paper and chemicals, under your own working conditions.
2. It allows you to accurately fine-tune your result up or down the available tone scale and to expand or contract how much scale it occupies (alter contrast) according to the needs of subject and interpretation.

In fact as an experienced zone-system user you should be able to look at any subject and 'previsualize' how it might be recorded in tone values on the final print, then steer the whole technical process to achieve these chosen qualities.

Adams intended the zone system for black and white photography using a large-format sheet-film camera. Ability to individually process negatives and the kind of performance you get from monochrome films and printing papers are in-built features. However, the zone system can also be used for roll or 35 mm film (page 157). For the moment, to learn how it works imagine that you are using individually exposed sheets of film and measuring exposure with a hand meter.

The zones

The essence of the system is that you look at each subject as being a series of brightnesses, from its deepest shadow to brightest highlight, and relate these to a set scale of tones. As shown in Figure 7.11, the zone system uses eight grey zones (I–VIII) plus total black (0) and total white (IX). Zone V is mid-grey – the tone you would normally pick for subject brightness about midway between darkest and lightest

Fig. 7.11 The Zone System. A full
tone range black and white
photograph can be re-arranged as a
scale of eight tones between
maximum black and clearest white
(approximated here in printer's ink).
Each one-stop change of exposure
shifts representation of all your
subject tones up or down the scale
by one tone zone. Top picture:
exposure gauged by one reflected
light reading off the top of the
waterline rock. This was
overexposed by one stop so that
instead of zone V (which all meters
normally give) the rock reproduces
zone VI. Bottom picture: the same
reading but underexposed by one
stop makes the rock zone IV, shifts
all tones to darker values

extremes and equivalent to 18% reflectance card. Other parts of the scene only half as bright would fall into zone IV or, if twice as bright, zone VI, and so on. Changing exposure by one stop reallocates all the subject brightnesses one zone either up or down the scale.

The span of ten different zones covers a subject brightness range of over 1:500, only rarely encountered in scenes backlit by some harsh light source. Eight zone-system zones (1:128), which is seven stops' difference, are taken to be more typical. This is just below the maximum subject range that normally processed film and paper will reproduce on a full tone range print, using a diffuser enlarger. See Figure 7.5. Your technique must be sufficiently under control for you to be sure that one chosen brightness really does reproduce as a chosen zone value on the final print. Then other brightnesses will also fall into predictable places along the tone scale. As a result, you can decide at the shooting stage which parts of a scene you want to make a particular zone and then previsualize how the whole print will finally look.

To achieve this, however, you must start by standardizing key aspects of techniques – effective film speed, development, printing – as they apply to your own equipment or working conditions. This preliminary work takes some time, but is a once-and-for-always operation.

Personalized film speed

The manufacturer's recommended ISO speed ratings and development time assume 'average' subject and lighting, typical exposure measurement and the kind of negative which prints well in popular enlargers. Their assumptions may not apply to you exactly. The first step, therefore, is to assess the effective speed of each of the films you use. Do this by finding the exposure needed to record deep shadow detail as zone II (just perceptibly darker than the film's palest tone) on the negative in the following way:

1. Find or set up in the studio a contrasty scene with a span of eight zones. Check with your camera or hand meter – brightest parts should need seven stops less exposure than darkest shadow.
2. With the camera or meter set for the ISO speed printed on the film box, measure exposure for the darkest shadow where you still want detail to just record. Meters making a single subject measurement read out the exposure needed to reproduce this part of the subject as zone V. However, you want darkest shadow detail to be about zone II on the final print, so reduce the exposure by three stops (three zones) before exposing the picture.
3. Shoot four other exposures, rating the film twice, one-and-a-half, half and one quarter its box speed. Then give all your exposed film normal processing in whatever developer you have chosen to use.
4. When results are dry, judge carefully on a light-box which negative carries just perceptible detail in the shadow area you measured. The speed setting used for this exposure is the effective speed setting for your film used under your working conditions.

Personalized development time

Next, review your film development time. Exposure does most to determine shadow tone, but highlight tones are the most influenced by development. While you still aim to reproduce shadows just above the negative's palest tone you can decide to record highlight parts of your test subject as just below the film's darkest tone. The reasoning here is that you make maximum use of film tone range.

1. Make a series of seven identical exposures of your test subject, as measured with the film rated at your effective speed.
2. Give each exposure a different development time – one can have normal time, others 10%, 15% and 25% less and 15%, 25% and 40% longer. Be very accurate with temperature and agitation technique.
3. Carefully judge which test negative records brightest important subject details just short of being too dense to print with acceptable detail and contrast with your enlarger. Make trial prints as necessary, to check quality. The development time which gave the best negative is correct under your conditions for an eight-zone subject. (If this differs much from the development used when you established film speed you may have to rejig your speed rating. Retest for speed if necessary.)

Now you can start to shoot pictures with a more controlled technique, adjusting development when necessary to expand or contract tone range. Always begin by separately reading the exposure for lightest and darkest important detail in any subject. Then compare them (in number of stops) to discover what zone range your picture spans. If the range is high (over eight zones) there are three alternatives:

1. Sacrifice either shadows or highlights to improve tonal reproduction at the opposite end of the scale. For example, underexposing by one stop shifts all tones down one zone. This sacrifices shadow details which move off-scale to zone 0 or beyond on your print but lets in highlight detail to now record as zone VIII. Overexposing one stop shifts all tones one zone in the opposite direction, moving highlights off-scale but improving shadow tones which now print as zone II. To take this decision, you must look at the scene, previsualizing it on the final print either with its palest detail indistinguishable from white paper or its darker shadow detail featureless black.
2. If you do not want to lose detail at *either* end of the tone scale then earmark the film for reduced ('held back') development. You already know from your tests the development time needed for an eight-zone range. Go back to your tests to discover how much reduction in this time will contract the zone range by one zone. Do not overdo development control, though. Avoid changes from the manufacturer's regular development time greater than 40–50%, otherwise, as discussed on page 145, you get negatives too flat to print on any grade of paper. Also, since this amount of development reduction affects both shadow and highlight tones you have to start re-adjusting your effective film speed (downrating to allow for holding back).
3. Adjust subject lighting range by adding more fill-in or wait for a change in existing light conditions. Even adjust viewpoint so that your picture contains a lesser range of tones. As before, check out the effect by comparing separate light readings of darkest and lightest subject detail to discover the new zone range.

Fig. 7.12 Rejigging exposure and development to compensate subject contrast. Top centre and bottom centre: normally developed contrasty and flatly lit subjects, respectively. Top left: negative given more exposure and less development has less contrast. Bottom right: negative with less exposure and more development increases in contrast. Reproductions here can only approximate photographic film results

Your problem may be the other way around – an excessively flat-toned subject spanning perhaps fewer than six zones. Control this by either (2) or (3) but *reversing the suggested technique*. It will also help if you can change to a slightly more contrasty film such as one with a lower speed rating.

Including your printing conditions

It is true to say that, having got a really good negative with the right tone range and all the detail, your picture should almost 'print itself'. In any case, within the darkroom it is easy to work trial-and-error methods not possible when shooting. However, you can choose to adopt a similar zone system approach here as well, to establish personalized exposure and development times geared to your printing paper and enlarging equipment.

First, test for exposure with just a clear piece of film in the enlarger negative carrier. Set your most usual lens aperture (typically, two to three stops down) and expose a half sheet of normal grade paper with strips of six to eight test exposures, bracketed closely around the time you estimate will just produce a full black. Process the paper in your normal developer for its recommended time, then check your print to find the strip beyond which extra exposure does not give a deeper black. This is the paper's maximum black produced from clear (subject zone 0) parts of the negative. (All other tones should then follow on, up to something almost indistinguishable from the paper base from subject zone IX areas of your negatives).

Next, test for best print development time. Working with the clear film and giving the exposure time you have just established, expose a full sheet. However, before processing your paper cut it into nine equal pieces, each numbered on the back. You then develop each piece for a different period bracketed around the recommended time. For example, if the regular time for fibre-based paper is 2 minutes, range from 1 to 3 minutes at 15-second intervals. From the processed strips decide which time has just produced the paper's fullest black, and then make this your standard print development time for the zone system.

Putting the zone system to work

You have now standardized your technique, from film speed to print development. It forms a chain giving fullest tone reproduction from your materials (regard paper contrast grades and local printing-in or shading as extra adjustments for corrective or expressive use). Successful use of the zone system relies on your keeping this core technique very carefully under control. You should then be able to look at and measure a subject, decide and forecast the final print, and be reasonably certain of achieving it.

For example, you might be shooting a portrait in soft, diffused light. Delicate flesh tone detail is of utmost importance. For a Caucasian you might decide to make this zone VI (see the scale on page 150), in which case take a single meter reading of the face and increase exposure one stop. A dark-skin face would be better reproduced as zone V, achieved by giving the meter indicated exposure straight.

Perhaps the subject is a harshly lit building, mostly in shadow. You judge the shadowed parts as most important, but reckon it would look wrong to have them any lighter than zone IV. So read the shadow only and decrease exposure by one stop. Another treatment, if the building has an interesting shape, is to make it a silhouette. This means reallocating the shadowed walls as perhaps zone I by underexposing their reading four stops.

Suppose you now move around the building to a viewpoint from which there is a harsh mixture of important sunlit and shadowed areas. You want detail in both but start off reading the lit part. Consider making it zone VIII. Now measure the shadowed walls – perhaps this reads six stops more, a difference of six zones. Can you accept detail here as dark as zone II? (A print from the negative may be wanted for reproduction on the printed page, where good separation of tones in darker areas of the picture is always important.)

It might therefore be a better compromise to raise the whole picture by one zone, making sunlit walls zone IX and shadows zone II. Do this by reading sunlit parts and decreasing exposure three stops, or reading shadowed parts and increasing exposure two stops. Another option would be to avoid a contrasty negative by decreasing development by an amount which reduces picture zone range from six to five zones. (If you decide to do this, consider halving the ISO setting on your meter before taking final readings, or bracket at both settings.)

Finally, check out the blue sky behind the building. Will any building tone match the sky too closely so that in monochrome they run

Fig. 7.13 With an extreme tone range subject like this, decide at which end of the scale you can best afford to sacrifice detail. For the left-hand picture, sunlit paving was exposed to record zone VII although shadowed earth is lost into zones I and 0. In the right-hand picture, giving more exposure holds this shadow detail at zone II but the paving now reproduces beyond zone VIII

together, losing subject outline? Decide this by eye, or compare readings from blue sky and sunlit parts of the building. If you forecast that tones are too similar (for example, the sky is less than one stop darker, one zone lower), you could separate them by using a filter. Try a polarizer or a yellow or green coloured filter on the camera. Do not forget the filter factor if you are not metering through the lens.

Metering for zoning

If you use the zone system you fully appreciate the value of accurately reading light from chosen parts of any subject. Generalized readings are not very helpful. A spot reading system is ideal, but, short of this, be prepared to come close with the camera or hand meter or read off a handy visually matching substitute.

If you have a hand meter with a suitable large calculator dial you can make a simple 'zone scale' to attach to it. These small segments of tone, perhaps cut from your bromide paper tests, give direct visual readout of how different subject brightnesses will reproduce (see Figure 7.14).

Limitations to the zone system

The zone system offers a sound technical grasp of tone control, but you must also recognize its limitations. The system best suits black and white landscape and still-life large-format photography, where time permits careful measurement of different elements in the picture.

Many other picture-shooting situations are too fleeting to allow several local readings. Again, it is less easy to individualize degree of development when using a rollfilm camera or a 35 mm film containing up to 36 different shots. One solution is to pick development which suits the most important pictures on the film, then rely on adjusting the tone scale of prints from your other negatives through paper grades (see also page 166). Alternatively, fill a whole rollfilm with bracketed exposure versions of each picture. If your camera has interchangeable magazines, or you have several bodies, organize your shooting so that all pictures requiring the same amount of development accumulate on the same film.

35 mm format films are also more vulnerable to the side-effects of over- or underdevelopment as part of system control. For example, overdevelopment increases graininess, and although this may barely show in enlargements from 4×5 inch negatives, the same size prints from 35 mm quickly become unacceptable. You must remember that any change of film type, developer or use of an enlarger with a different light source means having to make new tests.

Colour films cannot be given adjusted processing to expand or contract tones as freely as black and white because of unacceptable distortion of colours. Zone system methods for colour negatives especially are limited to light measurement and exposure. (Here it can be argued that a trial shot taken on instant-picture material gives you an equally valid and faster tone value guide.)

However, even if you do not work the zone system in detail, understanding it will definitely help you previsualize the final monochrome print at the time of shooting. Remember the concept whenever you light-measure different parts of a scene. It makes you stop and think what will be the most suitable tones for each part you read, and, where necessary, to put aside exposed material for modified development. Also bear in mind that a full detail, full rich tone image does not always mean a great photograph. You must know when to

Fig. 7.14 Some hand meters have zone system settings built-in. Other dial types (right) can be adapted by sticking on tiny pieces of a bromide paper grey scale to represent zones I–IX. Zone V should be pasted over the normal-setting arrow. Each paler tone corresponds to higher light readings, darker tones to lower readings. Now, by measuring any chosen part of the subject, you can align its light reading with the tone you want it to be in your final print. (Assumes normal development)

Fig. 7.15 Zones can leapfrog when you use colour filters on coloured subjects. Left-hand picture here was unfiltered, the other exposed through a deep red filter. Notice how the bottoms of balconies are darker than blue sky in left version, but a tone lighter than sky on the right. Always previsualize zones looking through the filter

make an exception – break away from this 'look' if it is likely to work against the style and mood of a particular picture. The zone system is a technical control but not something that should ever control and limit you.

Tone changes after processing

You can alter tone values in a processed film by chemical or physical means to get better final image quality. Most chemical treatments are for emergencies when mistakes have been made or subject conditions were beyond the range of the film. Physical methods such as duping or masking (sandwiching the film with a weak positive or negative contact printed from it) are less drastic. They do not alter your original film image itself, which remains safe. Chemicals to reduce or intensify image tones often create permanent changes, so you should choose and use them with due care. There is always some risk of ruining the image through stains or some other chemical or handling mishap, so it is a sensible precaution to make the best possible print first, as a standby. Always start out with a film which is properly fixed and washed before treatment, and for safety test out one image alone first. If possible, preharden in liquid hardener. During reduction or

Fig. 7.16 When chemically reducing a film, check results visually by working near a light box or window (but avoid direct sunlight). Have a water supply nearby to rinse and halt the action when tone changes have progressed far enough

intensification keep the film agitated gently all the time it is in solution, and afterwards thoroughly wash it before drying.

Correcting dense black and white silver negatives

Negatives which are too dense might have been overexposed, over-developed or slightly fogged overall. Perhaps the subject spanned too great a tone range and was exposed mostly for midtones and shadows. Dense flat negatives can be duplicated (easiest by rephotographing at 1:1) onto colour slide film. The resulting negative will be more contrasty, and by careful choice of exposure important subject brightnesses may reproduce as properly separated tones.

Alternatively, chemically change the flat original negative in a *subtractive* type reducer. This removes nearly equal quantities of silver from dark, medium and pale tones, and so has greatest effect on pale tones, making the negative more contrasty as well as less dense. Farmer's one-solution ferricyanide reducer R-4a is a good choice (see formula, page 283). Treat the negative in a white tray containing the solution near a light-box so you can closely observe the reduction effect. Do not allow it to go too far, and remember that heavily reduced negatives tend to show a coarser grain pattern.

Dense but contrasty negatives, perhaps due to overdevelopment, are best reduced in a *proportional* reducer such as Kodak's R8. If subject highlights are very dense (an overdeveloped contrasty scene, for example) use a *superproportional* reducer instead. Super-proportional R-15 persulphate reducer removes more silver from dense areas than pale areas of your negative. Used carefully, it reduces the density and printed tone separation of subject highlights without much affecting shadow tones. (Formulae and method are in Appendix B.) If you are working on a negative 4 × 5 inches or larger it may be practical to reduce just chosen areas of the image by apply-ing one of these reducers locally, by swab or brush. Another approach is to reduce contrast by masking (explained on page 161).

Correcting dense colour negatives

Colour negatives (and dye image black and white negatives) do not contain silver. Therefore you cannot treat them in the chemical solutions used to reduce regular black and white negatives. A special dye reducer for C-41 process negatives made by Colorbrite uniformly lightens the three image dye layers so that colour balance and contrast remain unchanged. Carry out reduction in a series of stages, carefully checking your negative's appearance as it gradually becomes less dense. It is not easy to judge how far to go. If in doubt, always under-rather than overtreat your film.

Correcting dense colour slides and transparencies

Similar but different Colorbrite reducers are made for reversal film. One solution gives a general lightening effect, maintaining colour balance and contrast. If you want to reduce one dye layer more than another (to correct slight colour casts) there are separate yellow-, magenta- and cyan-reducing solutions. If you go too far you can turn to a Colorbrite intensifier which regenerates up to 90% of the original

Fig. 7.17 Colorbrite reducer applied in a band across a slightly dense colour transparency. If this is overdone, blacks become grey

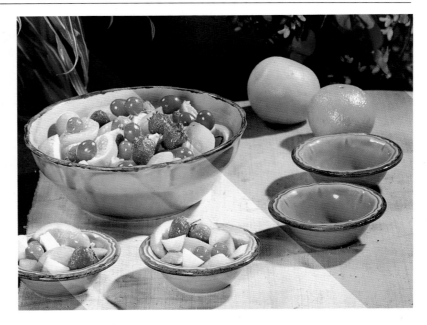

colour and density. Overreduction leaves poor blacks and degraded colours.

Alternatively, copy your dense transparency onto reversal dupe film (see page 249), giving an exposure which will produce lighter results. (As a guide, give one stop overexposure for every half stop the original was underexposed.) Once again, you reach the limit of this technique when shadow tones appear an unnatural featureless grey. You must also accept a generation loss – the kind of optical and tonal deterioration which happens when any image designed for final viewing is copied.

Correcting pale black and white negatives

The usual causes here are underexposure and/or underdevelopment or a very contrasty subject exposed mostly for midtones and highlights. Negatives which are severely underexposed with loss of shadow tones and detail are very difficult to salvage. You cannot put back information which has not recorded at all in the first place.

Various chemical intensifiers are designed to build up existing tone values in silver image negatives. They all increase graininess too. Flat, underexposed or underdeveloped negatives are best treated in a solution such as Chromium Intensifier IN-4. The intensifier bleaches the film, which you then wash and redarken in any fast-acting developer such as print developer (see page 283). Tones are strengthened in proportion to the amount of silver originally present, and you can repeat the treatment to increase the effect.

Negatives which are contrasty and thin will need the most density build-up in their palest tones. You therefore need a subproportional formula such as Kodak Intensifier IN-6 (see formulae). However, you can often get even better results by trying a contrast-reducing or a selective contrast-increasing mask used only on subject shadows (pages 161 and 164).

Fig. 7.18 A flat, underdeveloped negative intensified (right half) in chromium intensifier. Darkest tones strengthen most, increasing contrast

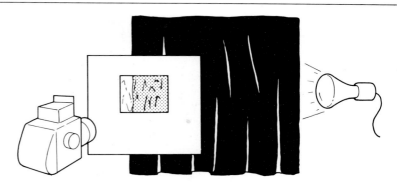

You may be able to press an extremely thin negative against white paper under glass and rephotograph it on reversal film. Another strictly emergency technique is to set up the film a short distance in front of black velvet (Figure 7.19). When you illuminate the negative obliquely from the rear with a hard light source even the slightest silver deposit scatters light and appears milky against clear parts you see through to the black velvet. The picture therefore appears positive and you can photograph it on reversal or negative film. Unfortunately, anything approaching normal tones (pale grey underexposed highlights, for example) may appear detailless grey, or even negative, when lit this way.

Correcting pale colour negatives

An underexposed or underdeveloped colour negative is unlikely to give a satisfactory colour print. Missing shadow tones reproduce darker parts of the subject as devoid of detail, and usually with a strong colour cast. Low contrast images 'mis-match' the quite critical relationships of negative and print material. For example, you will not be able to print with the same tone contrast or colour balance at shadow and highlight ends of the subject's tone scale. Try printing with a condenser enlarger (rather than the usual diffuser lamphead type used for colour). You may achieve best results by abandoning colour altogether and printing onto hard-grade black and white bromide paper.

Correcting pale slides and transparencies

There is almost no way to improve overexposed, overdeveloped or fogged reversal films because the subject's lightest detail is 'burnt out'. If results are also flat you can sometimes make improvements with a contrast-increasing mask (page 164). Even though you are only adding a weak black and white positive to the transparency to add weight to tones already there, results look much more acceptable. Otherwise, if the shot is important and unrepeatable you will need to have the best possible reversal print made – and then pay for this to be retouched.

Tone control by masking

This is the technique of sandwiching your deficient negative or transparency with a weak monochrome film image contact printed from it, and known as a mask. The two images registered together change the tone range of your result. For example, a negative with a weak positive mask will have most tone added to subject shadows, none to highlights. Its contrast is therefore *reduced*. However, if the mask is a weak negative it will have the opposite effect – having the two negatives together gives greatest tone build-up in subject highlights, *increasing* contrast.

Having made your negative or positive mask as described below, sandwich it with the original film image between two pieces of glass. Take great care to register them accurately. Avoid any dust or finger marks and seal up the edges of the glass. Then set up the sandwich in the enlarger negative carrier for printing, or over a light-box for 1:1 duplicating (see page 249).

Most contrast-controlling masks are pale, ghost-like images, far less dense than those they are masking. Anything stronger starts to give part-positive, part-negative 'special effects'. Masks are usually made on slow, low-contrast continuous-tone sheet film. For improving black and white originals you can use any suitable non-colour-sensitive material, which allows you to work in the darkroom under convenient bromide paper type safelighting. For colour film originals use a similar but panchromatic film such as Kodak's Pan Masking film. (Masks for colour originals are best made in monochrome as this alters tones without the complications of colour changes.)

Correcting excessive contrast (negatives)

Your colour or black and white negative may be too contrasty due to the extreme lighting range of the subject, overdevelopment or – worst of all – underexposure and overdevelopment. It gives harsh prints even with your most diffused, soft light head enlarger. In this instance you need to make a positive mask which ranges in tone from being

Fig. 7.20 Near right: an excessively contrasty negative. Far right: a contrast-reducing mask, contact-printed from the negative on normal-contrast sheet film. Non-colour-sensitive film was used here but pan film will do as well, provided you avoid safelight fog. Negative and mask sandwiched together give a lower contrast print. See also Figure 7.21

Fig. 7.21 Masking to reduce contrast. A contrasty negative with a density range of 1.8 (1:63) can be masked to a range of 1.3 (1:20) by sandwiching it with a pale, 0.5 density range, positive version. Mask adds 0.6 density to subject shadows but only 0.1 to highlights

Fig. 7.22 Two alternative ways of exposing an unsharp mask for a negative. Near right: under glass the original negative (N) is emulsion down on clear spacer film, above unexposed masking film (M) emulsion up. Alternatively have the negative emulsion up, without a spacer. Make the exposing light source oblique to the sandwich, which you rotate during exposure. Far right: exposing without movement directly below the enlarger as light source. Diffusion here is achieved by inserting a Kodak mask diffusion sheet, plus glass, between negative and unexposed masking film

transparent in subject highlights to pale grey in deepest shadows. See Figure 7.20. Judged by normal positive images, it needs to be under-exposed and underdeveloped.

The controlled way to set about masking is to use a densitometer. Then you can measure the density range of your original, compare this with what suits the printing paper and make the mask with characteristics to fill the gap (see Figure 7.21). However, a trial-and-error approach is often equally successful and makes masking easier than you might think. Try several bracketed exposures, always stacking the negative and unexposed film as shown in Figure 7.22. Use the enlarger as your light source. Process in a tray of diluted general-purpose negative developer giving only about 50% of the normal time (for example, 3 minutes in DK50 at 1:4).

The only way to find out which of the masks you have made is best is to try printing with it in place. Register the mask against the back of your negative and place the sandwich between glasses in the negative carrier. Expect the new printing exposure time to be about one and a half times what was necessary for the negative alone. The colour filtration for a colour negative should remain unchanged. Try your thinnest mask first. It is surprising what an improvement is produced, even with just the smallest amount of extra density in the shadows.

Contrast-reducing masks are best made 'unsharp', meaning slightly diffused. Figure 7.22 shows the technique. Consequently, although each mask carries a positive image any areas of fine detail only record on it as averaged, even tone. When mask and negative are registered together contrast is reduced in all areas except this very fine detail. Since your assessment of visual sharpness depends greatly on the contrast of detail, a print from the combination actually looks sharper than from the original negative. A soft-edged mask is also easier to register.

Correcting excessive contrast (positives)

Your reversal slide or transparency may be too contrasty, for reasons similar to those giving contrasty negatives. As a result, it may print too harshly onto reversal paper. To reduce contrast, this time you need a weak black and white *negative* as a mask. This is exposed on pan masking film following the same unsharp procedure described above. However, slides and transparencies often have highlight tones of slightly lower contrast than that of midtones. You saw how paler tones fall on the toe of the characteristic curve in Figure 4.15. So contrast reduction masking may improve most of the tone range but give overmasked and artificially grey-looking highlights.

To overcome the problem, you first make a 'highlight' drop-out mask from the transparency. This means underexposing onto lith film and processing in high-contrast developer to get a negative in which only highlight detail records, as dense black. Next, register the highlight mask and the original transparency and print your final contrast-reducing mask (unsharply) from their combination. This weak negative final mask therefore has clear areas corresponding to highlights. Now discard the highlight mask and combine original

Fig. 7.23 Highlight masking when making the main contrast-reducing mask for a transparency or slide.
1: original contrasty image on film.
2: underexposed high-contrast negative forms drop-out mask.
3: pale negative image printed from 1 + 2. Highlights, covered by drop-out mask, are just clear film.
4: when 1 is combined with 3 contrast is reduced throughout, except in highlight parts. (Mask densities here are greatly exaggerated relative to transparency)

Fig. 7.24 A: original transparency for masking. B: contrast-reducing mask made 'straight' from transparency. C: drop-out mask on contrasty film. D: mask made from combination of drop-out mask and colour transparency. Notice difference between B and D along rim of bowl. Strongest highlights are now unmasked transparency and contrast-reducing mask. The resulting picture has a generally reduced contrast range but still retains its purity of high-lights (see also 'flashing', page 166).

Correcting insufficient contrast

Occasionally, your negative or film positive is too low-contrast to print with a full range of tones, even using a condenser enlarger. The cause might be a low-contrast subject, atmospheric conditions or flat lighting, giving a low image brightness range; film which was slightly fogged; or overexposure plus underdevelopment. Here you need a mask to *increase* contrast, which must be negative for a negative or positive for a slide or transparency. Consequently, an extra stage is needed, making three in all:

1. Make an intermediate mask by sharply contact printing the original onto regular contrast film given normal development. The result should look like a normal monochrome positive (or negative) but slightly dense.
2. Contact print (1) onto another sheet of the same film. Have the intermediate mask pressed base side towards the film's unexposed emulsion. Give similar development to (1), aiming for a result which looks underexposed – clear film at one end of the tone scale and barely mid-grey at the other.
3. Tape (2) in register with your faulty original. You will see the improvement immediately. Sandwich the films between glass and print your final enlargements.

Selective masking

So far, most masks for tone control have affected the whole picture area, but sometimes you want to be much more selective and mask (or omit from masking) certain chosen parts. For example, the contrasty negative of an interior may include one or two dense, flat window areas where you do not want a contrast-reducing mask to operate. Alternatively, you may want to boost the contrast of just one or two figures in a crowd, or give emphasis to one red-coloured object in a colour shot. To do this, you must be able to decide freely where tone changes are to take place, and then use one or more of the following techniques.

Dropout intermediates

Following a similar procedure to highlight masking (see page 163), make a high-contrast intermediate mask. This blocks out one or other end of the original film's tone scale just while you are making your main contrast mask. The covered parts appear as clear film on the final mask, leaving the original unchanged. Images of all sizes can be selectively masked this way.

On the other hand, if your original picture is large format and the areas you want to leave unmasked are fairly simple in outline, you can paint a dropout intermediate by hand. Use fixed-out clear film taped over your original transparency or negative, and onto it paint liquid opaque to cover details not to be masked. You have total

Fig. 7.25 Preparing a 'handmade' drop-out mask using a clear sheet of film over your original film. With liquid opaque you can freely work over areas you want to remain unaltered when the rest of the image is masked. See text

freedom of choice here – areas need not be the lightest or darkest parts of the picture, or all have the same range of tones. As before, have your 'handmade' mask registered over the original when exposing your main contrast-controlling mask, then discard it and combine this main mask with the original.

Hand-bleaching the mask

You can make a whole picture contrast mask direct from the original tone-faulted image, but then bleach away parts of the mask image wherever you do not want masking to occur. Do this by applying silver bleach solution (such as iodine, see page 283) on a brush to any chosen part of the picture. Once again, this is only practical with large-format images and fairly simple outlines.

Selective colour masking

When you are masking a colour film image it is possible to alter the tone range of one colour only. You do this by exposing the mask through an appropriately coloured filter. For example, in a colour transparency of some blue flowers you may want to reduce the contrast of everything else in the picture. By comparison, the flowers will then stand out boldly in tone and colour. You therefore make a mask of the whole image (on pan masking film) but using a deep-yellow filter over the light source. As a result, blue parts of the picture record as clear areas on the mask. When mask and colour transparency are combined the flowers remain unaltered, while contrast elsewhere is reduced according to the strength of your mask.

Less extreme colour masking can also be used to compensate for inefficient dyes in the original colour film. For example, you might be printing from or duplicating a harsh colour picture in which greens and blues have reproduced too dark. It is then helpful to make a contrast-reducing mask through a pale red filter. Adding the mask then slightly darkens and subdues reds, effectively lightening greens and blues. Similar principles are used in the integral masking of colour negatives (see pages 94–95).

Electronic masking

Masking is much easier when your photographic image is in the form of a stream of electronic signals. This happens, for example, when a colour photograph is screened in the preparation of colour separations for reproduction on the printed page (see page 273). The original picture is scanned by blue, green and red sensors and their signals used to expose yellow, magenta, cyan and (mixed together) black printing separations on separate sheets of film. Electronically, it is easy to change from negative to positive images at the flick of a switch. The output from any one (or all) sensors may be negative but have a weak positive image superimposed to act as a contrast-reducing mask.

Similarly, the output of one sensor can be used to modify the signals sent to another sensor's exposing head. A weak positive signal from the green sensor added to the negative signal passing from the blue sensor to its exposing head automatically improves the blue record of magentas. Electronic masking facilities also make it extremely easy to improve tone contrast and colour accuracy when you edit and re-record video images, use a video printer to print chemical photographic negatives onto chemical photographic paper or print out recordings from electronic still-image cameras.

Enlarger and enlarging technique

Finally, do not overlook ways you can improve the printing quality of an excessively contrasty or flat negative by making simple changes in the printing darkroom. If you are trying to print a contrasty image in a condenser enlarger and do not have a diffuser head (such as a colour head) available, place tracing paper over the top of the condensers. This gives a dim but one-grade-softer light source. If this is not a sufficient improvement, try 'flashing' – evenly fogging the printing material to a small quantity of light.

A correctly flashed print changes only in subject highlights. Your normal exposure to the contrasty negative is too weak to give a developable image here. However, the extra photons of light the paper receives from flashing are sufficient boost for traces of subject detail previously 'sublatent' to develop up. Overdone, flashing gives a print with flat grey highlight detail and a fogged appearance, so there are limits to the amount of contrast reduction possible. You can also use flashing when printing onto reversal materials (i.e. colour prints from slides) or when duplicating contrasty transparencies. This time, flashing helps to bring up better *shadow* detail but overdone shadows start to look flat grey.

The amount of light needed to flash the emulsion after image exposure has to be found by testing. With colour printing try removing the film from the enlarger carrier, placing a 2.0 neutral density filter (factor ×100) under the lens and giving your paper the same exposure time over again. For black and white you can simply leave the negative in place and hold thick tracing paper about 3 cm below the lens. This scrambles the light sufficiently for the paper in the enlarging easel to receive even illumination. Try giving about 10–20% of the previous exposure.

To increase the printing contrast of a flat tone range negative, make any change which will harden the enlarger light source. Change from a diffuser to a condenser head. Better still, change to a condenser enlarger with a point source lamp. Alternatively, you can harden up a regular opalized lamp with a hole in opaque foil (see Figure 7.26), but make sure your negative is still evenly illuminated – you may have to raise or lower the lamp. The much dimmer image will have to be compensated for by a wider lens aperture or longer exposure time.

Summary: Tone control

● To control tone values, look after all the links in the chain – subject and lighting contrast; filtration; lens and imaging conditions; film contrast and grain; exposure accuracy; development; reduction, intensification or masking; enlarging conditions; print material; and final viewing conditions.

Fig. 7.26 Reducing the effective size of the lamp in a condenser enlarger lamphouse — gives harder illumination and a more contrasty print

- Typically, subject brightness range is compressed as recorded on the negative, especially shadow tones. It expands again to some extent (especially in darker tones) when printed. Quadrant diagrams prove the importance of correct exposure – partly on the toe of the film curve – to make proper use of the full tone range of the paper.
- Try to get your subject brightness range within reasonable limits in the first place by care over lighting. Compensate extreme contrast by reduced development (but overdone, your negatives will be too flat to print well). Gear exposure and development to your own printing conditions. Over- or underexposed negatives will not 'fit' any paper.
- Any *single* light measurement reads out camera settings which reproduce this part of the subject as mid-grey. You get greatest exposure information from several local area readings. Separately reading highlights and shadows shows whether subject contrast is within the range of the film. It warns you to compensate by lighting fill-in or adjusted development, or to accept loss of top or bottom of the tone range.
- The zone system helps you to devise your own practical routine for tone control. Subject brightnesses are previsualized against a range of zones (I–VIII), with mid-grey zone V, black (0) and white (IX). Changing exposure one stop shifts all subject brightness one zone up or down.
- To work the zone system you must have your exposure/development/ printing technique firmly under control. Then adjust one or more of these stages to get the best possible tone range reproduction for your particular shot. First establish the effective speed of your film. Find development times for high, medium and low subject brightness ranges to get negatives with the right tone range to print well through your equipment. Similarly, you can establish best paper development time.
- Use the zone system by picking a key subject brightness, deciding the tone it should reproduce and then exposing so you know you will achieve this precisely. You can also measure darkest and lightest important detail, and by picking the right exposure and development arrange that this just fills the full tone range offered by your printing paper.
- The zone system best suits sheet-film black and white pictures of inanimate subjects. It can be adapted to rollfilm and 35 mm sizes provided you can locate all pictures needing the same development together on the same roll. Even if you do not work every aspect of the system, remember the concept and train yourself to tonally previsualize your results.
- You can modify tone qualities at later stages to improve or salvage results. Use appropriate reducers to lighten dense negatives, slides or colour transparencies. Black and white film reducers also alter contrast – subtractive types increase it, proportional or superproportional reducers maintain or reduce contrast.
- Dense, flat colour transparencies may improve if duped. Treat pale black and white negatives in chromium intensifier or (contrasty negatives) use a subproportional intensifier.
- Masking to improve a contrasty film original means contact printing a very pale black and white film image of opposite tonality, then printing from both films sandwiched in register. Contrast-reducing masks are usually made unsharp to preserve contrast in details. Negative masks combined with contrasty colour slides and trans-

parencies are best left as clear film in delicate highlight tone areas, where contrast is lowest. Make a very underexposed, contrasty 'highlight mask' first, fitting this over the original before you expose your main mask.

● Contrast-boosting masks are pale black and white versions of the film image they are masking. You therefore need to go through an intermediate stage when mask making.

● Selective masks alter contrast in chosen areas of the picture. Make an underexposed contrasty dropout intermediate to block out whichever end of the tone scale you do not need masked. Alternatively, make your intermediate by opaquing-out these parts on clear film. Then print the main mask from your original plus the intermediate. You can also make a full image mask and bleach out unwanted parts by hand.

● Printing off a mask by coloured light produces a mask which is paler (or clear) wherever the original image is complementary in colour.

● Reduce tonal contrast at the enlarging stage by diffusing the light source or 'flashing' the paper to light. To increase contrast, change to a condenser head and more point-source lamp.

8
Subject problems

This chapter is subject orientated. It takes a cross-section of twelve kinds of subject matter from sports to simple astronomy, outlining some typical professional markets and the general organization and technical approach to the work, plus hazards to avoid. Of course, whole books could be written about each subject, but running them together here points up the different pressures and priorities they impose on you as a photographer. Perhaps you will never have to tackle all of them, but then you are unlikely to specialize in only one type of subject either, especially if you are just setting up as a professional.

It is dangerous to be too categorical about the technique used by different individual photographers. People have an idiosyncratic approach to equipment and working method. After all, it is *possible* to use a large-format camera for editorial photojournalism and 35 mm for still-lifes and architectural interiors. Similarly, some photographers heavily impress their own particular style on whatever they shoot, almost to the point of excluding the purposes for which the picture will be used. These, however, are the exception.

Generally, market forces, your own specialist subject experience and even equipment design determine why and how pictures are taken. Convenience and commonsense dictate your best technical approach. Most photographers tackle jobs in the way outlined here – just remember that no approach is set and immutable. New markets and new kinds of equipment mean that subject problems and their solutions change over a period of time. In any case, newcomers to photography should always question the way things were done previously, for breaking away and finding new visual solutions is one way of beating your own path to success.

Most commissioned photographic jobs have to fulfil some form of commercial need or requirement of communication. They also challenge you with extra constraints. The final image may have to fill a long low format, it may have to be quite small (calling for a simple, bold approach) or it has to work when converted later into stark black and white only. Even when you have not been *assigned* to photograph a subject as a job it is important to set yourself tasks or events is another way of making blur dramatize speed and isolating subjects from often distracting surroundings.

Despite autofocus cameras, experienced sports photographers often prefer to pre-focus on some key spot on the ground and shoot when the action reaches this point. Others pull focus by hand to keep the main element sharp – preferring the freedom this gives to the always centre-frame focusing of automation. Single-frame motordrive is an important aid because it becomes easier to keep your eye to the viewfinder between shots. Continuous-drive mode motordrive is mostly used in short bursts, unless you are going for a planned analytical sequence.

Never assume that by shooting a rapid series of frames you are *bound* to capture the vital moment of an event. Even at three frames per second, pauses between pictures are still around three hundred times longer than the moments being recorded. The mirror also locks up at fastest framing rates, making it difficult to work. There is really no substitute for foreseeing what will be the peak of action and learning to press the shutter just a millisecond or so ahead. In this, photography is like rifle shooting. See that you do not run out of ammunition (come to the end of a film) at some key moment. Remember how many frames are left, and have another body ready loaded. A bulk film back may be viable, although bulky and slower to reload in the field.

Photojournalism

Purposes

In-depth journalistic picture series are like essays or published articles, as opposed to press pictures which singly cover deadline news. The whole concept of photojournalism was pioneered in the late 1930s by magazines such as *Life* and *Picture Post*. A good *visual* story, strong photography with a point of view, plus intelligent layout on the printed page together form a powerful kind of communication. Equally, an extended photojournalistic project may end up as a travelling exhibition or a book of photographs.

Most subject themes revolve around human events – after all, most people are interested in people. The relationship of people to their environment, society, work, violence or some catastrophe are constantly recurring story lines. Some of the best journalists – like the best documentary writers – have been obsessed by their subject matter to the extent that it becomes a crusade rather than a job. (See the work of Farm Security Administration photographers revealing the 1930s plight of destitute US farmers, and Eugene Smith's book *Minamata*, on industrial pollution.)

Approach and organization

You must decide the theme of your story and give plenty of time and thought to the best approach. As far as possible, plan a mental list of vital pictures, so that your project is structured and shows various aspects of the subject and theme. At the same time, keep open-minded and aim to take a lot of pictures which can be edited down later. Good selection then allows you (or, more often, the art editor)

```
        _____
   ┌──⌒──────────┐
   │ PHOTOJOURNALISM │
   │ 2-3  35 mm camera bodies │
   │ Motor drive │
   │ Flashgun (GN 30-60) │
   │ Wide aperture   26 mm │
   │ lenses:         35 mm │
   │                 50 mm (2) │
   │                 70-200 mm │
   │ Tripod or clamp │
   └────────────────┘
```

to lay out pictures which determine the readers' order of viewing, make comparisons through being run side by side, and so on.

Perhaps you will want to show differences between young and old, rich and poor, or contrast people's public and private lives. People at work could be photographed to show both social life and working activity. At public events turn your camera on spectators and events behind the scenes as much as the scenes everyone else sees and photographs. A few of the pictures may have to be set up and organized, most others shot while your subject is unaware. This is not work for the shy photographer, yet you must still be sensitive, able to respond to small but significant events and reactions, and not steam-roller everything to suit your preconceived ideas.

Equipment and techniques

Mostly you will want to be inconspicuous, and merge in with the people around you. This means dressing appropriately and simplify-ing your camera kit which you carry in a bag not too obviously photo-graphic. 35 mm is the ideal format because of its compactness. Auto-focus is also helpful on occasions, especially if you must grab pictures without looking through the viewfinder (for example, over people's heads). Otherwise pre-set focus and also exposure settings by reading off substitute subjects such as your hand. Have two camera bodies, fitted with different lenses and motordrives. Be prepared to wind on manually in situations where motor noise will attract attention. Use existing light as much as possible but pack a flashgun for times when conditions and depth of field requirements are beyond even the fastest film, or when you must fill in ambient light to reduce contrast (page 122).

Most work will probably be done with a wide-aperture standard lens, but have a wide angle for interiors and whenever foreground detail should look large and dominate the general environment. Pictures taken close with a wide-angle lens add to a sense of 'being there' when you are among a crowd, and during a threatening situ-ation even increases the apparent aggression. Shooting from afar using a moderately long focal length 'puts together' elements in mid-distance and background. You can also use it for unobtrusive head shots some distance away (sometimes an easy option – you will get a less 'detached' perspective by shooting closer with a normal lens).

Portraiture

Purposes

Apart from mere physical identification, most deliberate portraits are shot either to flatter the sitter or to express individual character. Of course, these purposes are not mutually exclusive, but flattery portraiture is mostly commissioned by or taken for your actual sitter or his or her family or business organization. Sitters expect to be shown favourably, perhaps portrayed as they see themselves or hope others see them. However, with portraits commissioned by third parties such as magazine editors you can forget flattery and sum up a person as a character, even if this is cruelly revealing. It is helpful to know how a picture is to be used – perhaps framed in a command-ing position on a boardroom wall, reproduced single column or full reflectors to return light into the shadows and help to create catch-lights in both eyes is a typical starting arrangement. As soon as possible, stop tinkering with the equipment and concentrate on your relationship with the sitter.

Weddings

Purposes

Photographing weddings is often regarded as a chore, but the fact is that within a family a wedding is a very special occasion. Consequently, covering such an event is a serious responsibility. Indifferent or missed pictures will deprive participants of important memories. Your work must be good enough to be framed and put in albums, and looked at over the years by different generations. Wedding photographs are a kind of time-warp within which families measure themselves, so results are of increasing value and interest.

Approach and organization

Meet the bride, groom and parents before the event to talk over the scenario. Clear permission with the religious or official authorities so that you know where photographs can and cannot be taken during the ceremony. Find out if there are to be any unusual events – for example, the bride arriving in a horse-drawn trap or the appearance of some invited celebrity. If the proceedings are to follow an unfamiliar ethnic procedure it is vital to learn the order and significance of each stage.

On the day itself remember that you are a part of the proceedings. Dress neatly, in deference to other participants, and arrive early. This allows you to assess potential backgrounds, lighting and best camera positions. Avoid backgrounds which are cluttered, ugly or inappropriate (church gravestones, for example). You can also start photographing the arrival of guests, preferably posed in groups. Follow this through with the arrival of key figures such as groom and best man, bride and father. Where there are noticeable differences in height it is best to step back and take full-length shots rather than half-lengths and close-ups.

After the ceremony there will be formal groups. Start with husband and wife alone, then work outwards, adding the immediate family and increasing numbers of close relatives until the final group includes most guests, if there is sufficient space. With the smaller groups, especially, pay great attention to detail. Make sure that men have jackets buttoned and no flapping ties, long dresses are arranged neatly, hair and head-dresses tidy. Later, complement these some-what cliché but popular pictures by taking informal shots at the wedding reception. See Figure 8.4. Similarly, look out for, and record, any unexpected event which people will enjoy recalling – the groom arriving by motorbike because of a car breakdown, the best man hunting for the ring, even just a pile of hats in a church porch, or puddles and umbrellas if it rains.

Equipment and techniques

A medium-format (preferably magazine-loaded) camera allows you

WEDDINGS
6 × 6 cm camera with 80 mm,
    150 mm, 65 mm lenses
35 mm camera with 35–135 mm
    lens
Flashgun, meter
Effects filters
Tripod

to work fast yet give excellent detail. This is especially important for groups. Use mostly standard and moderately long focal length lenses, the latter mainly for head shots and half-lengths. Have a wide angle for interior general views, but do not use it for shots of people or groups unless space limitations are desperate. A tripod is important. It sets the camera position so you can go forward and adjust some detail or tactfully ask people to change places or move closer. You must also have a powerful variable-output flashgun to deal with daylight fill-in problems – for example, people arriving at a doorway photographed from within the building. A few effects filters such as 'misty' diffusers are useful, along with pins and clips to help arrange dresses. A 35 mm SLR outfit with zoom or wide-aperture normal lens is the best equipment for candid shots at the wedding feast. It you have an assistant he or she can use this equipment to cover incidentals at the ceremony.

Landscapes

Purposes

Landscapes are photographed for a wide variety of purposes. Detailed, representative shots are needed as picture library material for travel, ecology and educational publications of all kinds. Many of these photographs have timeless qualities which make them sell over a long period. However, landscape also lends itself to personal expression and interpretation. It can be majestic and dramatic, undulating and gentle, an abstract mixture of patterns or stark slabs of tone. From early times creative photographers have recognized landscape's pictorial possibilities. Pictures on exhibition walls, published as book portfolios or framed prints, prove how landscape photography can symbolize concepts like ageing, rejuvenation, a joyful sense of life or mystery and gloom.

Yet again, the main point of a landscape photograph may be much more social documentary, with the significance in *what* it contains. Threatened coastlines, pollution from industrial plant, the carving up of countryside by new roads and other developments need to be brought to the attention of the public and those who make planning decisions.

Approach and organization

Landscape photography looks deceptively easy. After all, the subjects themselves are largely unchanging and always there. Yet your total experience of a landscape includes space, distance, air movement, sounds, smells – you look around you, and notice the changing juxtapositions of elements near and far as you walk. These things are difficult to sum up within one still photograph, unless in some way you can isolate just a part which will encapsulate the character of the whole scene. Perhaps this means a low-viewpoint, wide-angle shot which exaggerates jagged foreground rocks and, through differences of scale, emphasizes the depth and distance between them and distant, brooding mountains. Alternatively, it could simply be a bunch of wind-blown trees shown silhouetted against the horizon almost at the bottom of the frame, leaving most of the picture to contain a skyful of spiralling cloud.

(form and texture). For more technical publications important details must be stressed, and the architecture generally shown with less visual licence. Specialist readers need information on its structure and proportions.

Environmentalists may want photographs to show the relationship of a new building to its local community, perhaps stressing detrimental influences. Real estate agents want a highly complimentary portrayal, showing space and light, and all the best features, but with no signs of the cement works and fertilizer factory next door. If the purpose of the pictures is freer and mainly to express yourself it can be argued that you are very much in the hands of the original architect. Like photographing sculpture, it is not easy to take someone else's creative work to form original images of your own. The challenge is often to express the impressions the architecture makes on you as an observer.

Approach and organization

Your two most important controls are lighting and camera viewpoint. Make up your mind about the important features to show and plan the best time and lighting conditions to bring these out in your pictures. Unlike landscape photography, your choice of camera position may be quite restricted, and this then determines the time of day you must shoot. A compass and watch are useful tools in planning where the sun will have to be to pick out different facets of the building. Better still, keep returning to observe throughout the day how lighting changes the appearance of volume, surface, colour and shadow pattern. See Figure 8.9.

List the shots to do at any one time. This might include close-ups of embellishments at one part of the building and, at the same time of day, general views of a totally different part, because light will then just be brushing across large wall surfaces. Do not overlook the possibilities of exteriors at dusk. Arrange to have all the lights on early enough for you to shoot a series while natural light fades and the dominant illumination changes from outside to inside the building.

The main problem with exteriors is the weather, as well as irrelevant surroundings such as parked cars and building plant. Listen to the weather forecasts. For many situations soft but directional hazy sunlight is best. Totally overcast conditions are easily the worst because of their lifeless, tone-flattening effect. Avoiding unwanted elements is mostly a matter of devising the right camera location. Sometimes this is quite hazardous, but you may need to be above parked cars, traffic and people, or block them out by some foreground feature. All this is best worked out ahead, helped if you know how much you can include with each of your different focal length lenses. Architecture which is essentially low in structure with surrounding grounds usually looks more impressive from a high viewpoint outside the area. If necessary, turn to low-level aerial photography (see page 190).

The main difficulty with architectural interiors is the unevenness and mixed colour balance of the light and the need to include as much as possible. Your eye tends to scan an interior, and it is not easy to match this with any wide-angle lens which does not also distort shapes. Like landscape, you may have to seek out some part which epitomizes important features of the whole. Be prepared to shoot rooms from outside windows or from corridors looking through doorways. The normal content of rooms often looks cluttered in photographs, so expect to spend time removing or re-arranging items to avoid confusion and give a sense of space when seen from the camera's static viewpoint. As in still-life work, take out anything which will not be missed from your picture.

Equipment and techniques

A camera with movements is essential for serious architectural photography, although detail work can be carried out with any regular camera. Vertical lines shown strongly converging are acceptable for dramatic, linear compositions but they look wrong (or careless) when just off-true. In any case, you will need shift and swing movements to work from high or low viewpoints, extend depth of field over a chosen plane, etc. Your lenses – especially wide angles – must therefore offer really generous covering power (see pages 41–42).

Have a kit of lamps or portable studio flash to help fill in and reduce contrast and unevenness with interiors. For colour shots, have blue acetate so that, where necessary, you can match up lamps with daylight seen through windows. However, never overdo your extra lighting – often it is vital to preserve the existing lighting scheme as part of the character of the building itself. For this reason, soft, bounced illumination is often best. Take some blue-tinted domestic lamps to swap for lamp bulbs in any desk lamp, wall lights, etc. included in the picture if an orange cast here is objectionable on daylight film stock. You also need a powerful variable-output flashgun for situations where there is no suitable electricity supply. An instant-picture back helps you to preview whether fill-in is sufficient yet natural-looking. Remember that either tungsten light or flash can be used from several different positions during a time exposure (covering the lens in between) to fill in dark areas. Another way of working is to shoot at dusk and use tungsten light film – at one point your interior will be lit at the same intensity as the outside orangey daylight view.

Have filters which include a polarizer to control unwanted glare as well as darken sky tones. A strong neutral-density filter allows you to extend exposure (say, $\times 100$, a filter density of 2.0) so that in daylight shots moving people or traffic are so blurred that they do not record. Have light-balancing filters for daylight and for different forms of tungsten and fluorescent lighting, colour-correcting filters as needed for reciprocity failure compensation, and the usual contrast filters for black and white shots. A spirit level will let you check that the camera is truly upright, and a small hand torch helps to make camera settings in dim interiors or when shooting at night.

Built studio sets

Purpose

A set built in the studio to represent a room, patio, etc. has the advantage that it can be designed in every detail to suit a drawn layout. Sets range in complexity from a couple of simple wallpapered flats to three sides of an elaborate room. Building time and cost involved is often much higher than working in a real location.

Fig. 8.8 Some 'room' sets are incredibly basic, using three simple surfaces – the floor and two walls. This shot is geared to present a common decorative theme, and is 'propped' to maintain colour scheme rather than convey reality. (By Michel Tcherevkoff/The Image Bank)

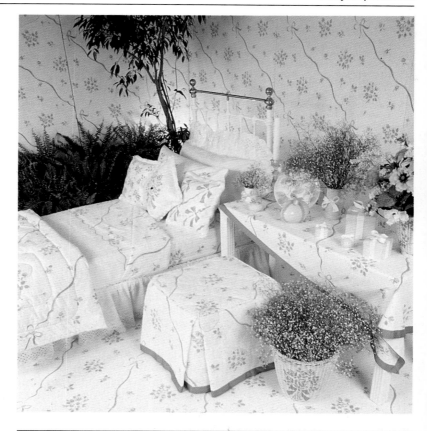

Fig. 8.9 Chateau in the Loire valley. Having set up for this viewpoint with a 6 × 6 cm camera and 40 mm lens, Charlie Waite hung on for over an hour until the expected storm appeared. The shot was taken just before the first rain broke up the reflections, and direct sunlight was blocked out

However, this is justified for jobs such as product advertising in bulk (for example, for mail order catalogues), where you want to shoot a series of kitchen suites or fitted bedroom units one after another, just changing the curtains and decorations. A built set may also be the only practical way you can put together a historical scene, such as a Victorian kitchen for an editorial feature on nineteenth-century recipes. The accessories can come from television/film prop hire or loaned or brought from dealers. The main advantage of a well-planned set is that you have greatest possible freedom of camera viewpoint and lighting. The absence of a 'ceiling' and fourth 'wall' gives plenty of space for equipment outside the picture area, and complete control over every element shown.

In macro form there are similar advantages when you photograph scale models for architects, town planners, exhibition designers, etc. The usual purpose here is to give a realistic preview of something which has not yet been constructed. You must therefore match the technical accuracy of the model with properly worked-out lighting and a 'human eye' viewpoint for the camera.

Approach and organization

Set building may take several days – far longer than the photography. Sets are best constructed from clamped-together 'flats', like theatre and television scenery (see Figure 8.10). Working from the angles of

Fig. 8.10 Simple corners of 'rooms' can be quickly constructed from wooden flats, G-clamped together and propped from behind.

view of your lenses for normal or steepened perspective viewpoints, plan out the total size of the set on paper first. Leave sufficient gap between the flats and studio walls and ceiling to get in lights, reflectors, etc. The main danger is that a constructed, propped set becomes too perfectionist, and lacks the idiosyncracies and untidiness of an actual room. Results then look selfconscious and sterile, like a museum exhibit. Naturalness is also important in the lighting. Illumination should appear to come through windows (or imaginary windows in a wall unseen), not from a ceiling grid of top lights as in television soap opera.

With scale models, take particular care over the height and direction of the 'day' light. Ths needs to comply realistically with any compass bearing marked on the model, not shine from one or more impossible quarters. If a model building has to be shown internally illuminated, as at night, use scaled-down sources which light limited areas just as they might be in reality. Fibre optics (page 134) are the easiest way to 'pipe-in' light to different areas within a small model.

Equipment and techniques

Apart from having a studio of sufficient size and with good access, you need basic carpentry and general do-it-yourself skills to construct flats. Whenever possible, incorporate standard builder's doors and window frames. Clamps and clips can take the place of nails and screws, provided they are unseen. If the budget is sufficient you may be able to have a stylist to decide and track down necessary props. There is little point in not using a large-format camera. You are certain to want camera movements to give the freedom to shoot from a higher or lower viewpoint without always showing vertical lines converging. Have plenty of studio lighting units – tungsten or flash – to light various areas of the set. They can also give general soft light, bounced off the studio ceiling and perhaps walls behind window frames. Have a sufficiently high level of illumination so you can stop down for sufficient depth of field without reciprocity failure. Remember that with flash you can fire and recharge again several times during one exposure.

For scale models, it may be physically easier to work with a medium- or small-format camera, unless you need comprehensive movements. For realism, scale down your viewpoint to match the model. For a 'standing spectator' viewpoint (say, 1.6 metres above the ground in a 1:50 model) have the centre of the lens 3.2 cm (1.6 m divided by 50) above the base. A wide angle is the most useful lens. Stop down fully, because shallow depth of field is the biggest give-away that the subject is not full size.

Studio still lifes

Purpose

Still lifes (inanimate objects) cover everything, from factual records of technical subjects to abstract images intended purely for mood and atmosphere. Your subject may be some form of merchandise for advertising, or perhaps the need is for a 'scene-setting' editorial illustration or cover shot to suit the theme of a magazine article or section of a book. It may be a collection of shapes and forms you put together for a picture which is complete in itself, as a piece of fine art or a social or political statement. Sometimes a plain background is necessary, for clarity of outline. However, more often you have to devise a background or setting which positively contributes to picture content, helping to put your subject in context without dominating it or confusing important features.

Approach and organization

By photographing a still-life subject in the studio you have a totally controlled situation. It is so open-ended that you can miss pictures by the sheer range of opportunities, skipping from one possibility to another. A disciplined approach is therefore essential. For example, decide the most important subject qualities (perhaps some aspect of form, shape, texture, colour) you need to show. Perhaps the subject itself will fill and bleed off the frame so there is no need for a setting, as in Figure 8.12; or the space around may be filled up with props, or an area of appropriate background. Simplicity is often best – the

STUDIO STILL LIFE
Large or medium-format camera
Normal and wide-angle lenses
Studio flash or tungsten lights
Meter, CC filters
Pola filter, camera stand
Instant-picture back
Fibre optics lighting

more you can take *out* of your picture and still make it work, the better. Where you have to include many items on a background it is often best to work them into a group which has a satisfying overall outline and shape. Build up the lighting gradually, starting by deciding the position and quality of your main source. Keep returning to the camera (on a stand) every time you adjust lights or the position of objects, to check how these changes look within the frame.

When shooting promotional pictures of products, food, flowers, etc. it is essential that the particular specimen in front of your camera is in immaculate condition. Special preparation for photography is advisable, although you must not break laws protecting the consumer from false appearances. It is legitimate, for example, to undercook food to retain texture and colour, 'shine-up' sausages and meats with glycerine or treat cut fruit with lemon juice to prevent discoloration. Food shots usually mean calling in expert help from a home economist who can prepare your dishes in the studio. Whenever possible, have two examples of each item made – one to set up, compose and light, the other to be substituted fresh just before shooting.

Equipment and techniques

The gradual build-up of a still-life picture suits the considered approach of a large- or medium-format camera. They also offer shift, swing and tilting movements. Use a normal or slightly longer focal length for most work, keeping close viewpoints with a wide-angle lens for rare dramatic effects. Studio flash is the best lighting equipment for any delicate subject matter which is easily heat damaged. Have a good range of light heads, especially softbox or large umbrella types. For subjects with highly reflective surfaces you will probably have to build a light-diffusing tent, while for exploded views items will have to be

Fig. 8.11 An exploded view of components must show them in true relationship to one another. Align and support them carefully; avoid shadows from blocks, threads etc. falling across the objects themselves. Later, supports are erased from the print by bleaching or airbrushing to give a plain white background

supported from behind or suspended from a gantry (Figure 8.11). Even quite small subjects often demand more studio space than you might expect. Remember, too, that still-life photography itself – with progressive refining of ideas and approach – can take far longer than most other subjects.

Natural history

Purposes

Natural history pictures span a vast range of subjects, from plants to birds, tiny insects to herds of wild animals. Mostly they are needed

Fig. 8.12 A still-life shot by Philip Fraser-Betts (for British Petroleum) making graphic use of simple shapes and colours. It is the sort of picture which can be used time and time again for brochure covers, exhibition displays and advertisements. Immaculate subject matter and tight control of lighting are vital. The tone range includes good shadow and highlight detail – without flatness – which reproduces well on the printed page

Fig. 8.13 Portable photographer's hide must offer ample space for you and equipment over long periods. A zoom lens is helpful here

for detailed factual information in educational publications (books, specialist magazines, exhibitions) as well as for general illustration. This is therefore another area where you can build up a long-lasting picture library. The secret of successful natural history photography is to show your subject and its environment accurately, but at the same time turn it into a creative picture which non-specialist viewers will also enjoy.

Approach and organization

This is an area where it is helpful to have special knowledge (as a biologist, ornithologist or zoologist) outside photography itself. You need to understand where and when to locate your chosen subject, best location and time of year, and (animals and birds, etc.) regular drinking or eating habits. Practise within an enclosed location such as a butterfly farm, plant sanctuary or safari park, where there will be a range of good specimens in a reasonably natural setting. Zoos are the easiest places for animal portraits, but these habitats are often ugly, and the inmates' behaviour usually quite different to that in the wild.

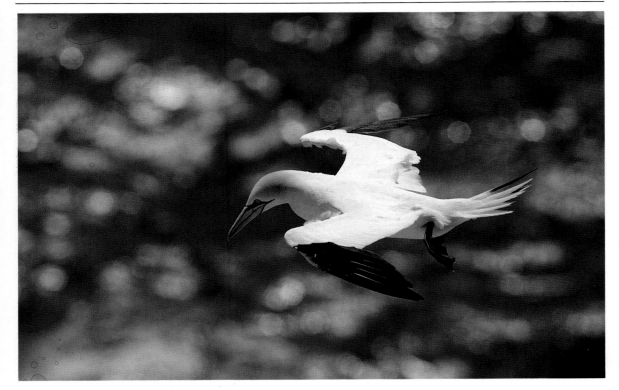

Fig. 8.14 Laurie Campbell stalked this gannet using a 600 mm f/5.6 regular telephoto lens. (Compare unsharp highlights here with the mirror lens shot on the front cover)

For animals and birds you need the ability to track down locations, perhaps with expert help. Then by stealth, anticipation and a great deal of patience you must photograph your subject from an effective angle and showing an identifiable activity. Sometimes it is more appropriate to work from a hide (see Figure 8.13) and watch and wait for your subject. Unless your hide is a permanent feature it may have to be assembled gradually over a period of time so that the animals and birds accept changes taking place. Then whenever you go to the hide take someone with you who soon leaves, making your prey think the hide remains empty.

With flowers and plants choose perfect specimens in their natural setting and photograph to emphasize their form, structure and colour. It is often helpful to include a scale for sizing – show this along one edge of the picture where it can be trimmed off later if necessary. With all natural history work there are two golden rules. Always log details of what, where and when you photographed; and do not damage or seriously disturb the plants or creatures which form your subjects.

Equipment and techniques

Most subjects are best photographed using 35 mm equipment, giving you the benefit of its range of lenses. Long focal length lenses are particularly important for wild life, giving a good-size image from a distance and picking out subject from background by shallow depth of field. Mirror-type designs are the lightest to carry and hold. Even so, a lightweight but firm tripod is essential. If your camera or hand

NATURAL HISTORY
35 mm camera
Macro, normal, 80–200 mm
    zoom, 500 mm mirror lenses
Spot meter, motor-drive
Tripod and clamp
Flashgun, remote control
Notebook

meter takes spot readings this is especially helpful when birds and animals are moving against changing backgrounds. Autofocus also helps in these circumstances.

You need a macro lens for insects, flowers, etc. A flashgun (on an extension lead) is also important for close work, allowing you to shoot at a small aperture to improve the shallow depth of field and freeze movement. Make sure that lighting direction will enhance form. Flowers often need card outside the picture area to act as a wind break when you are shooting outdoors. However, try to avoid card backgrounds – the trick is to include some information on habitat in your background but without confusing detail.

With subjects such as birds frequently returning to a nesting or feeding place you can gradually build up a motor-driven camera system clamped in some nearby position. Include flash if necessary. Then trigger the camera by radio or infra-red pulse (page 54) from a remote hide where you observe the action through binoculars. Sometimes you can use an infra-red trigger beam across the path of the subject itself so that it keeps taking its own photograph. At night you can photograph light-shy creatures with the flash filtered down to emit infra-red radiation only and expose on infra-red film (see page 125).

Underwater subjects

Purposes

Most underwater photography is intended to show fish and plant life for general informational purposes in publications, like many other natural history subjects (see page 185). However, you may also have to take underwater pictures of products, ranging from industrial equipment to fashions, as well as special editorial feature illustrations. Yet another facet is record photography of wrecks, for archaeological or marine engineering interests.

Approach and organization

You can photograph small objects, fish and plants in a glass-sided aquarium. As Figure 8.15 shows, decide and place your background and keep moving fish within your depth of field by narrowing the tank's front-to-back depth with an extra sheet of glass. True underwater photography, however, means shooting with you and your equipment also submerged. Apart from having waterproof equipment, the main problem is the optical changes created by imaging through water instead of air. Underwater, subjects appear closer and larger than they actually are. This upsets distance-guessing and focusing, but otherwise the camera is affected in the same way as your eyes – camera lens angle of view is reduced by about 25% (see page 46).

Second, light rapidly reduces in *intensity* and changes *colour content* (losing red) as depth increases. For greatest penetration, work at around noon, when sunlight is at right angles to the water and there is less reflection off the surface. Work out the depth at which you will be photographing. Down to about 30 feet the blue-cyan cast can be corrected by filtering, so prepare your camera with, say, a colour-correcting 30 or 40R filter. If you must shoot general views (for which only daylight gives broad enough coverage) try to keep to shallow

Fig. 8.15 An aquarium adapted for photography. Pick a suitable muted colour non-reflective backdrop. Black card around the camera prevents reflection of you and your equipment. Use main and fill-in flash from well to the sides for controlled illumination

UNDERWATER
35 mm auto-exposure camera
with motor-drive in
underwater housing
21 mm lens
Action finder
Underwater flash on long
extension

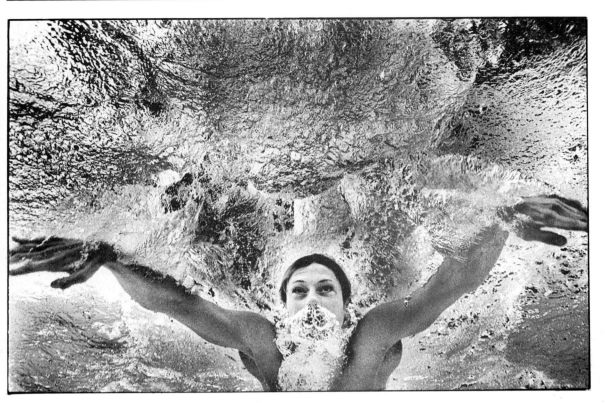

Fig. 8.16 A new angle on the butterfly stroke, showing how an Olympic swimmer expels air underwater. Chris Smith took this sports shot sitting at the bottom of the pool with an underwater 35 mm camera and 35 mm lens

waters. For close work, and at depths where only blue twilight remains, flash and battery lamps are the only satisfactory way to show subject colours. Never underestimate the potential dangers of diving and photographing underwater – always have at least one other person present.

Equipment and techniques

Underwater direct viewfinder cameras are small and handy but relatively primitive, especially for close work. An underwater housing for your 35 mm or rollfilm regular camera is expensive and cumbersome but you then have the imaging accuracy of an SLR and the ability to use your range of lenses. Remember that a housing with a domed port gives least optical distortion (page 46). Wear the smallest-volume face mask so that you can get your eye as close as possible to the camera eyepiece. If possible, change the regular SLR pentaprism for a sports action optical finder which lets you see the whole focusing screen from several inches away.

A wide-angle lens is by far the most useful choice underwater. It allows you to get everything in from a shorter lens-to-subject distance, so you suffer less light-loss and contrast-flattening scatter from all the particles of silt and plankton suspended in the water. An extreme focal length type, such as a 21 mm on a 35 mm camera, reduces its angle of view underwater to that of a 30 mm lens in air. Lack of visibility underwater also means that flash on the camera gives results like looking into fog. So have a waterproof flashgun on a long-jointed arm

Fig. 8.17 SLR camera in underwater housing, with flash on long adjustable extension arm. Flash should not be directed from the camera, but from well to one side

Fig. 8.18 Shallow-water diver working with a 35 mm camera in an underwater casing. Water quickly filters out longer wavelengths from daylight, giving this typical blue/cyan cast. Fit a compensating reddish filter, or use flash instead

which positions the light well to one side of the lens axis and closer to your subject. As a general guide underwater, do not try photographing subjects further away than about one quarter of the greatest distance your eyes can see.

Aerial subjects

Purposes

Air-to-ground photography at low altitude is used for pictorial shots of architecture and estates, records for traffic surveys, city planning and proposed new developments. It also forms a platform for press photography when covering large open-air events. In archaeology, aerial pictures (taken at dawn and dusk, when sunlight rakes the ground contours) often show up evidence of early structures invisible at ground level. Similarly, colour-filtered black and white shots or infra-red colour pictures in flatter light (during the middle of the day) reveal patterns in crops denoting earthworks and geological changes beneath the soil, as well as crop diseases. All these pictures are valuable for research, information and education. At higher altitudes, specialist aerial survey photography forms a vital reference for preparing accurate maps for resource planning and military purposes. (This merges into remote electronic imaging from satellites.) Air-to-air pictures of aircraft, ballooning, etc. are used for technical record, sales and general press pictures.

Approach and organization

The camera can be flown at low levels (up to 300 feet or so) in a model aircraft, balloon or kite and operated remotely from the ground. However, for more accurate, sustained work you need to be up there aiming the camera from a helicopter, fixed-wing aircraft or balloon. Helicopters are ideal for controlling your position in space but are expensive to hire and suffer from vibration. Air balloons make expensive, much less manoeuvrable but smoother camera platforms. You are most likely to do general low-level aerial photography from a light aircraft – preferably a high-wing type because this allows you maximum visibility. Have a window removed for oblique shots, and use an aperture in the cabin floor for vertical pictures.

To make best use of your hire costs, pick weather conditions which give the lighting you need. For example, air is clearest after a cold front has passed. Work out the time of day for the best direction and height of sunlight for your subject. Plan with the pilot the best flying height (links with focal length), provided that this complies with regulations such as a minimum 500 feet (150 metres) over country, 1500 feet (450 metres) over towns. The lower the height, the less light-scattering haze between you and your subject, so you get greater tone contrast and purer colours. Fix up a clear means of communication between you and the pilot. His cooperation and understanding of your needs are vital.

Equipment and techniques

Model aircraft, balloons and kites are able to lift a 35 mm motordrive camera, triggered by radio or controlled through the tethering wire. You operate the camera when it is seen to be pointing in the correct general direction. However, if your balloon or kite is powerful enough it will be practical to fit a miniature closed-circuit television camera to the still-camera eyepiece and so check what you are shooting from a monitor at ground level.

The best equipment for working from a full-size aircraft for general oblique photography is either a hand-held rollfilm aerial camera (see page 45) or a 35 mm SLR with normal and moderately wide-angle and long focal length lenses. Small-format cameras have the advantage of wider maximum apertures. Depth of field is not a problem, and this means that the best automatic exposure programme to use is shutter priority. Keep to 1/1000 or 1/500 second minimum, and let the camera's light reading control *f*-number.

Cushion the camera with your body or support it in a special hanging cradle – do not rest it on any part of the vibrating aircraft body.

Fig. 8.19 As when shooting still-life, try to choose lighting in aerial photography which picks out the folds of the land. Clear visibility is vital, especially when shooting against the light

Fig. 8.20 Camera-raising stands and platforms. Where you cannot be alongside the camera yourself, use video to monitor viewpoint (on mast and balloon here)

1500 ft (min)

500 ft

200 ft

60

50

22

16
14

8

Ceilings (feet)

Fig. 8.21 Video camera being fitted to a 35 mm SLR in place of removable pentaprism. Exact frame content can then be observed on a distant monitor

Filters are important to emphasize tone contrasts in black and white photography, and correct colour balance for colour work. An ultra-violet absorbing filter is best fitted as standard along with an efficient lens hood.

Vertical survey cameras are most often clamped on shock-absorbing supports looking downwards from within the aircraft fuselage. Typically, they shoot pictures 23 cm square on wide rollfilm, through a glass plate pressed hard over the emulsion and engraved with crosses at 1 cm intervals. By recording lens focal length aircraft height and ground speed as data alongside each frame you can make accurate measurements of ground distances from the processed film. It is vital that the aircraft flies at a steady height and speed over carefully planned flight lines so that by triggering cameras at timed intervals you get each shot overlapping in subject content by at least 30%. You can view prints or transparencies from such a series through a stereo viewer (page 52) or lay them out in an overlapping mosaic, from which maps are prepared.

Night skies

Purposes

Serious astronomical photography is mostly for experts, scientists with access to specialist equipment. However, as a non-expert you may want to photograph night skies as dramatic backgrounds for advertising products, fashion, etc. or as part of landscape or architectural pictures. (Remember that when star pictures are reproduced in print any specks of light smaller than the dots of the half-tone screen will disappear; see page 269).

Approach and organization

For best detail, pick a clear atmosphere and shoot in a rural area, well away from towns or highways, which will spill light upwards. If there is a product to be shown against the sky this can be lit independently by flash. Where you want some suggestion of detail in the landscape, take a series of pictures in clearest atmosphere at twilight (dawn or dusk). Stars appear at a constant intensity as the sky lightens or darkens, so the scene goes through a whole range of different lighting balances. The moon, like the sun, appears less bright when near the horizon. With careful planning you can record the moon with its surface detail at dawn or dusk, and still show most of the landscape detail (most realistically shot with the land one and a half to two stops underexposed).

Equipment and techniques

Long focal length lenses enlarge up moon detail but, curiously, have little effect on the image *size* of individual stars because of their vast distance away. Shooting with a telephoto simply limits your field of view. For starry skies it is often best to use a medium- or small-format camera with a wide aperture, normal or wide-angle focal length high-resolution lens. Then you can enlarge up from this picture later. Remember that the colour of starlight, and also the moon when high in the sky, is effectively the same as sunlight. Use daylight colour film.

Length of exposure may have to be found by trial and error, although most TTL meter systems will measure exposures of several minutes. Test exposure with the camera programmed for aperture priority, then time the exposure it gives and bracket around this with further shots. The longer the exposure, the more faint stars will record and bright stars flare. However, in practice, exposure is also influenced by four factors:

1. Blur caused by rotation of the Earth;
2. The light-gathering power of the lens (not *f*-number in this instance);
3. The reciprocity failure of your film (see page 73);
4. The general background brightness of the sky which gradually accumulates as light on the film, swamping detail.

The amount that the images of stars move during any given exposure depends on the part of the sky and your lens focal length. The pole star appears to remain stationary while all other stars rotate about it, 360° in 23 hours 56 minutes. As a guide, stars are likely to record as streaks instead of dots in a 1 second or longer exposure with a firmly clamped 500 mm lens. To keep all star images still, borrow an equatorial telescope mount which has motors and gears to gradually pan the camera against the Earth's rotation.

Another special feature of astronomical work is that a lens's starlight-gathering power depends on the *area* of its effective aperture, not its relative aperture (*f*-number). The wider the 'hole', the more photons of starlight the film will accumulate in a given time, irrespective of focal length. So a 500 mm lens at *f*/11 (effective aperture diameter 45 mm) becomes faster than an 80 mm *f*/2 (effective aperture diameter only 40 mm). This applies for point sources such as stars; for extended sources such as comets or nebulae the relative aperture is important.

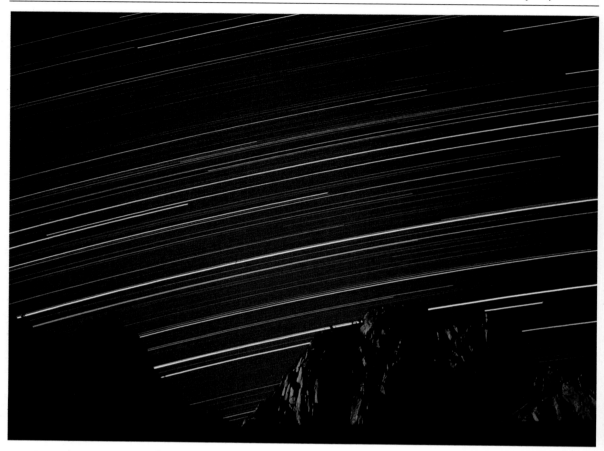

Fig. 8.22 The tracks of satellites, planets and stars recorded by a static camera during an exposure of several hours. Photographed from a high altitude in the mountains, the clear air allowed hundreds of tracks to record without light-scatter destroying contrast. Most of the colours here are normally unnoticed when you see objects only as specks of light (Marion Patterson/Science Photo Library)

Summary: Subject problems

● In sports photography you need subject knowhow and anticipation, patience and fast reaction. Pick moments of human tension and reactions. A good viewpoint is vital, plus a good range of lenses – mostly telephotos. Go for movement and dynamic action, often through controlled blur, dramatic angles, correct choice of moment. Do not rely on autofocus and motordrive to create good pictures.

● A good photojournalistic picture story needs research, ample shooting time to express a point of view and sympathetic final layout. Often the best work is people based. Adopt a positive, determined approach yet remain sensitive to significant events. A small-format inconspicuous camera kit and use of existing light will least influence your subject matter. Close viewpoint and wide-angle lens give a sense of dramatic involvement and overcome lack of distance in tight situations. Standing back with a telephoto closely relates near and far components.

● Portraits (for flattery or character) might be shot in the studio or in the sitter's own environment to add to content. Decide what features and postures to emphasize. Camera viewpoint, your personal direction of the sitter, lighting and surroundings are all important but never so fixed that they prevent freedom to relax and relate as person to person.

Work with a longer than normal focal length lens, using studio flash or existing light.

● Weddings are undervalued but responsible occasions for a photographer. Contact the people concerned, go over the details, plan your key shots. Dress appropriately. Pick the best possible backgrounds. Work calmly but authoritatively, covering formal and informal elements. Have a medium-format camera and tripod for groups, hand-held 35 mm for incidentals.

● Landscape photography ranges from a personal art form through pictorial travel illustration to objective geographic records. Pictures can symbolize abstract feelings, concepts or document social ecology. Plan the work, picking weather and time of day (lighting), distance and viewpoint. Medium- or even large-format cameras offer best tone qualities and detail. Do not overlook filters.

● Architectural photography ranges from the needs of real estate, architects or environmentalists to being a subject of form and texture for self-expression. Time the best lighting for chosen viewpoints – avoid flat, overcast conditions. Check the external appearance of lighted buildings at dusk. Expect to simplify internal furnishings, and counter lighting which is excessively uneven or of mixed colour temperature. Have a camera with movements, and include a high-quality wide-angle lens, flashgun or lamps and filters.

● Studio sets, built from flats, allow unobstructed use of lighting and camera viewpoint. Chosen props mean that you control every detail but avoid a false 'museum' look; do not overlight. For realism with scale models, accurately scale down your viewpoint and maximize depth of field. Use a camera with movements.

● Still lifes (advertising merchandise, technical records, editorial or poster illustration) need a disciplined approach to a totally controlled situation. Decide important subject qualities, pick appropriate non-confusing props and background, build up your lighting. Simplicity throughout is often best. For most work, subject matter must be immaculate. Have prepared foods made up professionally, undercooked for optimum appearance. Expect to use studio flash and a camera offering movements.

● Natural history illustration needs to combine scientific accuracy with strong visual qualities and is helped by specialist subject knowhow. Research best natural location and timing to suit subject habits. Pick an informative activity and background. Long focal length lenses are often vital. For some animals or birds, shoot from a hide or use a remote-controlled or subject-triggered camera. Tackle flower/insect close-ups with a macro lens and an off-camera flash. Log subject information.

● Underwater photography ranges from simple aquarium shots to pictures shot at depths. Subjects appear closer and larger, and lens angle of view is narrower than on land. Natural light dims to blue-grey monotone (correctable by filter down to 10 metres, 30 feet). Use flash to reveal true colours, but position it well off-camera. Shoot with a wide-angle medium- or small-format camera in a domed port underwater housing. Do not expect subject detail much beyond one quarter as far as you can see.

● Aerial photography includes obliques of architecture, highways, archaeology, etc.; vertical surveys for map making; air-to-air shots of other aircraft. Appropriate choice of lighting, filtration and special (infra-red) film helps reveal features not normally visible from the ground. Work from a helicopter or high-wing light aircraft, timing your flight according to light and weather. Use a rollfilm aerocamera or 35 mm SLR, working shutter priority mode (1/500 second or faster). Survey cameras, set vertically within the aircraft and fired remotely, record speed and height data alongside the image.

● Night-sky pictures for general purposes are best shot in clear air, far from town lights. Dawn and twilight offer greatest choice of landscape/ starlight/moon balance. For starry skies, use medium- or small-format equipment with a good wide-aperture normal lens and daylight colour film. Exposures beyond a few seconds blur from Earth rotation (unless you have an equatorial mount). Other limitations are film reciprocity failure, the area of your effective lens aperture, and ambient light within the sky.

9
Processing management

Beginners process their films in individual handtanks and their black and white prints in open trays. However, as your volume of work grows and you start to use a range of critical colour processes, you need to think how processing should best be organized. It may be sensible to send everything out to a professional laboratory, split it so that you still process black and white films and prints, or perhaps aim to become self-sufficient in all your processing and even offer a service to others. The reasons for going it alone in any process include quicker turnaround, tighter quality control and long-term saving of costs. Against this, you must afford the necessary equipment and the expense of running it. Most important of all, you must be able to consistently produce results at least as good as you can buy from an outside laboratory.

Good processing management means understanding all the current ways of processing quantities of films and papers, monochrome and colour. This chapter starts off with the main processes themselves and the practical handling points you have to watch. Then it looks broadly at different kinds of equipment designed to get chemicals to act on film or paper – conveniently, consistently and economically – whatever the process. You should also be able to regularly check out your processing in some way which will detect changes and trends before they noticeably start affecting pictures. So you must know the best practical ways of process monitoring for quality control. The chapter also discusses how money can be saved by replenishing developing solutions to extend their working lives and by recovering silver by-products from used fixers.

The processes themselves

Processing is rather like modern convenience cooking. The required ingredients are pre-packed, being built into the chemical solutions and light-sensitive emulsions; the procedure is set out by the manufacturers as a sequence of stages. You do not need to understand the chemical detail of what is going on, but it is essential to arrange that

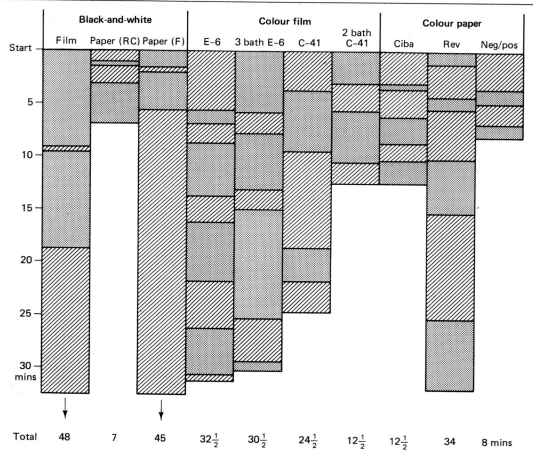

	Black-and-white			Colour film				Colour paper		
	Film	Paper (RC)	Paper (F)	E-6	3 bath E-6	C-41	2 bath C-41	Ciba	Rev	Neg/pos
Total	48	7	45	$32\frac{1}{2}$	$30\frac{1}{2}$	$24\frac{1}{2}$	$12\frac{1}{2}$	$12\frac{1}{2}$	34	8 mins

Fig. 9.1 Comparison of the number of stages (including rinses and wash) and total time required for different film and paper processes. Notice the variation in the processing times for fibre-base (F) black and white prints, against plastic based prints, monochrome and colour. As processes are updated they steadily take less time, require fewer stages

each solution is in good condition and has its proper effect. This means organizing timing, temperature and agitation throughout the correct order of steps required for each process. If something goes wrong, you can ruin expensive solutions or be left with images which are too pale or dense, wrong in contrast, off-colour, uneven, stained, scratched or impermanent. In some instances (steps in the wrong order, for example) there may be no final image at all.

Figure 9.1 summarizes some common sequences of stages for various types of film and paper processing. At one time there were almost as many different colour processes as brands of colour materials. Today these have become rationalized, so that virtually all reversal colour film except Kodachrome needs the same process E-6 and colour negative films C-41. Neg/pos colour paper uses process EP-2 and reversal paper either R-14 or (Cibachrome) a dye-bleach process. Shorter versions of several of these processes are available, for example combining certain stages. Some are designed to speed production from mini-lab equipment; others are for convenient one-shot processing by amateurs, rather than longer-term storage in the tanks of large processing machines.

Unless a radically new and important material requiring a different process comes onto the market, manufacturers prefer to make changes gradually, through adjustments to chemical kits in tandem with emulsion updates. This is because machines in commercial laboratories are dedicated to one or other process at a time. Paper processing can always be rationalized 'in house' according to the material the laboratory chooses to print on. However, if customers' films start to arrive needing all kinds of different processing chemistry, costly investment in new machinery may not justify handling the new product.

Chemical solutions often vary in dilution (and sometimes in content) according to whether you intend processing in small tanks or trays, deep tanks or processing machines with varying kinds of agitation. Machines are convenient but expensive, and suit some situations and processes better than others. First, bear in mind the different procedures and limitations in processing various kinds of exposed photographic material. The processes summarized below are typical current types. But all of them change in detail from time to time, mostly to reduce times and generally make them more convenient to use.

Black and white silver image negatives

Black and white negative films need only the simple sequence of developer, stop bath, fixer and wash, although they must be handled with the same physical care as is necessary with any other materials for top-quality results. You have a wide choice of developers, from softworking speed-reducing types such as Perceptol through general fine-grain developers D76/ID11 and HC-110 to high-acutance or speed-enhancing types and high pH extreme contrast solutions like line or lith developers.

Not all of these will suit all films, of course. Specialist purposes apart (lith films, etc.), decide the two or three developers which, combined with the few films you use most, best suit subject conditions and the required image 'look'. For example, in low-intensity, low-contrast lighting conditions ISO 400/27° film can be pushed to ISO 3200/36° in speed-enhancing developer provided that you accept coarse grain and loss of tone delicacy. The same film in D76 gives a better compromise between speed, grain, resolution and tonal quality, and is more easily fine-tuned for different subject contrast conditions by adjusting development times. You might, however, prefer a high-resolution developer like Rodinal for least grain and maximum tone gradation on slow film, or go for a 'gritty' grain effect by combining it with fast films (see *Basic Photography*, Chapter 11).

Sometimes your choice is influenced by the need for a developer which offers you a range of characteristics according to dilution, or perhaps you have to process on location so it is essential to work on a 'one-shot' basis, discarding the solution after use. On the other hand, for studio work, you might have a developer you can keep using for 3 months (with replenishment) in a deep tank. Unlike colour, black and white film processing offers great freedom to choose results through type of solution relative to type of emulsion as well as dilution and timing. It is also possible, with most formulae, to work at any temperature between 18° and 24°C and fully compensate by adjusting time.

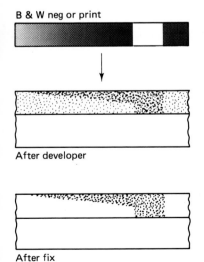

B & W neg or print

After developer

After fix

Fig. 9.2 Basic schematic diagram of black and white processing. Development reduces light-struck halides to black silver. Fixing causes the remaining halides to become soluble, so they can be removed from the emulsion by washing

Colour slides and transparencies

The first stage of reversal processing (Figure 9.5) forms a black silver negative in each of the film's emulsion layers. (It is the *remaining* emulsion which later stages turn into a colour positive, then remove all the black silver.) You can therefore adjust the time of this first development to compensate for up- or down-rating of film speed when shooting, rather like black and white work. Similarly, the degree of development alters the contrast of your result. However, remember that the range of adjustments open to you is much more limited, for unlike a black and white negative, the processed film is your finished picture. Beyond a certain point the image looks 'wrong', with coarser or flatter colours, pale shadows and a tendency to take on a colour cast which differs according to brand and type. Again, unlike black and white, there is no ability to *choose* developer for finer grain, greater acutance, extra speed, etc. Temperature is also much more critical.

In the E-6 process, designed for the great majority of films having colour couplers within their emulsion ('integral colour couplers') the next stage chemically fogs all remaining silver halides in the film. Then colour developer turns these halides into black silver, forming by-products which join with different colour couplers in each layer to create yellow, magenta and cyan dye images. Colour formation in this way is known as chromogenic development – dye amounts are in direct relation to the amounts of silver the colour developer forms. Sophisticated chemical cross-reactions (such as developer inhibitor release, Chapter 5) enhance image quality at this stage, so colour development must function strictly to specification.

The next stages remove unwanted residues, i.e. the black silver negative and positive images which together still make the film totally opaque. This is done by bleaching the silver back to silver halide and then fixing. (On shortened three-bath E-6 processing bleach and fix are combined, using more complex formulae to preserve their properties when together in solution.) The later stages of bleaching can take place in normal lighting because there is nothing light-sensitive left to fog. As the black fades, you start to see colours for the first time. Soluble by-products and absorbed processing chemicals are then washed out. Finally, a stabilization bath leaves the film in a chemically buffered state which improves image dye resistance to fading.

If all this sounds complicated, it involves far less stages than the older but still-used Kodachrome process. Kodachrome has no couplers built in, so each emulsion layer has to be *separately* fogged and *separately* yellow, magenta and cyan colour developed. Some twenty stages (including coloured fogging light) make factory machinery and technical staffing essential.

Colour negatives

The first stage here (Figure 9.7) is colour development, forming black silver and the three different-coloured dyes wherever the emulsions were affected by light. During development (and subsequent silver removal and stabilization) fine changes also occur to the integral colour masks (page 94). Properly carried out, this should give a colour negative matched in contrast range and different

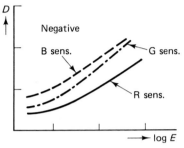

Fig. 9.3 Mis-processing can produce 'crossed curves' in the response of (top) colour reversal, and (bottom) colour negative film. The slide here will have a magenta cast to shadows, cyan cast to highlights. Colour prints from the negative will show an increasingly greenish cast in darker tones when correctly filtered for palest parts of the picture

absorptions of blue, green and red light to 'fit' the characteristics of the same maker's neg/pos colour printing paper. Departures from normal (such as lack of tight temperature control, or pushing or holding back to adjust for different ISO speeds or for different lighting contrasts) produce problems at the printing stage. Such negatives *look* all right to the eye but are mismatched to the paper. They may have crossed curves (Figure 9.3), which means that prints have one colour cast in highlights and pale tones and another, different cast in dark tones and shadows. No one set of filter settings can correct this during enlarging. Absolute consistency of film processing is therefore important.

Chromogenic (dye image) monochrome negatives

Dye image monochrome films contain couplers in their several emulsion layers and so conveniently allow you to give the same chromogenic processing as colour negatives. Results are a warm, brownish black – the combined dye layers give a rich tone scale and allow good exposure latitude. However, since image colour is not related to subject colours you can freely alter development times to make ISO speed and contrast adjustments. Where colour processing is not available you can give the film regular black and white processing instead. Negatives then consist of black silver instead of dye. Speed is reduced and grain in overexposed areas is more noticeable than dye image results.

Cross-processing of films

Treating films in a processing sequence designed for another film type gives a variety of results, illustrated in Figure 9.4. This is one way of producing 'off-beat' colour images – results are typically harsh contrast negatives or flat degraded slides. Sometimes you may use the wrong combination by error. If the result is a black and white negative from colour film you may at least be able to make black and white prints. E-6 or C-41 films given black and white processing can often be salvaged as colour negatives by bleaching the black silver to a silver halide, fogging it to strong light and then giving full C-41 colour negative processing. Check with the manufacturer of your film for current information. All forms of misprocessing understandably

If this film:	Is given this processing:	The result will be:
Regular B & W	E-6 or C-41	Clear film
Slide (E-6 type)	C-41	Contrasty, unmasked colour neg
	B & W neg	Pale B & W neg*
Kodachrome	E-6	Clear film
	B & W neg	B & W neg with backing† dye still present
Colour neg (C-41 type)	E-6	Low contrast, cyan cast slide. No mask colour
	B & W neg	Ghost-thin B & W neg* with mask colour

Fig. 9.4 What happens when you put film through the wrong process. 'Regular' black and white means silver image films, not dye image types designed for C-41

* May be possible to salvage as a colour neg. See text.
† Removable in film strength rapid fixer plus 8 grams/litre citric acid.

Fig. 9.5 Cross-section (simplified) of reversal colour slide film incorporating couplers. 1: emulsions receive image formed by camera lens. 2: after first (B & W) development. Black silver created where B, G or R sensitive emulsions respond to image. 3: after remaining halides are chemically fogged and developed in colour developer. Black silver and either yellow, magenta or cyan have formed in each layer. 4: after bleaching and fixing away all black silver. Only the dye images remain; when viewed against a white light source they reform original image colours

Fig. 9.6 Pos/pos colour reproduction with dye-bleach paper. 1: slide, projected by enlarger. 2: simplified layers, already containing dye with silver halides, exposing to image. 3: after development, black silver negative images form in each layer according to emulsion response. 4: after silver/dye bleaching. Dyes remain only in areas unaffected by development. The print reproduces the colours and tones of the original slide

Fig. 9.7 Neg/pos colour reproduction. 1: original image exposed in camera. 2: after colour development the colour negative film carries black silver plus yellow, magenta or cyan coupled dye where emulsion layers have responded to image colours. 3: after bleaching and fixing away black silver. 4: the resulting colour negative. 5: negative exposed onto colour paper, then colour developed. Black silver and a coupled dye form according to each emulsion response to exposure. 6: after each bleaching and fixing. Seen against its white base, dye layers reform colours of original camera image

upset the film's ISO speed rating. If you use this technique on purpose you must make tests to discover effective film speed.

Black and white prints

Fewer developers are designed for printing papers than for films, and they are all more active and fast-working. Choice centres on the 'colour' of the black silver image they produce more than any other factor. Regular, PQ type developers give a neutral black on bromide papers, either fibre or RC (plastic) based. RC papers develop much faster because of developing agents already incorporated into the emulsion which hasten the start of visible image formation. The non-absorbing base also minimizes carry-over of chemicals so that further stages – especially final washing – are much shorter.

Other restrained type developers for chlorobromide emulsion papers give results ranging from cold black to rich brown, according to formula. A few MQ/PQ 'Universal' developers are intended for black and white film *and* paper – they are used less diluted for prints. Generally, you should keep print-development times constant. Too little development gives grey shadows and weak darker tone values; too much begins to yellow the paper base and veil highlights due to chemical fog. After development, stop bath and acid hardening fixer can be the same formula as for films, although the fixer is used at greater dilution.

Colour prints from negatives

The two-solution process used for neg/pos materials is like a truncated form of colour negative film processing. All colour printing papers have an RC base. During the critical first stage the colour developer produces black silver in exposed emulsion layers and by-products which react with different couplers in each layer to give cyan, magenta and yellow image dyes. See Figure 9.7. This is followed by a bleach-fix stage to convert the silver into soluble compounds you remove in a final wash.

There is no flexibility in timing, and in professional processing kits the developer temperature is critical. However, some colour print kits designed for amateurs are specially formulated to be run at any temperature between 20° and 38°C, while others can be used to process both colour negatives and colour prints, although the total processing times needed are then slightly longer. It is very important that processing gives print-to-print consistency. Variations create images with colour shifts, poor tone range and stains. This can totally confuse your attempts to control results on the enlarger through filtration and exposure (see Chapter 10).

Colour prints from slides

Pos/pos colour prints made direct from colour slides and transparencies are processed in two quite different ways, according to paper type. The two most used materials are (1) Cibachrome, requiring dye-bleach processing, and (2) reversal paper, requiring a quite different processing sequence, similar to slide film.

Cibachrome material has fully formed cyan, magenta and yellow dye layers already present in the red-, green- and blue-responsive emulsion layers. See Figure 9.6. You expose it to your colour slide image through the enlarger. The first stage of dye-bleach processing uses a black and white developer to form a negative black silver image in each emulsion layer according to its response to the light. The second chemical step is a bleach which removes the silver *and the dye where silver is present.* At the next step the by-products of bleaching are made soluble by fixing and finally removed by washing. The remaining unbleached dyes leave you with a positive colour image matching your slide.

The advantage of dye-bleach material is that ready-formed dyes are purer in colour and more permanent than those formed chemically (chromogenically) by coupling. Images have bold, rich colouring well suited to display prints of commercial subjects. However, the material is quite slow to light, due to the light-stopping power of the colouring present, and the bleach chemical is more toxic than most other photographic solutions (see page 206). With some dye-bleach processing kits you can alter the black and white development to adjust contrast. Diluting the solution decreases print contrast and extending the time increases it.

Reversal colour paper has conventional emulsion layers incorporating couplers and needs reversal processing via a longer series of steps than dye-bleach. The various stages are effectively the same as shown in Figure 9.5. First, a developer forms black and white negatives then, after a stop bath, the remaining emulsion is fogged and colour developed into black silver plus positive dye images. Later stages bleach/fix and wash away all silver and finally stabilize your print. The chemical solution temperatures are very critical and you are not recommended to control contrast by adjusting first development or to alter the timing of any stage. (Remember that you can also make prints from slides via internegs; see page 248.)

Points to watch

Whatever process you intend to carry out, the key aspects to organize properly are:

Temperature; timing; agitation; physical handling without damage; and the condition of chemicals.

Temperature

This must be tightly controlled if you expect to handle critical processes with any consistency. Large volumes of each solution hold their temperature longer than small ones, although much depends on the ambient room temperature and how much solution surface area is exposed to the air. Small quantities for 'one-shot' use can be brought to correct temperature quickly, but equally they soon change again if poured into a tank or trough which is colder or warmer. Temperature-controlled water or air-jacketing of solutions plus any separate container for the material you are processing helps to avoid problems.

For black and white hand-processing the temperature needed is within the range of normal (temperate zone) room temperatures. If you have to use a temperature higher or lower than specified, a time/temperature table or graph (Figure 9.8) for your particular solution shows how to adjust timing in compensation. However, do

Fig. 9.8 Time/temperature graph for a black and white developer which gives correct density and contrast when used for 4½ minutes at 20°C. Between 16 and 24°C temperature changes can be largely compensated for by altering time

not exceed upper or lower limits – some chemical components of any one solution will be more affected than others, so that processing characteristics change. Colour processing generally functions at higher. temperatures than black and white and within narrower tolerances. Variations outside the limits laid down affect the rates of development in different emulsion layers, so you may get a faulty colour balance.

One way of working when conditions make it impossible to maintain one temperature is to use the 'drift-by' technique. This means warming the solution to, say, the upper limit temperature for the start of the processing step, so that although it gradually cools it does not drop below the lower acceptable limit by the end of that step.

Timing

Accurate timing is as important as accurate temperature. Times given for each step when you hand-process include a 10-second drain period for films (20 seconds for prints) to avoid carry-over of chemical into the next solution. Timings are usually different when you process by machine, depending on how the film is agitated in your type of equipment (see page 210). Increases or reductions in the timing of black and white development (not colour development) stages are the best way to push or hold back films to compensate for under- or overexposure. Colour slide films can be pushed up to two stops or held back for one stop without much side-effect, provided that this also suits subject contrast. You can go even further with black and white films. In both instances fast films designed to give the option of push-processing are the most responsive.

Agitation

Controlled agitation, especially in developers, is much more important than it may at first seem. To give too little produces uneven action and insufficient density in negative highlights. By-products diffuse from emulsions too slowly, forming streamers. Too much agitation can create uneven 'flow marks', particularly in films carrying perforations. Over-agitation also allows more fresh developer to reach the emulsion than is intended for the process, giving extra highlight density. In colour films too much agitation disturbs the way by-products are produced in emulsion layers, giving excessive dye formation. All these points are looked after in well-designed processing machines or deep tank lines using automatic nitrogen-burst agitation (see page 209). Agitation is often the source of inconsistent results if you are distracted or careless when hand-processing. Follow precisely the agitation specified for your particular processing solution or kit.

Physical handling

Do not forget that you are basically dealing with a thin layer of gelatin, absorbant to liquids (unintentional as well as planned) and especially delicate when wet and swollen. Troubles can begin with liquid splashes or damp hands before processing or clumsy loading of reels or clips. The material might be damaged from contact with the side of the tank during agitation or poorly maintained rollers in

Fig. 9.14 Replenishment technique. 1: dip a container into the tank of processing solution. Remove more liquid than the measured volume of replenisher (R) you have prepared. 2: pour in all the replenisher. 3: top up again by returning some of the solution you removed originally, then discard the surplus

terminal state of exhaustion and must be thrown away. The whole point is to keep it working consistently for as long as possible, so that you get greatest value for money.

Equipment

Highly controlled *machine* processing is ideal for the least flexible, temperature-critical processes such as colour negatives and prints and reversal colour films and prints. It also suits black and white RC prints. On the other hand, the variety of developer/emulsion combinations you can pick from for black and white negative and fibre-base printing paper still makes hand-processing attractive. Hand-processing is also the easiest way to vary development times for individual sheets or rolls of film, as required for the zone system (page 151).

If you are thinking of some form of machine-processing look first at your volume and pattern of throughput. For small quantities and occasional use a small unit using one-shot chemistry will be best,

Fig. 9.15 The advantages of hand processing and machine processing

For hand-processing	For machine-processing
● Flexibility	● Consistency
● Low capital cost	● Convenience
● Less money committed to chemicals	● Speed of through-put
● Can stand idle at times	● Low cost per film/print (if sufficient quantities)
● Suits process manipulation	● Less labour-intensive
● Less risk of mechanical damage	● Can handle long rolls of film/paper

especially if you can also use the same chemical kit for, say, colour negatives and colour prints. At the other extreme, a large, fully automatic machine accepts exposed material in the darkroom at one end and returns it back dry to the normally lit workroom at the other. However, this equipment will prove inconsistent as well as ruinously expensive to run if you have too little to put through it. Figure 9.15 compares the technical and economic features of manual and machine-processing.

Fig. 9.16 Producing large black and white prints (photo-murals). Lengths from a roll of bromide paper can be overlapped for image exposure, using your enlarger horizontally. Bottom: hand processing by rolling the paper in a sink filled with (diluted) developer. To remain manageable the paper is always rolled towards you. Then the roll is up-ended, reversed, and rolled towards you again

Processing in trays

Manual processing in open trays or troughs is still appropriate for small volumes of black and white non-panchromatic prints or sheet films. It is very flexible: you can easily check results under safe lighting during processing and use relatively small quantities of chemicals, including short-life lith developer. Equipment is cheap. Very large prints can be rolled through a trough of diluted developer as shown in Figure 9.16. However, trough or tray processing is messy, unhealthy (you breathe in chemical) and not very consistent. Solutions oxidize quickly and it is easy to contaminate one with another. All colour work and any processing needing total darkness is too awkward and unpleasant to be handled this way.

Tanks and tank lines

Small roll or sheet film hand tanks are the cheapest reliable method of processing one to three films at a time (see *Basic Photography*). The next step up is to have a run of deep tanks, each 15 litre capacity (Figure 9.17) set into a temperature-controlled water or air jacket. Each tank contains a separate chemical solution, according to the process you are running, plus a rinse/wash tank. You can process individual sheet film in hangers, agitating them by hand and moving them from tank to tank in darkness. Quantities of sheet film, rollfilms in reels and printing paper can be handled the same way in purpose-made racks. A single rack will accommodate up to 20 or 30 reels of 120 or 35 mm film, or 24 sheets of 4 × 5 inch film.

The best form of deep-tank agitation comes from a gas distributor grid which goes along with the rack. The grid is piped to give out timed bursts of (inert) nitrogen gas to agitate whichever solution you are using. Consider gas burst agitation essential for deep-tank colour processing. Tank lines are fairly cheap to set up and run for any

Fig. 9.17 Basic 15 litre tank line. Water jacket (J) encloses all tanks and is fed from thermostatic mixing valve (M) which also supplies wash tank (W). Temperature monitoring unit T has probe directly below critical developer tank (1). If temperature drops, monitor causes solenoid (S) to inject additional hot water. Nitrogen gas passes through electronic valve (V) regulating the frequency and duration of each gas burst. It then supplies flat tube distributor (D) moved from tank to tank along with rack (R) of films on hangers (H). After first stages demanding total darkness you pass the film rack through a trap to other half of unit, in room lighting. Here another gas distributor can take over

process and allow sufficient throughput for smaller professional users. However, someone has to be present to manually handle every batch – reversal processing is especially hard work. You must take care over process control (page 215) and replenishment if you want consistency. A series of large batches easily bring on exhaustion effects with only 15 litres of solution.

Drum processors

The heart of a drum processor is a light-tight cylinder you load with paper (or film in a suitable adaptor). All processing stages then take place in normal light. The cylinder rotates on motor-driven rollers within a water jacket and you pour in a small quantity of processing solution through a light-trapped funnel (Figure 9.18). Within the

Fig. 9.18 Drum processor. Drums accept print or film (roll or 35 mm on reels) loaded in the dark. Storage containers, graduates of chemical, and drum are all half-submerged in temperature-controlled water jacket. Drum couples to motor unit through magnetic lid. Lever (L) is used to tilt drum at end of each stage, discarding used solution down drain. The next chemical is then poured into funnel (F) while drum continues to rotate

turning drum the solution spreads rapidly and evenly over the surface of the emulsion. Drum movement gives controlled agitation; your thermostatic water jacket controls temperature. Notice how, unlike tank processing, where material is totally immersed in solution and given intermittent agitation, drum processors give intermittent immersion and continuous agitation. This may mean changing timings, even though solutions and temperatures remain the same.

Drum processors work on the discard principle – at the end of each step you tilt the drum, throw away the used solution, then return it to the cradle and pour in the next liquid. A few models can be programmed to work automatically, but most are labour-intensive. However, a drum processor is versatile and reliable and also the most economic way to process occasional large colour prints, although it is slow and inconvenient for large quantities of paper or film. Maximum capacity per loading ranges from four to 20 prints 8 × 10 inches or two to ten 120 rollfilms, according to drum size.

Automatic processors

With fully automatic, programmed processors you are moving up into the big league – financially and in terms of throughput. The cost of equipment may be ten times as much as a manual drum system. The four main types are known as rotary discard, roller transport, dip-and-dunk and continuous-strand machines, according to the way they move the film through solutions. Most need large and therefore expensive tanks of processing chemicals which makes them uneconomic to run unless you process *at least* a hundred films or 50 prints per week. They are ideally suited to multiple-stage, rigorously controlled colour processes – you can safely leave them like washing machines and do other jobs while they are at work.

Rotary discard machines

A rotary discard or trough processor is similar to a scaled-up drum machine. However, as Figure 9.19 shows, you clip the films or papers to be processed to the *outside* of an appropriately designed cylindrical frame, emulsion outwards. Typically, a batch ranging from one to 12 rolls of 35 mm film can be loaded at one time, working in the dark. Then you close the lid and work in normal light, starting a pre-set programme which rotates the frame and pumps up a small quantity of the first solution into the trough. At the end of each stage a drain automatically opens to discard the solution. Then rinse water or other chemical solutions are pumped from their holding tanks and discarded in turn to complete the process. Finally, you open the unit and, like a drum processor, remove the still-wet material for drying.

The advantage of a rotary discard machine is its versatility. With a range of tanks holding the chemicals for different processes and appropriate timing programs (switch-in computer chips) you can be processing colour prints one moment and E-6 films half an hour later. The timing of any stage can be overridden for pushing or holding back films. A jacket around the trough as well as the compartment enclosing tanks of solution is thermostatically heated. The one-shot processing means that there is no need for replenishment and minimal risk of cross-contamination. However, chemical costs are quite high if

Fig. 9.19 Rotary discard processor. Exposed material in batches (lengths or sheets of film, or sheets of paper) wrap around open spools which rotate in an enclosed trough. With the lid shut, solutions are pumped up in turn from temperature-controlled reservoirs. See text

you put a lot through the machine. To save money, chosen solutions (for example, bleach or fix) can be re-routed after discharge into a holding tank for repeated use or silver recovery (page 219).

Roller transport machines

These machines contain dozens of slow-moving rollers, turning continuously to transport *individual* films or sheets of paper, usually up and down along a sequence of deep tanks. They are mostly designed to be built through the darkroom wall (Figure 9.20) and into a lit area. You feed your material through dry receiving rollers in darkness and receive it back dry from the delivery end of the machine

Fig. 9.20 Roller transport processing machine, showing the path taken by sheets of material. This one is designed for colour paper — similar types made for films differ in their roller surface and dryer detail

where it has finally passed through an air-jet drying unit. The large-volume tanks are thermostatically controlled; the rollers give continuous agitation. Roller speed is the same in all tanks – for the longest stages of processing you have tanks which are deeper or longer than tanks for short stages. You can run the whole machine slower or faster while films to be pushed or held back are passing through the developer stage.

Roller transport machines are very convenient to use. You can feed in a mixture of sheets or lengths of film (or sheets or rolls of paper) at any time, unlike batch-loaded processors. However, each machine tends to be dedicated to a particular process. Changing to another is possible but may mean draining and changing expensive volumes of solution, which can be a major operation. Typically a 24-inch wide roller machine designed to process neg/pos colour prints at 20 cm per minute can turn out up to 120 prints 8 × 10 inch every hour.

In deep-tank roller transport machines the chemicals have to be very carefully replenished, usually by automatic injection. You should check process performance every day. With so many rollers in direct contact with the gelatin emulsion regular cleaning and good maintenance are vital. Otherwise chemical by-products, flakes of gelatin, scale or grit build up on rollers and damage everything you put through. Roller units lift out of the machine as a series of racks. On some processors you must remove racks from developers and rinse them at the end of each day, leaving the surface of the chemical covered by a floating lid.

A few smaller-capacity benchtop roller processors for prints use long shallow trays instead of tanks. They work on the principle of batch chemistry. Here you discard and replace the two litres or so of solution when a given maximum amount of material has passed through (say, 25 Cibachrome prints, 8 × 10 inches). A small 10-inch wide machine working at 8.5 cm per minute takes an hour to output this number of prints. See Figure 10.7.

Fig. 9.21 Dip-and-dunk film processor. Machine stands entirely in darkroom — gantry contains elevator (shown in action, right). Pumps circulate chemicals. Drying cabinet, nearest end, accumulates finished work

Dip-and-dunk film processors

Also known as a 'rack and carriage' or 'rack and tank' processors, these are effectively a robot form of deep-tank hand line. As Figure 9.21 shows, the machine stands in the darkroom and films are suspended from hangers on a motorized lift/carriage unit over a series of tanks. The machine lowers hangers into solution, gradually inches them along the full length of the first tank, then lifts and lowers them into the next solution. The longest stages have the longest tanks, and the solutions are thermostatically heated and pump circulated. Films on their hangers finally pass along a drying compartment. There is no risk of damage from poorly maintained rollers with a dip-and-dunk processor. Mechanically, the equipment is fairly simple but requires a lot of space (with good headroom) and large volumes of solutions. Machines are also dedicated to particular processes. You can put through material of mixed sizes at any time by attaching a rack of films to the transport mechanism at the start point of the process. Output ranges from about 40 to 100 rollfilms (120) per hour, according to the size of the machine.

Continuous-strand processors

Machines of this type are designed for processing long lengths of film (aero-survey or movie films, for example) or paper (output from

Drying   Wet processing

Fig. 9.22 Continues strand processor, working from a bulk reel of exposed film

rollpaper printers). They work like roller transport deep-tank units but only have rollers at the top and bottom of each tank (see Figure 9.22). To start up, you must thread the machine with a leader and then attach to the end of this the material you want to process. Other lengths of the same width are attached in turn to the end of previous material, forming one or more continuous strands passing through the machine at constant speed and rolling up dry at the other end. When used for prints, really accurate instrument control of image exposure and light filtration is essential, for it is not very practical to put through test exposures.

You must take the same care over solution replenishment and cleanliness as for deep-tank roller transport processors, although the equipment is internally much simpler. Agitation takes place through movement of the material you are processing through the tanks, but some processors inject gas-burst agitation into key solutions as well. Each machine is dedicated to a particular process. Solutions are continually replenished and recirculated through filter and heater units by pumps. A large paper-processing machine of this kind can produce about 500 8 × 10 inch colour prints per hour.

Making a choice

There is clearly a great difference between a simple hand-tank and a fully automatic processing machine, although they can both run the same process. Similarly, every update in a process which can shave off a few minutes (or, better still, combine solutions without loss of quality) means a substantial increase in output from the bigger machines. Before deciding on what equipment to buy (or whether to use a reliable custom laboratory instead) think hard about each of the following.

Pattern of workload

Is this steady and consistent, or varied and erratic? Do you want facilities that are flexible, or need to churn out steady quantities using one process only? How important is speed? Would it be best to buy something that has greater capacity than your immediate needs, with an eye on the future? (Perhaps you could also do some processing for other photographers in the first instance.)

Cost

This is not just the capital cost of the equipment but the often high-priced chemicals it uses, plus servicing and spares. Cheapest outlay is on labour-intensive facilities like a hand-tank line, but this will take up a lot of your time. Paying someone else to work it could prove more expensive than an automatic machine.

Installation

Do you have enough darkroom space, suitable water supplies, sufficient ventilation – especially where dye-bleach processing will take place? There may be tough restrictions on the effluent you can tip down the drains, which works against drum discard and trough processors. (Some chemical kits include a neutralizer that you mix

E-6
7091

C-41
6131

7352

Red　　　　Green　　　　Blue

Fig. 9.23 Manufacturer's processed control strips for (left) colour reversal film, (centre) colour negative film, and (above) neg/pos colour paper, shown actual size. The spots on the reversal film earmark the steps you must measure for D_{min}, LD (low density), HD (high density) and D_{max} readings. These are compared against readings you make from identically exposed strips you put through your own processing solutions. See Figure 9.28. On the print control strip you measure high and low density patches for each of the three colours, plus the black patch for D_{max} and the white patch for D_{min} (or 'stain'). Courtesy Kodak Ltd with discarded bleach before disposal.) Will the floor stand the weight? Large tanks of chemical or wash water are very heavy. Is the ceiling high enough? Apart from dip-and-dunk needs, large roller processors must have sufficient headroom to enable you to pull out racks vertically for cleaning.

Troubleshooting

Are you the type to conscientiously maintain good batch-to-batch quality on the kind of equipment you intend to have? For example, it may be best to choose some form of one-shot processing if you are likely to forget to replenish. Are you prepared to wash out racks of rollers thoroughly or trolley-in a heavy cylinder of nitrogen? Above all, if results come out with increasingly green colour casts or some other unexpected effect, will you wish you had used a laboratory or do you have enough persistence and interest to track down the cause and correct it? This is where some form of process monitoring will let you know what is going on. Monitoring can reveal subtle changes before they start to noticeably damage your results and become difficult to rectify.

Process control

The best way to monitor the total effect of your processing system – solution condition, temperature, timing, agitation and general handling – is to put through some exposed film. Then by comparing your results against some of the same film processed under ideal conditions variations can be measured. To do this job properly, you need the following items:

1. An exposed test piece of film or paper to process, plus another identically exposed to the same image and correctly processed;
2. A densitometer instrument to make accurate readings of results; and
3. The monitoring manual issued by the film/processing kit manufacturer to diagnose likely causes of any differences between your results and the reference film.

None of this is cheap, but it is a form of insurance which becomes more valid, the larger the scale of your processing. However, there are also some short cuts, as you will see shortly.

Process-control strips

These are strips of film or paper a few inches long, exposed by the film manufacturer under strictly controlled conditions and supplied ready for processing in boxes of 10 or 20 or so. Different strips are made for each black and white and colour process in which process control is normally practised. These are normal contrast black and white negative film; reversal colour film; negative colour film; neg/pos colour paper; and pos/pos papers. Each strip has been exposed to a scale of light values (Figure 9.23). Colour strips also contain some coloured patches and (sometimes) a head and shoulders colour portrait image. One strip in each box has been processed by the manufacturer under ideal laboratory conditions to act as a comparative standard.

K O D A K
Control Strips
(for B / W film)

Kodak

L D

H D

7093

Fig. 9.24 Manufacturer's processed control strip for black and white film. The two measurement patches, for low and high density readings, also give density difference figures. See plots, Figure 9.27. Fog level is read off the clear part of the film

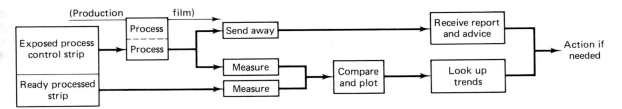

Fig. 9.25 Process control. One of the pre-exposed strips is processed alongside your normal production batch. You then send it away for analysis, or make your own comparison against the manufacturer's ready processed version

You must store unprocessed control strips so that changes in the latent image cannot occur. They are best kept in a freezer at $-18°C$ or lower. (Allow them time to return to room temperature before use.) The idea is that one control strip is processed at regular intervals alongside the batch of film you are processing, then checked against the manufacturer's reference strip. Intervals may be once a day, once a week, or even with every batch of film, according to your pattern and volume of processing.

Comparing your processed and reference strip side by side on a light-box will show you any gross processing errors at once. The eye is quite good at making comparisons, and visual assessment alone may be adequate for confirming that everything is reasonably on-line with black and white negatives and even colour slides and prints. However, you cannot easily judge colour negatives in this way, nor can you detect the slight drifts (especially colour) which forecast more serious problems ahead.

To get more information without purchasing further equipment you can subscribe to the manufacturer's laboratory check service, as offered by Kodak, Agfa and Fuji. Here you regularly post off processed strips which are analysed for you and any urgent remedial advice telephoned back. You also receive a routine graphic readout and written interpretation of every strip sent in. A service of this kind is excellent, but there is always a delay. Having your own measuring/analysing equipment on hand allows you to make processing corrections immediately.

Fig. 9.26 Densitometer for measuring film or paper density values. Area to be measured is located over reading spot on base of measuring unit D. Readout appears on panel alongside head, and a series of comparative readings can be plotted out on printer (P) as a chart, like Figure 9.27 or 9.28

Reading results

To accurately make spot density readings off the tone or colour patches on your process-control strip you need an instrument called a densitometer (Figure 9.26). This has a transmission illumination head for films (passes light through the film base from below) plus a reflection head which bounces light off print surfaces at a fixed angle. Light-sensitive cells receive the light and make a direct reading of black and white density or they read through appropriate blue, green and red filters in turn to give separate values for yellow, magenta and cyan layer image densities in colour materials. Density values appear on a readout panel.

For black and white film checks you measure two marked patches on the tone scale (Figure 9.24), one a high-density area and the other low. Do this for your reference and your newly processed strips. Then, using a pre-printed chart, mark in the *differences* between reference and processed strip readings for various patch readings; see Figure 9.27. The result is often called a 'clothes line plot'. Over a period of time the plotted line will show variations, which should

Fig. 9.27 Monitoring chart for a black and white negative process. Top section would be filled in with high and low density values for the manufacturer-processed reference strip (Figure 9.24). Strips were processed 2–3 times a day, and their high and low density readings logged. The density differences between the two readings were then plotted relative to the DD of the reference strip. The bottom plot shows how far low density readings vary from the low LD of the reference. Downward trend revealed by process strips 11–13 here was countered by added replenisher

remain within the tolerance limits recommended by the film manufacturer and marked on your chart.

To check out colour, you need more information. With reversal slide processing, for example, plot readings of minimum density (for stain), a lowish-density patch (for speed), a high-density one (for colour balance and contrast) and a maximum density (for fog). These are repeated for each colour layer, making a total of 12 readings per reversal film control strip. The difference between each reading and that of the equivalent part of the reference strip is logged on a special chart. The procedure is much easier if your densitometer feeds a computerized plotter which memorizes reference strip values and translates each reading you make directly onto a printed-out chart. Plots made over a long period can be stored on floppy disc.

Deciding what it all means

Your process-control chart is designed to make variations stand out clearly. Unless something disastrous has happened (developer contaminated with bleach/fix, for instance), plots should not vary greatly. Trends are more important than individual values. Plots which show upward trends indicate overactivity, with too much dye formation in colour materials. Downward trends usually suggest the need for replenishment.

The manufacturer's manual for the process will reproduce similar patterns and print advice alongside on action to be taken. Some computer software programs automatically display warnings and written advice on a VDU when fed with your readings. You can also extend the memorized fault-tracing program with your own experience, so that it ultimately recalls what you did on your own equipment the last time this trend occurred. Sometimes a process

Fig. 9.28 Monitoring chart for a colour negative process. Reference values for the manufacturer-processed strip appear in left-hand column. For each strip put through with film, blue, green and red readings are made from each of high density, low density and D_{min} steps. See Figure 9.23. These are turned into density difference (top), low density (middle) and D_{min} (bottom) comparisons with reference values. Notice how the tolerance limits (shown by broken lines) become narrowest at D_{min}

KEY

——— Thin line — red
━━━ Medium line — blue
━━━ Thick line — green

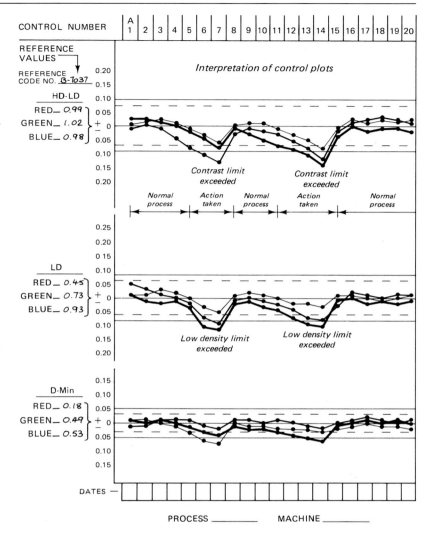

needs a little time to settle down after initial preparation. 'Starter' packs are needed to even out some solutions which are otherwise too 'raw' until a number of films have matured the chemical contents. Often, too, a process remains steady although not matching your reference strip. If processed pictures look good it may be better to leave this situation unchanged rather than tinker and possibly over-adjust. Always make any adjustment gradual and allow it time to take effect.

Silver recovery

Film fixing and bleach/fix solutions gradually accumulate an appreciable quantity of soluble silver salts from the materials they have been processing. Used black and white fixer can contain up to 4 g of silver per litre. It is possible to reclaim some of this metal from fixer solution and sell it to a silver refiner. Whether this is worth doing

Typical film appearance	Probable cause
Colour reversal film	
Too dark, with colour cast	Insufficient first development
Completely black	First and colour developers interchanged, or first developer omitted
Yellow, with decreased density	Fogged in first developer
Yellowish cast	Colour developer fault, e.g. too alkaline
Very light, blue cast	First developer contaminated with fixer
Too light overall	Excessive first developer
Contrasty colour negative	Contamination of first developer. Given colour negative processing
Blue spots	Bleach contaminated
Fungus or algae deposits	Dirty tanks
Scum	Dirt in solutions. Stabilizer needs replacement
Control plots showing:	
all densities up or down	First developer errors creating speed changes
all low, blue plot least affected	Excessive first development
Colour negative film	
Image light, and with reduced contrast	Underdevelopment
Image dense and very contrasty	Overdevelopment
Streaked and mottled image	Insufficient agitation
Heavy fogging, partial reversal	Exposure to light during development
Reddish-brown patches	Contamination of solutions
Completely opaque, or cloudy image	Bleach or fixer stage omitted
Colour positive, with strong cast	Given reversal processing
Opalescent yellow overall	Exhausted bleacher
Fungus, blue spots	As per reversal transparencies

Fig. 9.29 Colour film processing faults. (Some of these may differ in detail according to brand and type of film)

depends on the current value of silver, whether you have sufficiently large tanks and volume of throughput, the cost of the recovery equipment and the time and effort needed to use it. Consult a silver refiner or film manufacturer for current advice. The two most common methods are *metal exchange*, which removes silver but destroys the photographic properties of your solution, and *electrolysis*, which allows the fixer to be regenerated and re-used. Electrolysis is cleaner and less trouble, but needs more expensive equiment.

Metal exchange

When a base metal like iron is left in a solution of silver salts it slowly dissolves and is replaced by metallic silver. The best way of exploiting this in practice is to fill a large plastic container with steel wool (iron), such as pads made for floor-cleaning machines. These stand on a perforated platform a couple of inches above the container bottom, over an inlet pipe for the spent fixer. The solution rises to the top and is bled off to waste. As the steel wool is wetted by the (normally acid) solution it darkens and forms iron sulphide. Since it also gives off hydrogen sulphide you must do this somewhere safe outdoors. Over several weeks the steel wool converts to grey silver progressively upwards through your tank. When the top appears grey you scoop out the wool as almost entirely silver. Every 4.5 kg of steel wool yields about 10.5 kg of silver, which is dried and sold to a refinery. (Warning Do not empty pads and tightly stack them in air when they are only partly exchanged. After a while they may spontaneously catch fire.)

Electrolysis

Weak electric current is passed between two electrodes at opposite ends of a tank of exhausted fixer, causing silver to plate-out on the

Fig. 9.30 Two methods of
recovering silver from a spent fixing
bath. Metal exchange use iron
(steel wool). In electrolysis current
flows from anode (A), plating the
silver onto cathode (C)

Metal exchange   Electrolysis

cathode electrode. This offers you a convenient method of removing silver without contaminating the solution. As Figure 9.30 shows, the anode electrode is small and often made of carbon, while the cathode has a large surface area of stainless steel. Over a period of days the silver grows as grey scaling, which you eventually chip from the cathode and send for refining. You also need equipment to measure the silver concentration left in the solution. When this drops to about 0.5 g per litre the electrodes are removed and you add recommended fractional quantities (typically, 25–30%) of the original fixer chemicals and return the regenerated solution back to its original processing function.

Summary: Processing management

● Today's mainstream chemical processes for film are black and white negative, colour reversal and colour negative. Dominant print processes are black and white neg/pos, colour neg/pos, colour reversal and dye destruction (both pos/pos). Black and white processes allow you to freely choose developer, fixer, etc. Each colour process comes as a planned kit – sometimes amateur or professional, shortened or regular versions.
● The widest choice of developers exists for black and white processing. Differences include contrast, film speed, grain and resolution. Some are designed for you to dilute and use one-shot, others have long-life performance for use in a deep tank.
● Timing of the first stage of reversal colour film processing (black and white development) is adjustable to push or hold back film speed. Colour development times, during which couplers form dye images, are inflexible for colour films, but can be varied when developing monochrome chromogenic films. Finally, silver is bleached, fixed and washed out, and films soaked in stabilizer before drying.
● Monochrome print developers are chosen mostly for the image 'colour' they give, especially with chlorobromide emulsions. Fast-developing RC papers can be machine processed.
● You can colour print direct from slides, onto dye-bleach or chromogenic reversal papers. The processes are entirely different. Dye-bleach material, which already carries tricolour dyes, is given black and white development. Then you bleach all silver as well as dye wherever black silver was formed. Results have stronger, purer and more permanent colours than possible with coupled dyes. Reversal chromogenic colour papers need processing similar to slide films.

● For reliable processing look after temperature, timing, agitation, the state of chemicals and the way photographic material is physically handled. Temperature errors beyond acceptable limits change chemical characteristics. Timing is the best way to adjust processing. Insufficient agitation gives unevenness and weak maximum density, but too much creates flow-marks. In all processing, be accurate and consistent.

● Prepare chemical solutions safely, and according to detailed instructions. Do not risk contamination through insufficient rinsing of mixing gear, containers, etc. or sloppy working. Do not use any solution beyond its exhaustion point – use one-shot processing or log what you put through, then replenish or discard. Use replenisher formulated for your processing solution (or some fresh original solution, if recommended). Add it by topping up, or introduce a measured quantity, bleeding off surplus solution.

● Hand-processing of film in deep-tank hand-lines and black and white prints in trays is labour-intensive but justified for small quantities of work. Deep tanks need gas-burst agitation for consistent colour processing. Machines are ideal for larger volumes and the most rigorous colour processes, but automatic equipment is costly to buy and often uses large tanks of (expensive) chemicals.

● Drum processors accept paper (or film) for one-shot processing. Basic types are manually controlled, convenient for small batches of material only, but versatile and relatively cheap. More expensive rotary discard machines hold larger batches of material emulsion-outwards on a cylindrical frame rotating in a trough.

● Roller transport processors run continuously, accept individual sheets or rolls, and most types work dry-to-dry. But they are dedicated to one process at a time. Deep-tank machines are expensive to buy and fill with chemicals. Some benchtop versions for print processing use smaller quantities of chemical in throw-away batches. All roller units must be cleaned frequently and properly maintained.

● Continuous-strand processors are large-capacity machines accepting lengths of film or paper joined head-to-tail. This material is drawn through a sequence of deep tanks and dryer, using a minimum of rollers. Machines are process-dedicated, with solutions automatically replenished, heated and circulated.

● In choosing processing equipment, consider whether your work pattern is varied or regular. Are you prepared to pay for convenience, capacity and speed or go for cheaper but more labour-intensive methods? Work out cost of chemicals, servicing, etc. as well as capital investment. Check that you have the right space, ventilation, water supplies. Will your housekeeping and processing control be good enough to ensure consistent results? Can you troubleshoot when something goes wrong?

● Process control allows you to monitor your entire system by regularly processing pre-exposed control strips, then comparing results against a manufacturer-processed strip. You can send off for regular analysis or get results on the spot using a computer-aided densitometer and a process manual.

● Cold-store your unprocessed control strips. Use a densitometer to measure transmission density (for films) and reflection density (for paper). Colour materials are measured using tricolour filters. Black and white densities are read off high- and low-density marked patches, colour print results off D_{min} and D_{max}.

● Variations between your densities and those measured off the reference strip are plotted on a process-control chart. Check the pattern produced for trends – upwards, too active, downwards, too exhausted.

● Silver recovery from large-volume spent fixer or bleach/fix solutions may show a profit. Metal exchange (for example, making the solution bleed off through steel wool (iron) pads) destroys its photographic properties and gives off fumes. Electrolysis cleanly plates out silver and allows fixer regeneration, but needs more expensive equipment.

10
Colour printing

This chapter assumes that you are experienced with black and white work but are approaching practical colour printing for the first time. Colour is more demanding because you need all your monochrome skills (cropping to improve composition, judging correct exposure, shading and printing-in) plus the ability to assess 'off-colour' results and make corrections. You must also work in dimmer safelighting and more tightly control exposing and processing conditions. It is important that your colour vision is normal, so have your eyes tested if you find colour differences very difficult to detect.

Starting with types of equipment and practical facilities, the chapter first takes you through pos/pos printing (from slides). From this it is easiest to grasp the practicalities of filtration if you have not printed colour before. However, if you are more concerned with neg/pos printing, turn directly to the next section, which also starts from first principles. The use and advantages of different kinds of colour analyser come next, plus ways of printing additively. Various 'cross-over' techniques are discussed, such as printing transparencies from negatives and negatives from slides, as well as slide duping and making prints direct from other prints or artwork. Finally, you have to decide the advantages and disadvantages in doing your own colour printing instead of using an outside laboratory, in the light of your own type and volume of work.

Equipment

To colour print you need an enlarger with a lamphouse which not only evenly illuminates the film in the carrier (as in black and white) but can also be altered in colour content. Colour adjustment is vital to give you *flexibility* – within reason, you can match the colour balance of the film image you are printing to suit the batch of colour paper, compensate for enlarger lamp characteristics, etc. Above all, it lets you fine-tune your record or interpretation of the subject. There are two main ways of controlling illumination colour:

1. Giving one exposure using yellow, magenta or cyan filters in the light path; or
2. Giving three different exposures, separately through blue, green and red filters.

Subtractive filter ('white light') heads

Most colour enlargers work by introducing different strengths of yellow, magenta and cyan filter between lamp and negative. The cheapest arrangement is a lamphouse drawer into which you can fit several acetate CP filters chosen from a set of 20 or so, see Figure 10.1. However, it is much easier to use a 'dial-in' colour head, by which three calibrated dials each slide one deep-coloured yellow, magenta or cyan filter increasingly into the light beam. This part-tinted light is then thoroughly scrambled by bouncing it around a white-lined box and passing through a diffuser, so that it reaches the film carrier perfectly even in colour.

The stronger the yellow filtering you use, the more blue wavelengths are subtracted (absorbed) from the white enlarger light. Similarly, magenta filtering subtracts green and cyan subtracts red. You can watch the light changing colour as you turn the dials. Altering each control *singly* from zero to maximum units tints the light increasingly yellow, magenta or cyan; increasing filtration on *two* controls together gives blue, green or red. If you advance all *three* controls the light just dims without appreciable colour change. (This is because, when equal, they simply form grey neutral density.)

There is normally no reason for using all three filters at once in a subtractive filter head – they just waste light and extend your exposure time. So if during printing you make changes which bring three values into use you should 'subtract neutral density' by taking away the lowest value setting from each, making one of them zero, see Figure 10.3.

Additive heads

A few enlargers and printers do not use a variable-strength filtering system. Instead they have deep red, green and blue filters, one fixed

Fig. 10.1 Subtractive filtering lampheads. Left: basic system using filter drawer between lamp and negative. You need a wide range of Y, M, C acetate filters of different strengths from which to make up a suitable filter pack. Right: dial-in filter head. Each dial controls the strength of one colour filter and is calibrated in relative units, which vary slightly according to manufacturer. See also Figure 10.4

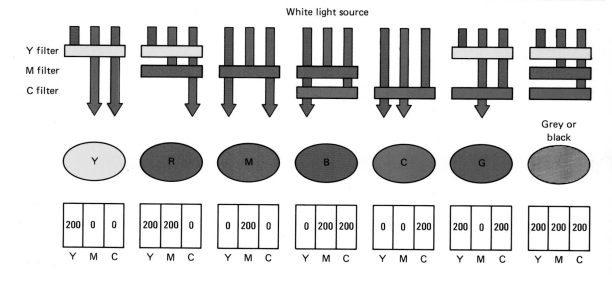

Fig. 10.2 Above: an enlarger colour head may have only three filters, but by adjusting dial-in controls you can change the light through a wide range of primary and complementary colours. Each primary colour is made by dialling-in two filters at a time (shown maximum here). Never use more than two filters at once

Fig. 10.3 Eliminating neutral density. Left: colour head settings here are utilizing all three filters. Left, below: to avoid unnecessary neutral density the lowest setting has been subtracted from all three controls. Colour remains the same but light is brighter

Fig. 10.4 Mechanical arrangement inside dial-in head, for raising and lowering the filters into light beam when finger dials (left) are turned. Matt white light-mixing box scatters and directs light through diffuser (bottom) to evenly illuminate negative

Fig. 10.5 Turret of strong B, G, R filters under enlarging lens for additive colour printing. Notches (not shown) tell you the colour and accurate positioning of each filter in the dark. See page 244

over each of three lamps or flash tubes or rigged on a moving carrier which positions one filter after the other across the light beam. Every print is given three exposures, and by varying the times for each colour (with flash the number and strength of flashes) you control the effective colour of the light. Additive printing can therefore be said to expose each of the red-, green- and blue-sensitive emulsion layers of the colour paper separately. It is an old system which still suits some automatic or electronically controlled equipment, as all adjustments are made by timing. The biggest disadvantage is that by having a *sequence* of three exposures, shading and printing-in become difficult.

Enlarger essentials

A typical colour head enlarger uses a tungsten halogen lamp with built-in reflector. (More light is needed than given by most black and white heads, due to losses later in the filtering and light-mixing optics.) Power to the lamp should be through a voltage-stabilizing transformer which smoothes out any dips or surges of current caused by other electrical equipment nearby, producing changes of lamp colour temperature. Next in line come three strong yellow, magenta and cyan filters. These slide into the light beam by amounts controlled by three finger dials on the outside casing or solenoids in circuit with some electronic system such as a colour analyser (see page 240). The effect on printing light colour depends on how much of each filter enters the beam – a 130Y filter pushed across one-fifth of the light beam has a 26Y effect. Values are shown on finger dials or diodes, typically between 0 and 130 or 200 for each hue.

Filters themselves are *dichroic* types, glass thinly coated with metallic layers which reflect the unwanted parts of the spectrum and transmit the remainder, instead of filtering by dye absorption of light. This gives them a 'narrower cut', a more precise effect on wavelengths, avoiding the usual deficiencies of dyes (page 94). They are also more fade-resistant – important when you keep introducing part of a filter into a concentrated light beam. The head also contains two permanent filters. One is a heat filter to subtract infra-red wavelengths and avoid film overheating, the other an ultra-violet one to absorb any unwanted ultra-violet from the lamp. There may be a separate drawer or shelf within the lamphouse where you can fit an additional CP acetate filter when the filtration you need is beyond the range of the dichroic system. This is occasionally useful for effects or when printing from early unmasked colour negatives.

The light beam is thoroughly mixed and passed through a diffuser large enough to cover the largest size film carrier you will want to use. The remainder of the enlarger – column, movements, timer, masking frame – are basically the same as for black and white printing.

In fact, most enlargers use interchangeable colour or black and white heads. You can even use a colour head for black and white printing – its characteristics are like those of any other diffuser light-source enlarger. Dial out all colour filtration, or use the yellow and magenta filters to control variable contrast monochrome paper (see *Basic Photography*).

Always fit the best enlarger lens you can afford (Figure 10.6), preferably one of at least four elements. All modern enlarging lenses

Fig. 10.6 Modulation transfer function curves for two 35 mm format enlarger lenses. Lens A is a top-of-range design, giving consistently high image quality. Lens B is a budget-price type. However for small enlargements of only × 4, viewed from normal reading distance, values of 10 lp/mm are the most relevant. Here results are never less than 70% contrast. See also Figure 2.15

Fig. 10.7 Bench-top colour paper processing machine, showing the path taken by prints through troughs containing developer and bleach/fix. Washing and drying takes place outside machine. See Figure 10.8

are fully corrected for colour, but it often helps to buy one with a wider maximum aperture than for black and white work. This makes focusing of masked negatives easier to see and more critical. However, always aim to expose with your lens stopped down to about the middle of its *f*-range for best performance.

Other basic facilities

Figure 10.8 shows most of the other basic items you will need. A colour analyser is a worthwhile investment. Once calibrated, it gives you a good starting point for filtration and exposure settings for each image (see page 240). As with black and white printing, rigorously separate 'wet' (processing) from 'dry' activities (handling of films and exposing prints). You will be working for longer periods than when film processing, so equip the darkroom with safelighting and efficient ventilation. Safelights for colour printing must be far less bright than monochrome types, passing a mixture of wavelengths to which the eye is sensitive but print material emulsions are least responsive. The result is a dim amber. Special filtered sodium safelights transmit a yellowy-brown line spectra (Figure 10.9) to exploit a narrow gap between colour paper's red and green sensitivity. These are somewhat brighter than tungsten safelights but more expensive, and they take 10 minutes or so to reach full power. Use a sodium type for general illumination, plus tungsten safelights in key areas such as above the

Fig. 10.8 Basic one-person colour printing darkroom (print drying undertaken elsewhere)

Relative sensitivity

Wavelength (nm)

Fig. 10.9 Safelighting for colour printing. Top: spectral sensitivity of the paper's three emulsions. Bottom: spectral emission from sodium-type safelight. A filter within the unit absorbs the two shaded bands. Peak emission therefore matches the 'gap' betwen green and red paper sensitivity. However, level of brightness must remain low to avoid fogging from lower energy bands

processor, darkroom door, etc. Safelight fog usually gives neg/pos papers pale bluish highlights, uncorrectable by enlarger filtration.

Make sure your printing darkroom is properly ventilated, with air preferably being drawn out of the room through the wall behind the processor. Aim for 10 room air changes per hour; with dye-bleach processing the recommended rate is 15 changes per hour. Health and safety equipment should also include protective gloves for chemical handling, eye wash and a fire extinguisher.

Prepare some well-illuminated white-light area where you will always judge your colour tests and prints. This can be near a blackout blind you open to let in daylight. Better still, because it is more consistent, have a bench with daylight matching lamps or tubes over-head. The spectral output of fluorescent tubes is often shown by a 'colour-rendering index'. The closer the CRI is to 100, the more suitable the tube is for colour viewing. Do not use anything less than 90 CRI. If you know that finished work will be shown only in tungsten lighting, use lamps of this colour temperature instead.

Print materials

Colour print materials are of three main types:

1. Chromogenic neg/pos such as Ektacolor or Fujicolor, designed for printing from negatives;
2. Chromogenic pos/pos, reversal material such as Ektachrome or Fujichrome papers; and
3. Dye-bleach pos/pos material such as Cibachrome.

Both (2) and (3) are for printing from slides or larger format trans-parencies. Each material needs completely different processing (see page 203). For paper prints use material with an opaque white, resin-coated base, but several types are also made on translucent or trans-parent base versions, used for display transparencies, visual aids, etc. (see page 248). Most printing papers come in a selection of surface finishes – typically glossy, lustre or semi-matt – with no choice of contrast grades.

Fig. 10.10 Colour printing suite for three colour enlargers, sharing one high-output roller-transport paper processor. Machine outputs dry prints to an area where there is white light illumination to judge results

All colour printing materials have multi-layer emulsions sensitive to the three primary colours of the spectrum. However, unlike camera materials, most papers have emulsions in reverse order, with the red-sensitive cyan-forming layer on top. A slight amount of image diffusion is inevitable in the bottom layer but is more hidden if this is yellow instead of the heavier cyan. Emulsion colour sensitivities have steep, well-separated peaks corresponding to the maximum spectral transmissions of the three dyes forming the film image. Remember, printing paper does not receive light from the same wide range of subject colours as camera film – everything is already simplified to combinations of three known dyes. In part of the spectrum (Figure 10.9) print material sensitivity can be sufficiently low to permit the use of safelights which would fog colour film.

Characteristics of the same manufacturer's colour negative films are taken into account in the design of neg/pos print materials. The two are 'keyed' in terms of contrast and the effects of integral colour masking used in the film (pages 94–95). Cross-printing maker A's negatives on maker B's paper may need heavier filtration, but the result, with its mixed use of dye characteristics, can suit your style of work.

Because of slight variations in manufacture, some brands of colour print material are labelled with filter and exposure changes relative to other batches, like sheet colour film. So be prepared to adjust filtration and/or timing between finishing one packet and starting another if they are different batches (see Figure 10.21). Whenever you buy a stock of paper try to ensure that it is all from the same batch. Take care over storing printing materials too. Like all other colour emulsions, they need properly controlled conditions. Keep your stock sealed and located in a refrigerator at 10°C or less, but prevent moisture from condensing on the cold emulsion surface by allowing it time to reach room temperature before use.

Fig. 10.11 Recommended warm-up times when you remove printing paper from cold store

Paper size	Form of packing	Time to reach 21°C	
		From 2°C	From 10°C
20.3 × 25.4 cm (8 × 10 in)	100 sheet box	3 hours	2 hours
40.6 × 50.8 cm (16 × 20 in)	50 sheet box	2 hours	2 hours
8.9 cm (3.5 in) × 240 m	Roll	6 hours	4 hours
20.3 cm (8 in) × 80 m	Roll	7 hours	4 hours

Pos/pos colour printing

The two main advantages of printing from positive film images instead of negatives are:

1. You can see what you are aiming to get. The film is easy to judge for colour balance, portrait expression, lighting, etc. Your print should retain the best of these features yet also allow you to manipulate cropping, colour and density.
2. Working this way should give you the best of several worlds – you can not only make prints but have a transparency which can be projected and which is also the preferred form of colour image for mechanical reproduction on the printed page.

However, transparency film has no integral masking, and its

Fig. 10.12 Technique for getting maximum test information from one full sheet of colour paper. Use four hinged flaps of opaque card (white on top) so only one-quarter of the paper (P) is exposed at one time. Set filtration for the film type as recommended by paper manufacturer. 1: Lift flap one and expose three bands for different exposure times, shading with card. 2: with all flaps protecting the paper, switch on the enlarger again. Shift the masking frame so that the strip of image exposed at stage 1 now falls on flap two. Increase or reduce filtration by appropriate units in one direction. 3: switch off enlarger, lift flap two, and expose three exposure bands again. Continue for flaps three and four. Processed sheet will show four filtrations at three exposure levels. Keep notes

Fig. 10.13 A result of using the test technique above, printing a transparency on pos/pos Cibachrome paper. Nearest strip, right, was filtered 20Y; then 20Y 40C; then 60Y 40M; and finally 60Y 40C. Each strip received 7 seconds exposure bottom, 14 seconds middle, and 21 seconds top. From this it was decided to filter 20Y 10C and give 20 seconds contrast is greater than a negative because it is designed to look good as an end in itself rather than suit colour paper. Both these features limit your print quality. For example, contrasty slides, especially when due to harsh lighting, can give disappointing results. Print material processing also involves more stages (chromogenic) or is more toxic (dye-bleach) than neg/pos paper (see page 233).

The best kind of slide for printing pos/pos is moderate or low in contrast, evenly lit and not overexposed. In fact, the deeper colour highlight detail of slight *underexposure* is often an advantage because you can lighten results somewhat during printing, but nothing can bring back the bleached detail of an overexposed image. Make sure your film is spotlessly clean. Any debris on the slide prints as *black*, which is much more difficult to spot-out than the white specks this would produce on neg/pos prints.

Practical procedure

Set up your film in the enlarger, stop down and initially set the filtration as recommended by the paper manufacturer for your brand of slide. Test first for correct exposure, then for colour. Have some device which covers the paper in the masking frame and lifts one segment at a time. If possible, keep repeating the same part of the image by repositioning the masking frame. If you do not have an analyser you can get correct settings most quickly by giving each segment different filtration *and* a range of exposures. See Figure 10.12. Vary each band of exposure by about 50% around what you estimate (or measure) to be correct. Try to keep exposure time within 5–30 seconds, making changes outside this range by altering lens aperture instead. This way you avoid colour shifts due to reciprocity failure (see page 73).

Process your material (Chapter 9) and examine dry results under your standard viewing light to judge density and colour. Remember that the darkest segment has had least exposure (Figure 10.13). Isolate your best exposure result and compare colour with your transparency. If the test looks, say, too yellow, reduce your yellow filtration. If it looks too green, reduce yellow and cyan equally, but if one of these is down to 00 filtration already you can add magenta instead. Avoid having a neutral density situation through using all three filter colours (page 226). Filtration changes of 10 units have a barely discernible effect. Expect to alter 20 units at a time, or 30–40 for more effect – all bigger steps than you normally need in neg/pos colour printing. Get used to making notes of filter and exposure time settings on the back of prints or in a notebook. Having reset your

Fig. 10.14 Controlling results in (white light) colour printing

Required effect on final print	When using pos/pos printing materials	When using neg/pos printing materials
Lighter image	Increase exposure or (locally) print-in	Reduce exposure or (locally) shade
Darker image	Reduce exposure or (locally) shade	Increase exposure or (locally) print-in
Less blue	Reduce M + C, or increase Y	Reduce Y, or increase M + C
Less green	Reduce Y + C, or increase M	Reduce M, or increase Y + C
Less red	Reduce Y + M, or increase C	Reduce C, or increase Y + M
Less yellow	Reduce Y, or increase M + C	Reduce M + C, or increase Y
Less magenta	Reduce M, or increase Y + C	Reduce Y + C, or increase M
Less cyan	Reduce C, or increase Y + M	Reduce Y + M, or increase C
White borders	Fog paper edges	Cover paper edges with easel masks

filtration, check whether the changes will necessitate any adjustments to exposure. Calculate this from the manufacturer's table (Figure 10.18) or read it with an analyser.

Shading and printing-in

The technique for darkening or lightening chosen parts of the print appear strange at first if you are used to printing negatives. You shade pale parts to make them darker and give heavy areas more exposure to lighten them. Print borders, where edges of the paper are under edges of the masking frame, come out black. White borders must be fogged in after image exposure, covering the main area of the print with black paper just as you would if printing *black* borders neg/pos (see *Basic Photography*). You can make local colour corrections by shading with filters. For example, if part of an outdoor shot includes shadow excessively blue-tinted by blue sky, shade this area with a CC 10Y filter. (Do not use CP acetate – this upsets definition when used between lens and paper.) If your shading also makes the shadow *darker* than you need, lighten it back by printing-in the area with extra exposure through a hole in a card covered by the same filter.

If prints show excessively harsh contrast you may have to lower the contrast of your slide by masking it with a faint black and white contact printed negative (see page 162). As a quicker solution (although more limited in effect), try 'flashing' the paper after exposure. Remove the film from the enlarger, cover the lens with an ND2.0 filter and repeat your exposure time. With dye-bleach materials you may be able to dilute the developer solution to reduce image contrast.

Making a pos/pos 'ring-around'

Making a print chart such as Figure 10.15 helps you as a beginner to recognize the direction and degree of filtration needed to correct errors. Pick a slide which includes some pastel hues and grey or white. An easy-to-judge subject such as a portrait with softly lit Caucasian skin tones works well. Make the best possible correctly exposed and filtered small print first, then increase filtration (or reduce complementary colour filtration) by steps of, say, 20 or 30 units and make other small prints with casts progressively in the directions magenta, blue, cyan, green, yellow and red. Mount them on card, each captioned with the amount of filtration you must subtract from your enlarger setting to get a correct print. Have the chart near your print viewing light to help to identify the hue and strength of colour casts when judging test strips from any other slides.

Neg/pos colour printing

The advantage of making colour prints from colour negatives rather than slides is that you get better results from a wider range of subject lighting conditions. The information encoded within a properly exposed integral-masked colour negative allows you to make greater adjustments of colour and tone during printing, without unwanted side-effects such as poorer shadow or highlight quality. However,

Fig. 10.22 Colour print viewing filters. You need a set of six of these triple filter cards. Each card has filters which are the same colour but differ in strength. Pick the filter which best corrects test print cast

part of a sheet of colour paper). The patch which prints most neutral grey guides you to the filtration needed. All the devices described below are designed for neg/pos printing, and most also work for pos/pos printing.

Viewing filters

If you view a faulty test print through a filter of appropriate colour and strength you can tell the best change to make to enlarger filtration. Look through CP acetates, as used for filter drawer enlargers, or buy sets of similar filters (Figure 10.22) in cardboard mounts. Have the print under your standard viewing light and hold the filter about midway between print and eye. Do not let it tint everything you see and do not stare at the print through it for more than a few seconds at a time – keep flicking it across and back. Viewing too long allows your eye to start adapting to the colour.

If your test print is too 'warm' in colour, try looking through blue, green or cyan filters; for 'cold' prints, try yellow, magenta or red. As with colour transparencies (page 116), viewing through a filter tints the appearance of highlights far more than shadows. So only judge appearance changes to your print's lighter middle tones. Having found which viewing filter makes these tones look normal, read off the required enlarger filter changes printed on its cardboard mount. (Neg/pos colour printing changes appear one side and pos/pos changes on the other.) Alternatively, if you are viewing through CP filters and printing neg/pos the rule is: *remove from the enlarger filtration the same colour but half the strength of your viewing filter.* For example, if a test print with a green cast shows corrected midtones viewed through a 20M filter, remove 10M from the enlarger. If this is impossible, add 10Y + 10C.

Electronic analysers

There are a great number of electronic analysers available. All make tricolour measurements of your negative or slide and read out the most likely filter for your enlarger and paper batch. They also measure exposure. Most analysers are for 'on-easel' use – they have the advantage of measuring the same image light that will eventually expose the paper. Some analysers are 'off-easel'. They work separately, like a densitometer used for process monitoring (page 217), and allow you to measure your film images outside the darkroom before printing. One skilled user can therefore serve a number of enlargers.

Off-easel analysers have to be programmed for the characteristics of the enlarger through which your film will be printed. Then they compare readings of each negative against a memorized standard negative for which correct filtration and exposure are known. This kind of equipment best suits large laboratories employing many staff and turning out volume work such as printing amateur films, aerial survey pictures, etc. The best off-easel analysers incorporate a video image display (see page 242).

Using on-easel analysers

A unit such as that shown in Figure 10.23 sits on the bench beside your colour enlarger. The plug-in probe, which rests on the masking

Fig. 10.23 On-easel colour analyser, with image-reading probe. Rows of knobs under the readout window are for pre-programming. Four-way switch on left is selector for measuring the three colours, and the brightness, of the image to be printed

frame, has a small spot-reading aperture. This ducts light through a fibre-optic tube to light-sensitive cells inside the unit. A choice of either blue, green, red or colourless filters are brought into play over the cells by turning a four-way selector marked Yellow, Magenta, Cyan or 'Exposure'. The analyser again works by comparing its tri-colour readings from the film image you are about to print against memorized readings from an image for which you know the filtration and exposure.

You must start by programming the analyser for your 'standard' image. This should be on the same type of film as you will be printing, and preferably shot under similar lighting. Set up the film and its known filter settings in the enlarger, focus the image and stop down to the *f*-number used when you last printed it. Then position the probe to receive light from an area chosen for reference – preferably a mid-tone grey or a pale Caucasian flesh tone (see below). Selecting 'Yellow', press the yellow programming button until the read-out diodes show zero. This procedure is repeated for the Magenta and Cyan controls. Using the 'Exposure' selector setting, press the exposure programming button until the read-out shows the number of seconds you gave for a correct print. Now the analyser is ready to use. Further programming adjustments are only needed if you change paper batch, enlarger lamp or lamphouse light-scrambling box.

Set up your unknown negative in the enlarger, position the probe to read an appropriate mid-grey or flesh tone and switch to yellow assessment. Change the enlarger's yellow filtration until the analyser reads out zero. Then follow a similar routine to adjust magenta or cyan readings (remember to eliminate neutral density). Finally, switch to exposure and read off the number of seconds to give.

If your enlarger filtration is altered electronically it is possible to link the analyser to the head so that settings are made directly. Plug-in modules can be pre-programmed for any different paper batch characteristics you may have to use. You can also switch your analyser circuitry from neg/pos to pos/pos printing mode.

Spot or integrated readings

Spot-reading negative analysis, like spot-reading camera exposure, is very selective and accurate provided that you intelligently choose which part of the picture to read. Your master negative and the unknown one to be printed should ideally contain directly comparable subject matter. A mid-grey is ideal, for even Caucasian skin tones can vary quite widely. Often, if you are printing a picture you shot your-self it is possible to read from something remembered as a reasonably mid-tone grey. (Never analyse from dark shadows or specular high-lights – both extremes of the tone scale can be deceptive for colour.) The most difficult images to read are unfamiliar technical subjects, paintings, artwork, etc. Here it helps enormously to have included a grey scale (page 150) in your picture to give the analyser something reliable to read. Place the card near the edge of the frame where you can crop it out and evenly light it at the same intensity and colour temperature as your main subject. When there is nothing tangible to measure, an integrated reading may give better results.

Integral readings are based on the assumption that if all the image light is scrambled, the resulting 'average' equals mid-grey. You take a

Fig. 10.30 Video colour negative analyser. Negative (in enlarger negative carrier) fits over light-box base. Internal video camera gives positive colour image on monitor. You adjust colour balance, and cropping, until video image looks correct

becomes easy to evaluate picture content, portrait expressions, etc. and you can zoom in to preview how different kinds of cropping might look.

These features alone make video a useful tool for selecting colour and black and white negatives for printing when contact prints are not available. For colour analysis, adjust filtration on the light-box until the picture on the screen looks at its best, then transfer these settings to your enlarger. Like all off-easel systems, video analysers have to take into account your enlarger characteristics and current paper batch data, programmed in and held in a memory. Equipment of this kind is still very expensive.

Printing additively

It is not essential to use yellow, magenta and cyan filters to control the enlarger light. Instead, you can give three separate exposures through deep blue, green and red filters and control print colour by the relative *time* you give through each one. As Figure 10.27 shows, you effectively expose the colour paper one emulsion layer at a time. Today only a few enlargers work on this 'tricolour' principle, although it still forms the cheapest way of colour printing using a black and white enlarger. (You only need three gelatin filters, held in sequence under the lens.) Some colour printing machines used in laboratories for both pos/pos and neg/pos work function this way. It is also used for photographic printing from electronically recorded pictures – the read-out from computers, frames from video tape or still-video floppy discs – because video channels work on the bases of BGR signals which can be separately displayed and exposed in sequence.

The best way to test for colour density in additive printing is to expose a 'patch chart'. For example, when printing a colour negative onto neg/pos colour paper, Figure 10.28 shows how you might first expose a whole test sheet through the *blue* filter for 10 seconds. Then without moving paper or image, give strip exposures of 10, 15 and 25 seconds with the *green* filter replacing the blue. Finally, give strip exposures of 5, 7 and 10 seconds at right angles to the green set through the red filter. The processed test then shows the results of nine different combinations.

After judging your result, adjust colour according to the principle that when working neg/pos you *increase* exposure through the filter(s) *matching* the unwanted print cast, or decrease exposure through the filter(s) *complementary* to the cast. So if the best patch on your neg/pos print is too magenta (i.e. too much light has affected the paper's green-sensitive emulsion), make the green filter exposure shorter.

Altering exposure through any one filter also affects overall density. Imagine that you have a neg/pos print given 15 seconds blue, 20 seconds green and 10 seconds red, which appears too blue. You might decide to compensate by increasing blue exposure to 20 seconds, so the previous exposures of 15 + 20 + 10 = 45 seconds are changed to 20 + 20 + 10 = 50 seconds. The increased total will mean that the print is darker as well. If you want it to remain the same density, each of these exposure times will have to be cut proportionally to keep the total 45 seconds, yet still give the required colour change. You do this by multiplying each exposure by the original total divided by the new total, which in this case is 45 divided by 50 = 0.9. So your final exposure times become 18 seconds blue, 18 green and 9 red.

On the other hand, if you just want to make your print darker or lighter without any colour change, do this by either (1) opening up or stopping down the lens aperture or (2) changing all three exposure times equally by multiplying or dividing them by the same amount. Remember that no subtraction of neutral density is needed in additive printing.

Batch changes (additive printing)

Packets of paper carry 'tricolour factors' for additive printing. These might read, for example. R60 G80 B60. When you change batches you use these factors to recalculate the three filter exposures just as you would for exposure time adjustments in white-light printing. In other words, to find each filter's new exposure:

$$\text{New exposure time} = \text{old exposure time} \times \frac{\text{new exposure factor}}{\text{old exposure factor}}$$

For example, if you previously gave 20 seconds green filter exposure using a box of paper stamped Green 80 and have to change to a new box with a 100 green factor, the new exposure to give is 20 seconds multiplied by 100 divided by 80, which is 25 seconds. Similarly, calculate new red and blue filter exposures from the factors for these colours also shown on the boxes.

Unusual printing equipment

Flash-source enlarger

An enlarger can have a group of flash tubes instead of a tungsten continuous light source. See Figure 10.31. Some tubes are permanently filtered deep blue, others green or red. You measure colour and exposure with an on-easel probe, having input paper characteristics data into its electronic control unit. Exposure is programmed additively, the number of flashes from various tubes contributing to final image colour. For example, to increase the yellow content of the light, red and green flashes pulse more often. Light from the multi-source head is then scrambled and diffused before reaching the film carrier. There are no moving parts – the analyser is wired direct to the head. In focusing mode most tubes come on and pulsate rapidly to give almost continuous light. Flashes can also be dimmed and fast-pulsed over a longer period to produce the same density and colour but allow you time to shade and print-in (not possible with other additive systems).

Roll paper holders

Instead of using paper in sheets it makes sense to print onto paper in rolls for large-quantity production. Rolls are cheaper to buy and easier to machine process than an equivalent number of sheet prints. Exposed material is fed through either a roller transport or continuous-strand processor (see page 213). You need a roll paper

Light-mixing box

Neg

Fibre-optic probe

Analyser probe

Electronics package

Micro computer

Multi-purpose LCD display

System controller

Fig. 10.31 Flash-source colour enlarger. On-easel analyser measures image colour and intensity. Microcomputer relates this to paper characterisitics, programs number of flashes from each (filtered) tube, and monitors total light via fibre-optic connection to head

Fig. 10.32 A roll paper holder in position on an enlarger baseboard. Unit has motor-drive. A white-faced blind covers the emulsion surface except during exposure

Darkroom

Workroom

Fig. 10.33 Roll paper printer. This is operated in a normally-lit room, but loaded and unloaded with colour paper from the back in darkroom. Lamphead (L) illuminates your negative and an internal lens enlarges image to a pre-set size on paper lying flat in base of unit. Colour and exposure analyser is built-in. Often such printers work on an additive basis, giving a sequence of three exposures; see page 244 easel to fit onto your enlarger baseboard in place of the regular masking frame. It accepts a paper roll loaded (in darkness) into a feed compartment on one side, led across under a maskable exposing frame and into a take-up compartment. A white-faced opaque blind covers over the paper emulsion. This protects it from fogging when you have white light on in the darkroom, and also allows focusing and composing the image under the enlarger. The blind opens when you are ready to expose, then afterwards closes and triggers the wind-on of a pre-set length of paper. All this is controlled by a hand switch or a foot switch on the floor.

Bulk-printing machines take the use of roll paper a stage further in terms of speed and convenience. See Figure 10.33. They can be loaded (in the dark, or using cassettes) and then used in a normally illuminated room like a work desk. Typical maximum paper capacity is 275 feet and you can turn out over 250 8 × 10 inch prints per hour. With any roll paper system you need a really accurate filtration/exposure analysing system if a variety of pictures have to be printed. If you want to see tests, make one exposure from a strip across every film image in the batch you have to print, then process this length of paper and assess results. Make notes of any necessary changes to the settings for each individual shot, then run off your quantities of prints.

Other colour-printing routes

Colour prints from flat copy

Pos/pos print materials are capable of being used in the camera because, like reversal film, they record a direct positive colour image of your subject. In practice, the slow emulsion speed (Cibachrome is about ISO 5) and the need for a mirror in the camera's optical system for a right-reading paper print limits this use to copying.

You can make direct prints from colour photographic prints, drawn or printed artwork and similar two-dimensional subjects, on equipment such as that shown in Figure 10.34. The copy camera part of the unit uses high-intensity lighting and reflects the lens image directly onto a roll of chromogenic reversal or dye-bleach paper. Each exposure is guillotined from the roll and passes directly into a roller transport processor forming the back part of the camera. Special copy paper materials are made, including high-contrast type for maps and similar line originals. The complete unit therefore acts like a very high-quality, bulk document copying machine. Different models are made with processors for chromogenic and dye-bleach materials, respectively.

Fig. 10.34 Principle of direct copying unit. Photo prints, artwork or simple flat objects are imaged direct onto pos/pos colour paper, which is then roller transport processed. Mirror between copyboard and lens is essential for right-reading results

Fig. 10.35 An overhead projector. Transparencies and objects placed on the lightbox are imaged large scale onto distant screen

Fig. 10.36 Internegative colour film. Characteristic curve of one of the three matching emulsion layers shows how correct exposure records your colour transparency shadows and mid-tones with lower relative contrast than highlights on the copy negative

Enlarged colour transparencies

To make large-scale display transparencies from colour negatives you enlarge onto special neg/pos print film having a translucent plastic base. The film is handled like paper in sheets or rolls and processed in colour paper chemistry, with extended times to boost contrast and colour density. Similarly, you can enlarge slides or large format transparencies onto translucent dye bleach film. All these results are used for rear-lit billboards, illuminated panels at exhibitions and in shops, restaurants, etc.

Chromogenic reversal material on a clear film base (Ektachrome Overhead, for example) allows you to print standard 10 × 10 inch overhead transparencies by enlarging directly from slides and other camera size transparencies. OHP transparencies are shown on an overhead projector (Figure 10.35) as visual aids for sales presentations, teach-ins, etc. These must be paler in colour and density than display transparencies. Tests should be projected for assessment.

Colour internegatives from slides

As an alternative to printing a slide or any other colour transparency directly onto a pos/pos material you can turn it into a colour negative, then print this on neg/pos paper. Results are excellent provided that you have a good-quality original and prepare your negative on internegative colour film designed for this purpose.

Interneg materials have three special characteristics:

1. Blue, green and red sensitivities in narrow bands keyed to the maximum yellow, magenta and cyan absorption of these colours by the image dyes in colour film. In this respect, interneg film is more like printing material than general-use camera films.
2. The yellow, magenta and cyan image dyes it forms chromogenically are (like other colour negatives) keyed to the response of neg/pos colour paper. However, interneg material has additional integral colour masking which compensates for deficiencies in the colour dyes of your *original* as well as the dyes formed within its own layers (see page 94).
3. By combining low-contrast and slower, slightly higher-contrast emulsions in each colour-sensitive layer, interneg film has an unusual characteristic curve, looking like that in Figure 10.36. Correctly exposed, the film records the shadows and midtones of slides within its low-contrast region (compensating for the inherent high contrast of images designed for projection). However, slide highlights fall on the steeper part of the curve so that contrast and brilliance here is largely retained. You avoid the veiled, flattened lighter tones which are often the hallmark of a copy negative. Results are similar to the use of a highlight mask (page 163) but built-in.

You can expose onto internegative 4 × 5 inch sheet film under the enlarger by contact printing or projecting an image to fill this format. Alternatively, use a copy camera arrangement. Here, for example, you can expose 35 mm slides onto 35 mm interneg film by means of 1:1 imaging over a tungsten light-box. See Figure 10.37. Try to avoid making your internegs smaller than the original and then enlarging them back as prints. Size change should be progressive for best optical

Fig. 10.37 35 mm copying systems. Left: simple tube attachment incorporating 1:1 close-up lens. (Transparency being copied is backed up by opal plastic diffuser, not shown.) Centre: copier containing flash unit and modelling lamp. Swing-over unit (M) is a meter with downward-facing sensor. Controls raise or lower internal flash tube to compensate for different density slides. Right: inverted head from a colour enlarger forms a tungsten light-box for copying. Controls here adjust colour balance

quality. Internegatives are processed with the same chemistry as that used for regular colour negative films.

Slides from slides and transparencies

Using low-contrast 35 mm reversal duplicating colour film, you can make colour slides from other slides and transparencies. Work with a 35 mm camera and macro lens in conjunction with one of the copying devices shown in Figure 10.37. The camera's TTL light reading takes close-up imaging into account. Some copiers contain their own light sources – either flash (suits daylight film) with modelling light for focusing and exposure-metering or a tungsten light enlarger lamp-house used upside-down. Simpler copying attachments have to be pointed towards a suitable source. They hold the slide at the far end of a tube containing optics for 1:1 imaging. Since camera and subject are firmly locked together you can hand-hold quite slow shutter-speed exposures. The most elaborate copiers incorporate a device by which you can introduce a small amount of even white light into the lens during exposure. This light has the effect of reducing recorded image contrast in the same way as 'controlled flashing' does during enlarging (see page 166). Overdone, shadows start to fog in and look grey.

No slide reproduced in these ways will quite match the sharpness and tone gradation of an original shot, so it is always better to run off a series of slides from the original subject if you know that several copies will be wanted. Nevertheless, you can definitely improve slides which have a colour cast by duplicating them through a complementary colour filter. For example, the green cast of fluorescent lighting is greatly reduced by a 20M or 30M filter. (Shadows tend to reproduce slightly overcorrected and highlights undercorrected.) You can also improve on a slightly dense, underexposed slide by giving extra exposure while copying it. Copiers have other useful functions for special effects such as sandwiched slides, double exposures, etc. Duplicating film is processed in regular colour reversal film chemistry.

Fig. 10.38 Correction of cast by slide copying. The slide, near right, was shot in fluorescent lighting and shows a characteristic green cast. The 1 : 1 copy, far right, was made through a CC30M filter

Fig. 10.39 Colour print from a black and white negative. The graduated coloured tones in the picture below were created by hand shading, then printing back with changes in the Y + M filtration. Effects are similar to selective toning but more muted and subtle. (By Tim Stephens, courtesy Faber and Faber)

Colour prints from black and white negatives

By printing black and white negatives on neg/pos colour paper you can produce results which look like toned prints. The image can be one colour overall or different areas of the paper can be given different colours or made to graduate from neutral to a colour (see Figure 10.39). Sandwich your negative with a piece of unexposed, processed colour negative film. Its yellowish mask avoids the need for heavy filtration to get a neutral result, so you then have a wider range of filter options for print colouring.

First, you must establish the filtration for a neutral black and white result. Make a series of exposure tests across several pieces of paper each given large (50-unit) filter changes. Then, depending on the colour and intensity of cast in your result, work back with progressively smaller changes until you reach neutrality. Now you select the image colour of your print by appropriate filtration – for example, reducing yellow or increasing cyan to get a warm tint. For a change of tint in chosen areas, shade these parts during the main exposure, then alter filtration and print them back in again. With care you can achieve quite subtle, graduated results, such a a winter landscape greeny-grey at the bottom becoming blue-grey towards the top. It is also possible to work by hand-tinting chosen areas of black and white (large-format) negatives, which then print in complementary colour.

Printing from electronically stored images

Some hybrid printers produce results on neg/pos photographic paper but work from pictures input as electronic signals rather than on film. For example, they accept recordings on still-video camera discs (page 103) or the output from computers. Before printing, the image can be stored in digital form and influenced in various ways. It can be adjusted in contrast and colour balance by a form of electronic masking. Several images can be merged or text added. It is possible either to reduce or enhance grain and also increase the edge contrast of image detail to improve visual sharpness. You can check all these changes on a video monitor. Finally, your image-enhanced picture is displayed on a high-resolution cathode ray tube (in the form of a colour negative). This is imaged onto regular neg/pos colour paper, given normal processing. By adding a scanning unit at the input end of the machine it will also work from photographic colour negatives and slides. Controls allow you to electronically reverse and mask slides so that both these types of original can be printed on the same roll of neg/pos paper.

Is it worth doing it yourself?

This chapter has ranged from the use of a basic colour enlarger to bulk roll paper printers and costly video analysers. The question remains, is it worth doing your own colour printing when many excellent custom laboratories offer this service? You must first decide whether there is sufficient volume of work to justify outlay on equipment and chemicals. Again, the job of top-quality professional colour printing is best handled as a full-time occupation – whoever does it really needs to keep in daily practice. (Both printing employee and the cost of setting up might be a shared facility by a group of photographers.) However, a small user-run darkroom is less likely to have all the quality control facilities of a commercial laboratory (see page 216). Also, as with film processing, your smaller throughput and less automatic equipment mean a greater risk of inconsistent results.

A good custom laboratory aims to give professional photographers as personal a service as possible. Often you can discuss test prints with the member of staff handling your printing, and the larger laboratories offer all kinds of specialist services such as montaging, duping, retouching, etc. On the other hand, colour printing 'in-house' means that you can most easily retain control over the complete job, from initial planning to final image. This is important when (1) you are aiming for a particular style or 'mood' or (2) pictures are highly technical and you need intimate experience of the subject to judge colour accuracy. Results are also seen more quickly, and you have greater opportunities to experiment.

When you are planning a colour job clearly establish what will eventually be needed – prints, transparencies for reproduction, slides, large display transparencies, black and white – in order to shoot on the most appropriate film material(s) in the first place. Someone may need black and white prints off pictures shot on reversal colour material. You might then have to mask before making black and white internegs, and results will inevitably be of poorer technical quality than if pictures had also been taken with black and white film in the first place. This highlights again the advantages of using a camera with interchangeable film backs.

Fig. 10.40 The main interconnecting routes between camera images (top) and final result (bottom). Best choices change from time to time as new technology develops. The CRT printer interfaces electronic imagery with chemical print materials, i.e. picture displayed on a high-resolution TV tube is lens-imaged direct onto photographic print material. Image can be displayed in positive or negative form

● Work out whether doing your own colour printing is viable. Is there sufficient volume to ensure consistency or justify capital cost and staffing? Own printing offers faster turn-around, tighter control of style, and greater accuracy with records of specialized subject matter. If you choose a custom laboratory instead work closely with their staff. When shooting pictures use camera material(s) which most directly give results in all the final forms you know will be needed.

11
Extending photography

This chapter contains three contrasting topics, illustrating how photography extends into widely diverse ways of communicating visually. The first part looks at homespun kinds of printmaking which rely greatly on manipulative skills and imagination but need only simple equipment. Results are generally 'one-offs' or, at most, limited editions. The methods actually described are do-it-yourself silver halide emulsion coating and gum-bichromate printing – both handmade processes still used by artist photographers today.

The second chosen topic is audiovisual production. Here, given professional facilities, projected slides plus sound offer you a powerfully theatrical way of presenting ideas to an audience. Third, and most important of all in terms of audience size, this chapter discusses how photographs get onto the printed page. The emphasis here is mostly on what sort of photographic originals reproduce best. Much of the vital reproduction work (colour scanning, screening, etc.) takes place before presses begin to turn and is handled electronically. Images in the form of electronic signals can easily be manipulated, transmitted and interfaced with other electronic equipment. So we come back to a recurring theme in this book – how today's chemical methods are gradually giving way to tomorrow's electronic ways of making pictures by the action of light.

'Handmade' image processes

Everyone buys printing papers as packaged products, ready for use. There is a range of types and surfaces, of course, but they all give an inherent quality to your pictures you accept as normal and 'photographic'. To get something physically different, look at the possibilities of preparing your own black and white materials instead. This can mean coating your own choice of paper (or any other suitable material) with a light-sensitive liquid such as silver bromide emulsion or bichromated gum.

Liquid emulsion

It is possible to mix up your own emulsion from chemicals such as silver nitrate, potassium bromide and gelatin (formula – page 284). However, preparation is time consuming and it is extremely difficult to get consistent batch-to-batch results. Instead, you can buy containers of ready-to-use gelatin emulsion such as Rockland Liquid Light. Then, working under bromide paper safe-lighting, you coat your chosen base material and allow it to dry before exposing it under the enlarger and processing (gently) in the normal way.

The type of surfaces you can coat include drawing paper, wallpaper, canvas, wood, plaster, most plastics and glass. Do not try to emulate the smooth qualities of commercial photographic paper. Your evenness of coating and the richness of image tones will not compare – and, in any case, there is no point. Use the 'handmade' look to your advantage. For example, coat a sheet of paper only in the centre and let the emulsion trail off into brush strokes around the edges. Try coating three-dimensional objects like egg- or seashells, fragments of stone, ceramic tiles or plates. Since the coating is thin and transparent it takes on all the texture and colour of whatever base material you use. (*Note:* Gelatin cannot be fire glazed into the surface of ceramics like normal ink-printed designs, which are applied by special transfer.) Choose a picture which suits the nature of the unusual base, both in subject matter and visual design. Highly textured materials need simple images. Sometimes it is worth converting your continuous-tone image into line first by copying it on lith film.

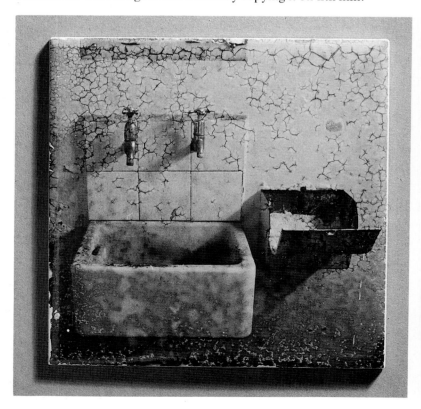

Fig. 11.1 This ordinary white ceramic wall tile was coated with ready-made emulsion, then exposed to a negative under the enlarger and processed in bromide paper developer. Rapid drying caused the emulsion to pucker and wrinkle, which helps to relate surface and image here. Pick subjects which relate in some way to the surface you print on. Try to display results lit in the same manner and direction as the original subject. (By Lorry Eason)

Fig. 11.2 For this picture, Lorry Eason brushed drawing paper over with liquid emulsion in a deliberately uneven fashion. Paper was left uncoated around edges. When dry the sheet was exposed under the enlarger, then processed normally

Fig. 11.3 Gum-bichromate print contact printed from an enlarged negative onto sensitized drawing paper. See page 261

Fig. 11.4 Coating and exposing a ceramic tile with ready-made emuslion. 1: liquefying the bought emulsion in hot water. 2: coating the prepared tile surface. 3: after drying, the sensitized tile is exposed (on black paper) to the image from the enlarger

The emulsion itself comes in a light-tight plastic container in solid jelly form. You have to turn it into a coatable liquid by warming the top part of the container in hot water (Figure 11.4). This only takes a few minutes, but in fact holding it at 50°C for about 3 hours improves emulsion sensitivity and maximum black as well as liquefying it. Do not let the gelatin warm beyond about 55°C or it 'overcooks' and loses adhesive power. With most papers and unprimed canvas you can coat the emulsion on directly, using a flat brush and criss-crossing your strokes. Small three-dimensional objects can just be dipped in emulsion. Always coat some emulsion onto one or more small extra pieces of the same base material, which you can then use later for exposure tests.

Direct application to an absorbent surface means that emulsion (and subsequent processing chemicals) penetrate deeply and improve image richness. However, it quickly uses up expensive emulsion, sometimes unevenly, and there is more risk of staining. So highly porous materials such as plaster and earthenware are best sized first with a thin coating of clear phenol varnish diluted 1:1 with naptha. Give primed canvas a coating of dilute flat wall paint.

Having coated your base surfaces in the darkroom, leave them for several hours in darkness until fully dry. Then use some test material first under the enlarger to make an exposure series. Process in regular print developer and fixer, wash gently and air dry. Once your final result is produced, materials such as ceramic or metal can be sealed over with matt clear varnish to help protect the image.

Gum-bichromate

The gum-bichromate contact printing process also allows you to pick your own paper or cloth base material. However, instead of silver you end up with an image consisting of watercolour or gouache in any hue you choose. This process also makes it easy to scrub out details or alter tones on individual prints, so that both in its physical handling and visual result the gum-bichromate process comes close to fine art printmaking. It is possible (but difficult) to produce a run of matching prints – so you will do better to regard each gum print as a one-off handmade image. Gum bichromates are low cost but labour-intensive, and their watercolour content gives interesting 'unphotographic' image quality.

No silver halides are needed. You coat good-quality drawing paper with gum arabic mixed with your choice of artist's water-based colour pigment, plus potassium dichromate which hardens the gum when

---

Gum*

Powdered gum arabic	350 g
Hot water to	1 litre
Powdered watercolour pigment as required for colour and density	

Sensitizer

Potassium dichromate crystals	50 g
Warm water to	500 ml

Store in dark-tinted container

Mix 2 parts gum to 1 part sensitizer before use

---

* Add anti-fungus agent if gum to be stored more than a few hours.

Fig. 11.5 Gum bichromate formulae

heavily exposed to ultra-violet radiation. (Dichromate and bichromate are equivalent photographically. Ammonium bichromate is occasionally used instead of potassium dichromate, being slightly faster but more expensive.) Light-sensitivity is far too slow to use for enlarging, so you work from an enlarged photographic negative contact printed using a bright ultra-violet-rich light source. 'Development' consists of gently washing away the pigmented gum from the unhardened lighter areas of the print.

Work from a final image size negative, either continuous-tone or half-tone screened (page 269) up to 250 lines/inch. You can make the former by enlarging up a slide onto 8 × 10 inch pan film, or start from an existing negative via an enlarged positive (on a sheet cut from a wide roll of darkroom film or even on RC bromide paper). Then contact print this back onto normal contrast non-colour-sensitive darkroom film. Subjects with soft, directional lighting give most detail. The printing negative should not have a density range much beyond 0.5 unless you intend printing with several layers (see below).

Size your paper surface first using one or two coatings of 10% gelatin flakes. Then tape the wet paper on all four sides onto hardboard and leave it to dry so that it stretches tightly. Mix your dissolved and cooled gum solution with pigment and combine it with dichromate solution under weak tungsten light. (You must *always* wear gloves when mixing or using dichromate – this chemical's toxic content can be absorbed through the skin.) Note down how much pigment your coating contains – you cannot judge final colour here because of the dichromate's orangey tint. Either lightly outline in pencil the area of paper you want to coat or treat the whole surface with your mixed warm solution, brushing it on with cross-hatch

Fig. 11.6 Gum bichromate printing.
1: taping the wet, sized paper to hardboard with paper tape.
2: coating mixture of pigmented gum and dichromate solution onto the dry, stretched paper. 3: when re-dried, paper surface is faced with film negative and thick glass.
4: long exposure to blue-rich light.
5: exposed print removed from board, floated face down in warm water. 6: gum, pigment and dichromate dissolve away where they received no light. Local areas can be swabbed lighter with cottonwool, or by brushing

strokes. Coat several sheets because you will want to use some as exposure test strips. Finally, leave your sensitized material to dry in the dark.

To expose, clamp the negative firmly down over the paper, under glass. Expose to a bright ultra-violet sunlamp, or daylight, for several minutes – if your negative is on RC paper give hours rather than minutes. Process by inserting the print into a tray of plain 27°C water, then letting it float undisturbed face down. Gradually, all the orange dichromate and unhardened gum dissolves out. Using a series of three or four trays, this takes 15–60 minutes. During processing you can work out dark shadows with a soft brush, or scrub out or texture entire areas with a stiff one. See Figure 11.3.

Most gum prints gain depth and contrast by several printings. You do this by recoating the dried print with sensitizer, drying and then exposing the same negative over again. (Some registration system is essential – you cannot judge the position of first image detail through the dichromate.) It is quite common to give four or more printings, varying the colour and intensity of your pigment. You can also print several versions of the image, such as one negative containing only contrasty shadow detail followed by another which is darker and has normal contrast. Colour-separation negatives (page 91) can even be printed in yellow, magenta and cyan, but use this process for effect rather than colour accuracy. The final dry print is quite tough and can be dry-mounted and spotted or locally tinted by watercolour on a brush.

Audiovisual

Audiovisual means the presentation of slides from several projectors (usually a programmed bank) synchronized with quality stereo sound on tape. It can be augmented if necessary by many 'bells and whistles' – movie projectors, video screens, lasers, smoke machines and other theatrical special effects. At its best, audiovisual offers a powerful and dramatic form of communication through pictures which dissolve, mix and snap change, and with image quality far higher than movie film or video can offer. It is more flexible too, for slides can be individually updated and parts of programmes reorganized at any time. Professional audiovisual is used for conferences and exhibitions of all kinds as well as for prestige tour introductions for visitors to corporate organizations, industrial plant, etc. Since the equipment

Fig. 11.7 Audio-visual presentation — flow of commands. The show is run from tape machine (T). This reproduces the sound track through speakers S, and also passes inaudible pulses to computer C. At each pulse the computer triggers the next programmed command to pairs of slide projectors (P) through dissolve modules. Computer can control 20 or more projectors

Fig. 11.8 AV production and show layout. Projectors may be stacked in twos and threes, focused in register onto various areas of the screen. Light-box benches facilitate slide sorting

takes time to set up and align, shows are best presented in a static installation built into some kind of auditorium.

Equipment

As shown in Figure 11.8, the heart of audiovisual presentation is typically a stack of 'carousel' 2 × 2 inch slide projectors. These are connected in pairs or groups to dissolve modules, which electrically fade down one lamp while fading up another, change slides during dark periods and (if projectors are fitted with shutters) make instantaneous cuts from one machine to another. The modules are controlled by a desktop computer fitted with audiovisual software.

Computer commands are made in 'steps'. You write into the computer all the projection situation changes needed at each step, i.e. which projectors are to be on, which are fading or dissolving and at what rate, etc. Information on hundreds of steps goes into the computer memory to build up your complete visual program, bit by bit. Then, to play back, each step is cued in sequence by signals you have laid on one track of a multi-track reel-to-reel tape recorder. Other (audio) tracks feed through an amplifying system to reproduce sound, and sometimes a track is also used to control house lights, curtains and effects.

Planning and shooting

The most basic way to get the 'feel' of audiovisual is to set up two projectors onto the same area of screen and dissolve images from one into the other. Notice the composite images formed midway by superimposition and how highlights come up before shadows. Next, by allocating different parts of the screen to different projectors (or to different pairs or groups of projectors) you can realize the possibilities of multi-images – a changing patchwork of different pictures one moment and the next a full screenwidth panorama appearing as one image.

Some audiovisual presentations can be planned in detail almost from the start. Having listed a rough outline on paper, you draw up a storyboard (Figure 11.9) containing almost everything that should appear on the screen before a single 35 mm slide has been shot. More often, subjects and situations have to be photographed as they occur, so you must remain flexible and work slides into a sequence afterwards. Even here, bear in mind the following points.

Fig. 11.9 Part of storyboard for an AV programme. There is no set way to lay out the various strands of the show, but the main aim is to plan the relationship of what you see and hear, on a time scale

Fig. 11.10 Pin-registered slide mount. Square pins within the mount engage in the 35 mm film sprocket holes, precisely locating the picture in the glass window area

1. The need to keep all pictures horizontal (or all vertical) format;
2. The value of sequences in which the camera stays fixed while changes of position, lighting or expression occur with the subject;
3. Any change of viewpoint into or out of a scene (by moving or zooming) should usefully maintain one element in the same part of the frame, or keep a strong horizon in the same position;
4. The importance of creating visual continuity between shots of quite different subjects, perhaps through a similar picture structure or use of colour. However, do not try shooting action to emulate movie-making. Audiovisual cannot reproduce true movement beyond brief sequences – it is better at melting and weaving high-quality *still* pictures.

Most audiovisual photography is shot on 35 mm reversal stock using regular camera equipment. It is useful to have a motordrive for occasional rapid sequences and to help you to maintain the same composition between a series of shots which will dissolve into each other. Another aid is to have a camera body register pin adapted.

Fig. 11.11 Frames from an AV sequence in which the camera maintains a fixed position. Continuous dissolves between projectors accurately registered on the same area of screen make the main subject here seem to move against an unchanging garden background

ON SCREEN

IN SLIDE MOUNT

Fig. 11.12 AV images may be projected into the screen using (1) central area only, (2) equal pairs, (3) triples (masked to square or upright using slide mount mask B, below). With two projectors registered on each area, dissolves can be achieved; more projectors make faster dissolves and superimpositions possible. (4) Patchworking effect using pairs with 'hand cut' masks such as C below. These are made by drawing shapes in indian ink and copying on lith film. Make negative and positive versions so you can superimpose other pictures into the gaps. (5) Using a pair, each with a single edge vignette mask A. (6) When projectors are directed 'three-on-two', like (5) but adding centre ones having vignette mask D, you can form one long seamless image

This engineering conversion is expensive but ensures that the picture area of the 35 mm film always relates to the placing of the perforations in a precise and consistent way. You then use plastic audiovisual slide mounts which contain pins to hold every frame of film by its perforations. Given projectors which precisely locate the slide into the gate, one picture will register on screen with the next without variations, exactly as they were shot. This is vital whenever you want one picture to dissolve into another containing, say, the same background detail without that detail perceptibly shifting.

Rostrum duplicating

In professional audiovisual work it is unusual to project original, irreplaceable camera-shot slides. These are more often rephotographed onto duplicating colour slide stock. Copying also allows you some adjustment of colour balance, density and framing. Most useful of all, you can alter image *size*. Pictures can be reduced to occupy quarter frames (for patchworking) or, by enlarging one shot and splitting it over two or more frames, you will form one join-up widescreen image when these are all projected at once.

The copying set-up can be a vertical slide duplicator or even a 35 mm camera set up on an enlarger column over an inverted colour head (page 247). If possible, the camera body should be adapted to give other forms, there would be little market for professional photography. However, really good results depend on supplying the right kind of original in the first place and having it sympathetically reproduced by skilled print technicians. Some knowledge of the technical procedure helps when results are disappointing and photographer and printer start to blame each other.

Three systems

The three main methods of reproduction in the printing trade are letterpress, lithography and photogravure. Letterpress uses a raised printing surface (Figure 11.16), like a typewriter. It is the oldest form of printing, originated for letter forms and later for pictures hand-engraved on wooden or metal blocks – areas to print light being etched or gouged out. Letterpress is still used for some newspapers, magazines and books.

Lithography originated about 200 years ago when artists drew on the flat surface of limestone – a porous rock. It is based on the fact that greasy ink and water repel one another. Today called photo-lithography, it uses a thin porous metal sheet treated so that the areas to print dark will not retain moisture. The surface is then wetted, rolled over with greasy ink (which only holds in the non-porous areas) and printed onto paper. On the press the thin litho sheet is wrapped around the outside of a cylinder. It comes into contact with a water-damping roller, then greasy ink rollers, and finally a larger rubber roller which transfers the ink from plate to paper. (This 'offsetting' means that the litho plate never comes into direct contact with the paper, card, tin, etc. It can print at speed with minimum wear.) Most modern newspapers, brochures, posters, packaging and books (including this one) are printed by offset photolithography.

Photogravure works in the reverse way to letterpress. Areas to print dark are etched as hollows into metal, then filled with a thin ink and the whole top surface wiped clean. When the gravure surface comes into contact with absorbent paper, ink filling each hollowed-out cell is transferred into the paper fibres. Gravure cylinders are expensive and relatively slow to prepare, but they can give good-quality results on only average paper and stand up to very large printing runs. They are mostly used for weekly magazines, newspaper supplements, etc.

All three forms of printing are referred to generally as *photo-mechanical reproduction*. This term acknowledges both the photographic processes involved in preparing the printing surface and the machinery of the actual printing press.

Fig. 11.16 The three main methods of ink-printed reproduction. Although lithography here is shown transferring ink direct to paper, normally the ink image is taken off onto a large rubber roller which then meets the paper. This is called offset lithography

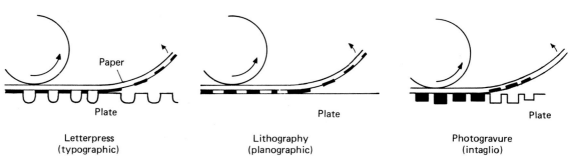

Letterpress
(typographic)

Lithography
(planographic)

Photogravure
(intaglio)

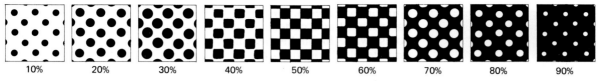

10%	20%	30%	40%	50%	60%	70%	80%	90%

Fig. 11.17 Halftone printed images appear to have a range of greys but in fact these are made up of pure black and pure white dots, in different proportions. The pattern above is about 16 times coarser than would be used normally. View the page from about 6 metres away to see these patches as a grey scale

Halftone dot

As you can see from Figure 11.16, letterpress and lith printing at least are all-or-nothing processes. The paper either receives a full loading of ink or remains white. To reproduce the range of greys in a photograph, *tones* are turned into a fine pattern of *dots* of different sizes. Take a look at any black and white photograph in this book through a magnifier and you will find that a mid-grey area is really a mosaic of black dots and clear spaces, about 50:50 in ratio. Darker tones have more black dots than white, while pale greys are the reverse. This use of halftone dot images is based on your eye's inability to resolve fine detail. Dot patterns of about 133 per inch (5–6 per millimetre) or finer merge into a tone at normal reading distance (see Figure 4.12). The same eyesight limitation is exploited when spotting prints and in additive screen colour films (page 95).

To turn the continuous tones of a monochrome photograph into a halftone screened image for printing, the picture can be copied through a soft-edged ruled grid (Figure 11.18). This turns image tones into many tiny equal-size but graduated 'pools' of light – bright pools from highlight areas down to dim ones in shadow areas. Copying is

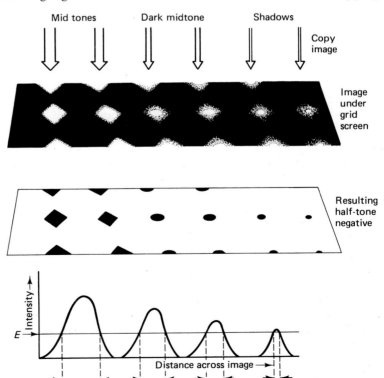

Fig. 11.18 How a halftone screen works. Image light from the photograph being copied passes through vignetted grid screen (typically 133 lines per inch). Highlights and midtones form brighter pools of light than shadows. Correctly exposed onto high-contrast film beneath the screen, the brighter the pool the larger the black dot recorded. This halftone dot negative is contact printed onto the printing plate

and printing (in register) from two versions of the same halftone image. One version may carry delicate highlight detail down to darker mid-tones; the other is paler and more contrasty, carrying well-separated tones from mid-tones into rich black shadows. Collectively, this duotone printing gives good tone separation over a much wider range of values than is possible from one impression alone. (It is similar to the effect of the black printer in colour reproduction and multiple build-up of dye in gum-bichromate printing.)

Anything from two to four or more impressions can be used, with corresponding increase in cost and ever smaller improvements in image reproduction. The separations can differ in density, contrast and the 'colour' of the ink in which they are printed. Inks can be different shades of neutral grey, black, brownish black, etc. When superimposed, these will reproduce most of the subtleties of even a rich chlorobromide photographic paper. Monochrome can also be reproduced using four-colour printing techniques. This makes sense when high-quality black and white and colour pictures must print on the same sheet. For monochrome the yellow, magenta and cyan impressions all carry the same image, and, together with the black printer, build up a good tone range in visually neutral density. However, unlike duotone, any misregistration or 'drift' during a printing run can introduce startling bits of colour or casts into a colourless illustration.

Scanners

At one time the conversion of photographic originals into halftone separations was all done by copying through a large process camera. A ruled screen held a set distance from the film gave the required soft-edged light pattern; in four-colour work contrasts and colour were adjusted by registering silver image masks with the original (see page 162). However, today most of this work is done electronically, using a scanner (Figure 11.23). Typically, an original colour trans-

Fig. 11.23 Components of four-colour separation scanner. Original colour transparency (T) or print is scanned by light source (L) in the input section. The signals produced are often stored and manipulated (see text) then exposed in halftone dot form onto photographic film in the light-tight output section. Normally a batch of original transparencies are all scanned at one time. The mirror moves up the transparent cylinder keeping pace with the analysing head. For inputting from paper prints a reflected-light scanning system, far left, replaces transmitted light. For electronic photography images the input can be direct from floppy disc, bypassing scanning parency is taped to a clear perspex drum and rear-illuminated by a tiny point of light. An extension of the cylinder in a lightproof housing carries the photographic process film ready to receive the four separation images.

As the cylinder rotates, the analysing light spot gradually moves along the cylinder, progressively scanning every part of the transparency. A light-sensor unit with blue, green and red receptors tracks along in parallel outside the cylinder and turns the changing light values it receives into one long stream of electronic signals. Meanwhile, at the exposing end of the cylinder a small beam of light (often a laser) focused on the separation film dims and brightens according to signals received. The exposing optics track along the rotating cylinder, gradually exposing each of the black and white film separations which will finally give yellow, magenta, cyan and black printing images.

The analysing unit (which, incidentally, also accepts prints, bouncing a light spot off the surface) feeds to the exposing unit through very sophisticated, computerized circuitry. Here the operator can electronically carry out almost limitless contrast masking and dye-deficiency masking. Actual screening of the separations can also be programmed-in. The system will electronically generate the required high-resolution dot shape to suit known printing/ink/paper conditions. Sets of separations can be scaled up or down in size by making the exposing cylinder a different diameter and other changes. It is even possible to elongate or compress one of the dimensions of a picture (for example, set horizontal enlargement greater than vertical) to squeeze your photograph into a different-shaped space in a page layout without cropping.

While a picture is stored in electronic form as digital pixel data, spots and defects can be removed and sharpness enhanced. Watching on a video display unit (Figure 11.24), you can greatly enlarge up the pixels containing blemishes, then 'patch in' colour and tone from copies of mixed adjacent pixels, so that when the image is returned to its original size the repairs are invisible. To enhance visual sharpness, the scanner's computer will step up contrast locally across the boundaries of detail, while leaving broader areas unchanged. You can also choose to soften detail in chosen areas; see Figure 11.25.

In fact, most of the special effects possible in television – posterization, bas-relief, 'pasting up' one image alongside or within another – can all take place between scanner analysis and separations exposure. It is therefore normal to check these changes on a colour VDU as the work proceeds. Rather like video analysis for photographic printing (page 242), any adjustments you made to the picture while viewing it can be programmed to make the corresponding changes needed on the separations.

Preparing four-colour and other separations is a specialized task, requiring costly equipment. Some firms specialize in 'reproduction' or 'origination' then pass on their product as film ready for other (printing) firms to use. Large printing houses have their own origination departments.

What the photographer should supply

Despite the aids and controls possible when reproducing photographs

Fig. 11.24 Video display unit and planning table. Having scanned and electronically stored colour separations, the photographic originals are set up in lit cubicle A. Here they are compared against electronic 'proofs' displayed on video screen V. Control cursor C relates to planning table (which has embedded mesh of wires). By moving cursor over drawn page layout any chosen area of displayed picture can be enclosed. Menu on computer, right, allows changes to be made to tone or colour balance, shape, page location etc. Finally the manipulated result is sent as signals to output exposing section of scanner, Figure 11.23.

Fig. 11.26 Frame-grabbing. Some methods of converting chemical photographic prints or film images to electronic form. Left: video camera on print copy stand. Centre: simple video copying adaptor for transparencies, using light-box. Right: unit for converting slides to video (also allows dissolves). All units output to videotape or floppy disc

Electronic and chemical photography

For the time being at least, electronic photography and chemical (silver) photography have separate strengths and weaknesses. Where the end result is to be hard copy (prints to hold in the hand or slides to project) there is still nothing to approach the colour, tone and resolution qualities of a chemical photography image. Where you need a video signal for soft display on one or many VDU monitors there is nothing better than an electronic image. This can be input from a still-video camera, scanner or graphics computer, via floppy disc, VCR, telephone or radio link.

It so happens that you can turn a chemical photographic image into an electronic one using some form of 'frame-grabbing' copy stand (Figure 11.26). However, it will not look as crisp and sharp on the video screen as it did in its original form. Similarly, you can turn a video signal into a hard copy paper print, using equipment such as a thermal printer (Figure 11.27) or CRT printer (page 251). However, despite steady improvements, the result will not be as sharp as a print from a chemical photographic original. Other factors are your time and the cost of equipment and materials, which alter with every new technical advance.

Electronic image recording increases the flexibility of chemical photography by letting it do things not otherwise possible. For example, a press photographer in the field can transmit electronic still pictures back to the newspaper's news desk via any cable or radio telephone. See Figure 11.28. Speed of communication here is of prime importance. The picture can be viewed on a video screen, sized,

Fig. 11.27 Principles of thermal printer making hard-copy colour prints on paper from electronic images. Receiving paper (P) fits under roll of transfer film with consecutive segments of cyan, magenta and yellow heat-transfer dye. Bar of heated pins responds to each row of scan signals from electronic image, transferring tiny spots of colour to paper. After each single colour is printed, the roll shifts relative to receiving paper, to bring next colour into same printing position

Fig. 11.28 Battery-powered transmitter allows electronic images from still-video floppy to be sent through any telephone system. Tiny monitor displays picture being transmitted. System cuts time between news photographer and picture desk

cropped, enhanced if necessary and passed on down the wire to the photomechanical department as electrical signals for direct conversion to halftone dot form. The photographer's work only turns into hard copy at the end of the line – on the newspaper's printed page.

Electronics also offer a convenient cost-cutting way of storing and distributing your pictures. A series of photographs (perhaps for instructional or reference purposes) can be transferred into video floppy discs in any required sequence. Further sets are made by duplicating the disc. Discs can be mailed anywhere for reading out on a monitor: in fact, they are so inexpensive, they need not be returned. Meanwhile, your original shots remain safely on file. Again, in medicine there are now many forms of examination, including ultrasound, computed axial tomography (brain scans and body scans) and nucleomagnetic resonance imaging, which read out pictures in electronic form. These are viewed in soft copy on a monitor and magnetically recorded, but can be retrieved using instant-picture material, heat prints or CRT-exposed chemical photographs to form hard copy for reports, etc. In police and security work thousands of mug shots can be stored on video discs or still-video floppies and coded for selective retrieval. Through a computer you can call up faces under dozens of different categories, which are then re-recorded and presented in sequence on screen.

Electronic still photography clearly has important commercial and industrial applications, especially where convenience and time-saving are more important than finest quality. As for general professional and amateur photography, quality will always be compared holding electronic hard copy and chemical prints from a conventional negative side by side. Resolution differences are largely a question of lines per millimetre versus pixel density. The quality of video images – and the capacity of computer memory to store and process the information they contain – increases by several orders of magnitude every few years. However, the difficulty in forecasting when electronic photography will 'catch up' with chemical photography is that the

Fig. 11.29 Some of the interconnecting electronic routes from camera and other recorded input (top) to different forms of output (bottom). The CRT printer gives chemical photography colour prints by direct exposure from a video display latter is a moving target. Silver halide technology is also advancing and improving with higher resolution, faster emulsions, better dyes and shorter processes. So for a long time the two forms of image recording will co-exist – chemical photography for its quality and responsiveness to craft skills (especially in the fine art area) and electronic photography for its convenience and easy interfacing with other electronic media.

Eventually, most still photography will be done by electronic means, but we will be getting our hands wet in 'archaic' liquid processing for some time to come. The essence of photography remains the making of pictures by light, and this will always rely, as now, on having 'a good eye'. Your ability to see pictures, organize subjects, viewpoint and lighting, and decide appropriate image sharpness and exposure still remains vital. It matters much less whether you image onto an electronic chip or chemicals coated on film.

Summary: Extending photography

● Several forms of 'handmade' printing allow you to break away from the regular appearance of photographic prints. You can coat prepared liquid emulsion on two- (or three-) dimensional surfaces. Relate image content to the texture and character of your chosen base – drawing paper or canvas, stone, shell, ceramic, etc. Size porous surfaces first. Warm the emulsion to liquify it before coating, then allow the surface to dry fully in the dark. After exposure and processing, apply a protective seal of matt varnish.

● Gum-bichromate is a non-silver process giving a final image in one or more chosen watercolour pigments. Coat your choice of (sized) paper with a gum/pigment mixture, sensitized with potassium dichromate. Contact print onto it from an enlarged film negative, using ultra-violet-rich light.

● During gum print 'processing' (hot water, diffusing out areas unhardened by light) you can lighten shadows or scrub out parts by hand. Prints are usually recoated and exposed several times over, to build up density or introduce further colours. Finish off with pigment applied by brush.

● Multiple projection of slides with sound (audiovisual) allows you to make dramatic high-quality image presentations for sales, entertainment or information purposes. Slide projectors with dissolve modules are commanded by computer. Each computer-memorized step is cued in sequence from signals on one track of your sound and effects tape.

● Audiovisual allows slide images to 'flow' – superimpose, dissolve, fade, animate, multiply or patchwork across a wide screen. Often it is best to plan and storyboard before shooting. Exploit viewpoint, framing, colour, focus, timing; but keep some elements constant (for visual continuity), others changing (to give variety and action).

● A pin-registered 35 mm camera back plus audiovisual pin slide mounts helps to give consistent registration of images on screen. Ideally, a precision slide-duping rostrum set-up allows you to adjust size (for patchworking or wide-screen composite projection). Duping can help to match up colour and density and avoids damaging original slides from overprojection. Make titles and soft- or hard-edged frame masks on lith film.

● After shooting, slides are sorted on light-boxes, rough-edited and loaded into designated projector magazines. Each slide-changing step is previewed on screen, computer memorized, then linked to tape voiceover, music and effects. A show's structure might be audio based or determined entirely by visual content.

● Audiovisual is more flexible and cheaper than film; visually more dramatic and stimulating than simple still-image projection. However, you cannot ape film with long stretches of animation. Audiovisual also has many mechanical elements which can break down. Shows are best run in static installations under supervision, or transferred (professionally) to videotape.

● The three main systems of reproducing photographs on the printed page are letterpress (raised surface), lithography (water-repelling greasy ink) and photogravure (ink-retaining hollows).

● For letterpress or litho reproduction continuous-tone photographs are converted into a fine pattern of halftone dots. Your eye's limited resolution reads purely black and white dots as a full tone range, according to ratio and distribution.

● Duotone reproduction of black and white pictures enriches tone range and density but needs at least two halftone separations and two runs through the press. The finer the halftone screen ruling, the greater the detail, provided that it suits the paper being used.

● To reproduce full colour requires at least four separations, printing in yellow, magenta, cyan and black inks. (Screens are rotated to different angles.) Scanners convert picture information into a stream of signals representing the four separations. While in electronic digital form, images can be masked for contrast and colour, sharpness-reduced or enhanced, retouched, changed in proportions and screened, then re-exposed back onto process film as halftone dot separations.

● Chemical and electronic photography images play different roles. Present chemical methods give best-quality hard-copy prints, electronics best (VDU) soft display. Electronics can input from camera chip, graphics computer, scanner, etc. Signals are transmitted via cable or radio link and recorded on floppy disc or video tape. Electronic imagery is important where speed of communication and retrieval are prime considerations, together with easy interfacing with other electronic systems.

● Electronic hard copy will improve, and, to a lesser extent, so will chemical imaging. Electronic and chemical systems will co-exist for some time. Chemical photography will always have its devotees wherever craft skills and handwork are more important than speed and economy (for example, fine-art prints). Provided that you possess an eye for an image, you should have no problems adapting to either form of recording technique.

Appendices

A: Optical calculations

Formulae below relate to lenses, and make use of the following international symbols:

F = focal length
U = distance of object from lens (measured from front nodal point*)
V = distance of image from lens (measured from rear nodal point*)
D = total distance between object and image, ignoring nodal separation
O = object height
I = image height
M = magnification

(*Warning: these distances are difficult to measure accurately with telephoto and inverted telephoto lenses, because the nodal points may be well in front or behind the centre of the lens. See page 28).

You can calculate focal length, or image and object distances, or magnification, when other measurements are known:

$$F = \frac{UV}{U+V} = \frac{V}{M+1} = \frac{MU}{M+1} = \frac{MD}{(M+1)^2}$$

$$U = \left(\frac{1}{M}+1\right) \quad F = \frac{D}{M+1} = \frac{VF}{V-F}$$

$$V = (M+1) \quad F = \frac{DM}{M+1} = \frac{UF}{U-F}$$

$$D = U+V = (M+1)U = \left(\frac{1}{M}+1\right)V = \frac{F(M+1)^2}{M}$$

$$M = \frac{V}{U} = \frac{I}{O} = \frac{D-U}{U} = \frac{V}{D-V} = \frac{F}{U-F}$$

Bear in mind that when you are using an enlarger or projector the 'object' refers to the negative or transparency; the 'image' is that projected on the baseboard or screen.

Depth of field

When the object distance is great relative to focal length, the simplest way to calculate depth of field is to work from hyperfocal distance (see Glossary). This gives sufficient accuracy for most practical purposes.

f = f-number

c = diameter of circle of confusion

$$H = \text{hyperfocal distance} = \frac{F^2}{f \times c}$$

Distance from lens to nearest part of object in focus $= \dfrac{HU}{H+U}$

Distance from lens to farthest part of object in focus $= \dfrac{HU}{H-U}$

Exposure increase in close-up work

Owing to the effect of the inverse square law when the lens is located much beyond one focal length from the image plane, exposure time indicated by an external meter should be multiplied by

$$\frac{V^2}{F^2} \quad or \quad (M+1)^2 \quad or \quad \left(\frac{U}{U-F}\right)^2$$

Supplementary lenses and focal length
Assuming that the supplementary lens is placed very close to the main lens:

S = focal length of supplementary lens†

When using a converging supplementary:

$$\text{Combined focal length} = \frac{S \times F}{S + F}$$

When using a diverging supplementary:

$$\text{Combined focal length} = \frac{S \times F}{S - F}$$

†In same units as F. If in dioptres, divide dioptre value into one metre to get S.

Cosine law
Illumination across the field of a lens reduces as the fourth power of the cosine of the angle made between the portion of field and the axis. This means that less light is received at the corners of the frame in the camera than at the centre – noticeably so with wide-angle lenses of non-retrofocus construction. With neg-pos photography the effect of the camera lens is often compensated for by the cosine law effect on the enlarger lens. But with pos-pos printing corner darkening is cumulative.

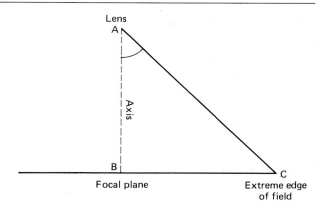

$$\text{Light fall-off at edge of field} = \cos^4 \hat{A} = \left(\frac{AB}{AC}\right)^4$$

B: Chemical formulae

Monobath

Single-solution combined developer and fixer for black and white films. Gives a set degree of contrast. Works on basis of active developer components developing fully during long inertia period before fixer begins to affect film. May cause dichroic fog with some film types.

Water (hot)	750 ml
Sodium sulphite (anhydrous)	60 g
Hydroquinone	30 g
Sodium hydroxide	25 g
'Phenidone'	3 g
Sodium thiosulphate (crystals)	150 g
Cooled water, to make	1 litre
Before use, add 40% formaldehyde	10 ml

Process to completion – about 6 minutes at 20°C.

Reducers for black and white silver image materials

Reducer R-4a is a subtractive reducer for over-exposure. Increases contrast, also removes veil due to fog.

Stock solution A
Water	250 ml
Potassium ferricyanide	38 g
Water, to make	500 ml

Stock solution B
Water	1 litre
Sodium thiosulphate (crystals)	480 g
Water, to make	2 litres

Mix one part solution A, four parts solution B and 27 parts water just before use. When reduction is sufficient, halt action by transferring film/paper to tray of running water. Finally wash fully.

Reducer R-8 is a proportional reducer. Reduces density and also slightly reduces contrast.

Water (about 32°C)	600 ml
Ferric ammonium sulphate	45 g
Potassium citrate	75 g
Sodium sulphite (anhydrous)	30 g
Citric acid	20 g
Sodium thiosulphate (crystals)	200 g
Water, to make	1 litre

Use at full strength. Treat negative for 1–10 minutes (18–21°C), then wash fully. For slower action dilute 1 + 1.

Reducer R-15 has a super-proportional effect, reducing mostly high density areas and therefore lowering contrast.

Stock solution A
Water	1 litre
Potassium persulphate	30 g

Stock solution B
Water	250 ml
Sulphuric acid (10% sol)	15 ml
Water, to make	500 ml

Use two parts A and one part B. Pre-treat negatives in liquid hardener, then wash. Reduce by inspection, then fix and wash fully.

Iodine bleacher

For total erasure of image, to 'shape-out' subjects on prints; can also be applied on tip of brush to convert black specks to white (these can then be spotted-in normally).

Warm water	750 ml
Potassium iodide	16 g
Iodine	4 g
Water, to make	1 litre

Keeps well. Apply undiluted with brush or cotton-wool. To remove the intense brown stain, rinse and treat in a small quantity of print fixing bath (10 minutes). Discard fixer. Wash fully.

Intensifiers for black and white silver materials

Intensifier IN-4 is a proportional type (chromium intensifier). Strengthens image without much change of contrast.

Stock solution
Water	500 ml
Potassium dichromate	90 g
Hydrochloric acid (concentrated)	64 ml
Water, to make	1 litre

Use one part stock and ten parts water. Pre-harden negative. Then bleach the black image in reducer, wash for 5 minutes, and redevelop in regular bromide paper developer. Work in white light (but not direct sunlight). Finally rinse, fix and wash. Can be repeated to increase the effect.

Intensifier IN-6 is a sub-proportional intensifier. Strengthens paler densities more than high density areas, so it reduces contrast. Works best with fast speed negative materials.

Stock solution A
Distilled water (about 21°C)	750 ml
Sulphuric acid (concentrated)	30 ml
Potassium dichromate	23 g
Distilled water, to make	1 litre

Stock solution B
Distilled water (about 21°C)	750 ml
Sodium metabisulphite	3.8 g
Hydroquinone	15 g
Wetting agent (Kodak Photo-Flo)	3.8 g
Water, to make	1 litre

Stock solution C

Distilled water (about 21°C)	750 ml
Sodium thiosulphate (crystals)	22.5 g
Water, to make	1 litre

For use add two parts B to one part A, stirring continually. Then, still stirring, add two parts C and one part A. Wash negative for 5–10 minutes, treat in hardener for 5 minutes, then wash again for 5 minutes before intensifying. Treat negative for up to 10 minutes (20°C) with frequent agitation. When using a tray, treat only one piece of film at a time and discard solution afterwards. Finally wash negative for 15 minutes.

Black and white silver halide emulsion

Chlorobromide enlarging type. Normal contrast, warm black tones.

Solution A

Water	750 ml
Gelatine	25 g
Potassium bromide	53 g
Sodium chloride	15 g
Cadmium chloride	2 g
Hydrochloric acid (30% sol)	2.5 ml

Solution B

Water	1400 ml
Silver nitrate	100 g

Solution C

Water	250 ml
Gelatine	150 g

Bring all the above solutions to 60°C. Then, under amber safelighting, add solution B to solution A in three separate and equal parts at intervals of 5 minutes. Some 5 minutes after the last addition, add solution C.

Ripening Hold the emulsion at 60°C for 30–45 minutes, covered from all light.

Coating additions Cool the emulsion (but keep it liquid enough to coat paper – about 40°C). Then make the following additions (quantities here per litre of emulsion).

Potassium bromide (10% sol)	2 ml
Chrome alum (10% sol)	15 ml
Formalin (40%), 1 part plus 3 parts water	40 ml
Alcohol (rectified spirit)	10 ml
Glycerine	10 ml
Sulphuric acid, 1 part in 10 parts water	3 ml

Once prepared, the emulsion can be stored in an opaque container in a refrigerator. For coating, follow information as for commercial emulsion, page 258.

Gum-bichromate formulae
See page 260.

C: Batteries

Batteries are vital power sources for most kinds of cameras, powerwinders, hand flash units, and exposure or colour temperature meters. So battery failures mean breakdowns that can ruin a shooting situation, especially when on location, unless you can anticipate problems. Each of the main types of battery has different practical characteristics.

Zinc carbon The oldest domestic-type batteries, as used for bicycle lamps etc. Low cost and best suited for functions where only intermittent 'bursts' of current are required. They lack staying power and are prone to leakage after exhaustion, through use, heat or storage.

Zinc chloride Fairly low cost. Useful as emergency supply for motor-drives, flashguns etc, but used regularly they are more expensive and less efficient than alkaline types. Prone to leakage – remove batteries when putting away the equipment.

Alkaline Much better staying power, as needed for micro-motors and camera circuitry, as well as flash units and meters. Virtually leak-proof. More costly than zinc battery types but have a longer working life. Good shelf life, and still work well at low temperatures. As with zinc batteries, voltage eventually falls off from initial output.

Nickel cadmium (Ni-Cad) These batteries are rechargeable. Batteries and charging gear are expensive, but with two batteries and a charger you should always have fresh battery supplies. However, Ni-Cads need charging more often than you would have to replace alkaline types, so you may be caught out by your batteries 'dying' on a shoot. Ni-Cad batteries do not have infinite life, and need recharging more frequently as they age. Since these batteries deliver high amperage they can give you shorter flash recycling times. But they can also damage components in some electronic circuits, and so should only be used if *specifically* recommended by the equipment manufacturer.

Mercury Used in some early electronic circuit cameras and meters, batteries of this kind give constant voltage throughout their full life. However, mercury batteries contain highly toxic chemical and are now illegal to manufacture in many countries. (*Spent batteries must be disposed of safely – never thrown onto a fire.*) Voltage is insufficient for some products of recent manufacture, although old equipment may *have* to be used with this battery type.

Silver oxide Modern replacement for mercury oxide batteries, but more expensive (and about twice the price of alkaline types). Very suitable for LED displays in camera viewfinders etc. Gives constant voltage throughout a long life. However, because of this an almost exhausted battery gives the same reading on a voltmeter as a new one – you cannot check whether batteries are fresh when purchased. Unlikely to leak.

Lithium Covers a number of individual types, all of growing importance. Has a long storage life. However, unless your equipment is specifically designed for lithium batteries their useful life may be short. They must be effectively leak-proofed – never leave an exhausted lithium battery in any equipment.

Storing batteries
Remember, batteries work by chemical reaction, which is speeded up by high temperature and slowed down in the cold. Warm storage reduces life – the spare batteries in your pocket are probably losing power almost as fast as those in your camera. At low temperatures batteries become sluggish. Outside on a cold day you may have to raise battery temperature with body heat to gain sufficient power to run your equipment. By the same token batteries sealed into a polythene bag and stored in a refrigerator or freezer have greatly extended shelf life.

Battery care
- Always check the polarity of batteries before fitting. Make sure they face the appropriately marked terminals.
- As far as possible, when you load a battery run a (cleaned) pencil eraser over both contacts. Complete the process by rubbing the contacts on clean paper. This can improve performance by 50%.
- Never attempt to recharge batteries other than Ni-Cad types.
- Don't attempt to open battery cases. Don't throw any battery into the fire. Keep batteries away from young children.
- It is always best to remove batteries before storing equipment for more than a week or so. Avoid leaving any exhausted battery in any equipment, and change your batteries at least once a year.

(Based on Photax data.)

D: Business practice digest

To run a photographic business successfully you have to master certain management skills, even though you may work on your own. Some of these activities are specifically photographic but most apply to the smooth running of businesses of all kinds. If you are inexperienced try to attend a short course on managing a small business. Often seminars on this theme are run by professional photographers' associations. There are also many user-friendly books and videos covering the principles of setting up and running your own business enterprise.

The main areas you need to understand are as follows.

Book-keeping

This may sound the dullest aspect of professional photography. But without well-kept books (or computer data) you soon become disorganized, inefficient, and can easily fall foul of the law. Good records show you the financial state of your business at any time. They also reduce the work the accountant needs to do to prepare tax and similar annual returns, and this saves you money.

Basically you need a separate bank account for your business activities. This alone gives you a primitive form of income and expenditure account. You should also have a financial diary or computer disc into which all receipts and expenditure are entered, daily. Do this conscientiously, because by recording everything each day you enable your accountant to prepare and check really accurate figures for your annual returns.

To cover small purchases – tools, tape, stamps, taxi fares etc. – withdraw a lump sum of cash from the bank. Keep this in a 'petty cash' box and gradually replace it with dated receipts as it is spent. As the lump sum runs low, total up the chits and file them, then draw this sum from the bank to re-establish the cash float. A petty cash system saves cluttering up your main records with small entries. It also points up the vital need always to retain every relevant receipt – big or small.

You also need to keep records of all your main items of equipment. This forms an inventory (against fire or theft), but more importantly you can agree a 'depreciation' rate for each piece with your accountant. For example, a camera may be given a reliable working life of five years, which means that its value depreciates by a set amount each year (effectively this is the annual cost to your business of using the camera, and part of your overheads when calculating trading profits for tax purposes).

Another vital record is your negative/transparency registers – perhaps one based on date order as jobs are done, and one listed in client name or subject description order. Good computer accountancy software will allow you to pick out all three types of information from the same data base.

Charging for jobs – costing

Knowing what to charge often seems more difficult than the technicalities of shooting the pictures. Charging too much loses clients; charging too little can mean periods of hard work for nil profit. Some photographers charge by knowing 'the going rate for the job', based on what competitors are charging and what your client will expect to pay. This may be valid in top echelons of the market, where time taken and materials consumed are minor elements in the charge relative to the visual approach and individuality of the photographer. However, for most businesses you need a more organized system of determining charges – based on costing.

Costing means identifying and pricing everything you have paid out in doing each job, so that by adding a percentage for profit you arrive at a fair fee. This should prevent you from ever doing work at a loss, and provided you keep costs to a minimum the fee should be fully competitive. Identifying your costs means you must include indirect outgoings ('overheads') as well as direct costs like film and paper. Typical overheads include rent; electricity; telephone; water; cleaning; heating; building maintenance; stationery; petty cash; equipment depreciation and repairs; insurances; bank charges; interest on loans; and accountancy fees. Also include the salary you pay yourself, as well as any staff. With costs spread over a working year (excluding your own and public holidays) you can work out a business cost per day, or even per hour.

When it comes to costing, you base your fee on three elements added together:

(1) What the business cost you to run during the time period you were working on the job.
(2) Direct outgoings which you incurred in shooting (such as the photographic materials; travel; accommodation and meals; models, hire of props, lab services, and any agent's fee).
(3) The percentage profit you decide the business should provide. Profit margin might be anywhere between 15 and 100%, and might sometimes vary according to the importance of the client to you, or to compensate for unpleasant, boring jobs you would otherwise turn away.

Often photographers charge by pre-agreed day rate plus the cost of materials and other direct expenses. Knowing what the business costs you to run, plus experience of how long it takes to set up and shoot and process various kinds of pictures, should allow you to quote a reasonably accurate final price. However, have some broad agreement with your client on the likely number of pictures you can be expected to complete in one day, bearing in mind the particular subject and shooting conditions.

Otherwise people often press you to produce quantity at the expense of quality. Then, later, they complain.

Commissioning forms
When someone asks to commission you to take photographs it is sensible practice to fill in a commissioning form. This has spaces for subject and location, likely duration of shoot, agreed fee and agreed expenses. It also specifies what the picture(s) will be used for and any variations to normal copyright ownership. Small print on the form spells out detail such as cancellation fees, the extent of a 'working day', and so on. Signed by the client it serves as a simple written contract. The form therefore avoids difficulties, misunderstandings and arguments at a later date – which is in everyone's interests.

Job sheets
One good way of keeping track of a job in progress (especially when several people are working on it at different times) is to use a job sheet system. A job sheet is a form the client never sees but which is started as soon as any request for photography comes in. It follows the job around from shooting through printing to retouching and finishing, and finally reaches the invoicing person's file when the completed work goes out. The job sheet also carries the job instructions, client's name and telephone number. Each member of the team logs the time spent, expenses, materials etc. in making their contribution. Even if you do all tasks single-handed, running a job sheet system will prevent jobs being accepted and forgotten, or completed and never charged for.

Invoicing
It often looks a trifle hasty to invoice your clients at the same time as sending the pictures. But then invoices sent months later may confuse their accounting system, and makes you look inefficient. Usual practice is to invoice about a week after delivery, and follow this by statements (just invoice number, date and fee) on the last day of each subsequent month. Some firms only pay on statements.

Uneven cash flow is the most common problem with small businesses. Clients (especially advertising agencies) are notorious for their delay in paying photographers. Often they wait until they are paid by *their* clients. It is therefore advantageous to have one or two regular commissions which might be mundane, but are paid for promptly and even justify a special discount.

Releases
Anyone who models for you for a commercial picture should be asked to sign a 'model release' form (see page 288: this can be photocopied off the page and used for jobs). The form in fact absolves you from later claims to influence uses of the picture. Clients usually insist that all recognizable people in advertising and promotional pictures have given signed releases – whether against a fee or just for a tip. The exceptions are press and documentary type shots where the people shown form a natural, integral part of the scene, and are not being used commercially.

Copyright
Be on your guard against agreements and contracts for particular jobs which take away from you the copyright of the resulting pictures. In most countries today the copyright in a photograph remains with the photographer (unless he or she is working as the salaried employee photographer). This is important when it comes to reprints, further use fees, and general control over who else may use a picture. If an agreement permanently deprives you of potential extra sources of revenue – by surrender of transparency or negative for example – this should be reflected by an increased fee. A commissioning form will help clarify the situation to both parties before you begin.

Promoting yourself
Like any other service industry, professional photography needs energetic marketing if it is to survive and flourish. The kind of sales promotion you need to use for a photographic business which has no direct dealings with the public naturally differs from one which must compete in the open market place. However, there are important common features to bear in mind too.

Your premises need to give the right impression to a potential client. The studio may be an old warehouse or a high-street shop, but its appearance should suggest liveliness and imagination, not indifference, decay or inefficiency. Decor and furnishings are important, and should reflect the style of your business. Keep the place clean. Use equipment which *looks* professional and reliable.

The business name, logo, notepaper and packaging design, along with all your printed matter, should have a coherent house style. Take great care over your portfolio of specimens of work too. Make sure this is well-presented, and specially selected and ordered to suit the interests of the particular prospective client. Include tear-sheets from publications etc. where your pictures have been used, to help inspire confidence. Talk clients through the collection of pictures, adding relevant information they will want to know. If you don't feel up to this kind of salesmanship then employ a good agent who will take the work around on your behalf.

Remember that you yourself need to project energy, enthusiasm and interest, skill and reliability. Take similar care with anyone you hire as your assistant. On location arrive on time, in professional-

MODEL RELEASE FORM

To

In consideration of your agreeing to pay me my fee for posing for photograph(s) taken or to be taken by you, I hereby acknowledge and agree:

that the entire copyright (which includes all rights of reproduction) in the photograph(s) belongs to you.

that you and/or your licensees or assignees are entitled to make whatever use of the photograph(s) and all reproductions thereof, either wholly or in part, in any manner or form whatsoever and in any medium and either separately or in conjunction with other photograph(s), part or parts of photograph(s), drawings or other forms of illustration you or they decide.

that the said photograph(s) whether or not retouched, altered or worked up, and all reproduction thereof, and any statements and/or words published in conjunction therewith or in relation thereto shall be deemed to represent and refer to an imaginary person AND NOT MYSELF

that unless my name is published, used or referred to in connection with the publication of the photograph(s), neither the photograph(s) nor any reproduction thereof nor any statement or words published or reproduced in conjunction with or in relation thereto shall be deemed to be attributed to me PERSONALLY.

* I am over 18 years of age.

* I am *not* over 18 years of age but my parent/guardian has agreed to my undertaking this work and to the use of this/these photograph(s) as mentioned herein. I have read and fully understand the terms of this contract. I authorize you to pay my fee for posing viz.

* to my agent/

* to me.. Address..

Signed.. Date of sitting(s)..

* Delete whichever does *not* apply   Job Number..

looking transport containing efficiently packed equipment. If you want to be an eccentric this will ensure you are remembered short term, but your work has to be that much better to survive such an indulgence. Most clients are arch-conservatives at heart. It is a sounder policy to be remembered for the quality of your pictures rather than for theatrical thrills thrown in while performing.

During shooting give the impression that you know what you are about. Vital accessories left behind, excessive fiddling with meters, equipment failures and a feeling of tension (quickly communicated to others) give any assignment a kiss of death. Good preparation plus experience and confidence in your equipment should permit a relaxed but competent approach. In the same way, by adopting a firm and fair attitude when quoting your charges you will imply that these have been established with care – and that incidentally you are not a person who is open to pressure. If fees are logically based on the cost of doing the job, discounts are clearly only possible if short cuts can be made to your method of working.

Glossary

aberrations Optical errors in a lens which limit its capabilities – causing the images it forms to differ from subject appearance, usually in small details.

accelerator Chemical ingredient of developer to speed up the otherwise slow activity of developing agents. Normally an *alkali* such as sodium carbonate, borax, or (high-contrast developers) sodium hydroxide. Also known as 'activator' or 'alkali component'.

acid Chemical substances with pH below 7. Because acid neutralizes an alkali, acidic solutions are often used to halt development – as in *stop bath* or *fixer*.

acutance Physical measure of how the transition from high density to low density reproduces in a developed film which has been exposed to a high contrast (test chart) subject.

adaption Ability of the eye to change its sensitivity to light (generally, or in different colour receptors). Adaption occurs naturally when there is a change in the colour or intensity of the subject light.

adaptor ring Narrow threaded ring which fits the front rim of a lens to allow use of accessories of a different ('step-up' or 'step-down') diameter.

additive colour processes Processes which represent subject colours by adding together different quantities of primary coloured light – blue, green and red.

additive printing Printing onto colour paper by giving separate blue, green and red light exposures.

AE Automatic exposure metering.

AE lock (AE-L) Control for holding a particular automatic exposure reading in the camera's memory.

aerial perspective Sense of depth conveyed by changes of tone with distance. Typically seen in a rolling landscape when atmospheric haze is present.

AF Autofocus.

AF converter Special tele-converter (typical power ×1.6), fitting between lens and camera body, which allows non-autofocus lenses to work in conjunction with an autofocus body. Glass elements within the converter itself shift to bring the subject into focus.

AF illuminator Infra-red source, in camera flashgun or built into body, used to illuminate subject and assist the image-measuring autofocus lens mechanism.

AF lock (AF-L) Locks an autofocus lens in its present focus setting.

alkali Chemical substances with pH above 7. Solution feels slippery to the touch, can neutralize acid. See also *accelerator*.

ambient light General term covering existing subject lighting, i.e. not specially provided by the photographer.

anaglyph Method of viewing stereo pairs by which left-hand and right-hand positive stereo images are presented overlapped and in contrasting colours (typically deep red and deep green). You view these results through spectacles with green and red eyepieces, so that each eye sees only its respective image and you experience one 3D picture.

analogue image recording An electronic waveform signal recording in which the degree of magnetism represents image strength. (Somewhat similar to a continuous-tone photograph, which uses a range of different densities to represent different brightnesses in the image.) See also *digital electronic recording*.

anastigmat lens Lens corrected to be largely free of astigmatism (totally so at one subject distance), and having minimal curved field.

angle of view Angle, formed at the lens, between lines from the extreme limits of a (distant) scene just imaged within the diagonal of the picture format. Varies with focal length and format size.

anhydrous (anhyd) Dehydrated form of a chemical. More concentrated than same substance in crystalline form.

ANSI speed number American National Standards

Institute number designating the light sensitivity of a printing paper.

anti-halation Light-absorbing dye present in film to prevent reflection or spread of light giving 'haloes' around bright highlights. Disappears during processing.

aperture preview SLR camera control to close the lens diaphragm to the actual setting used when exposing. For previewing *depth of field*.

aperture priority mode You set the lens aperture you require and the camera sets the appropriate shutter speed, to give correct exposure according to the camera's built-in metering system.

apochromat (apo) lens Lens highly corrected for chromatic aberration at three wavelengths (usually blue, green and red) instead of the customary two. Also dispenses with the need to correct your focus setting when taking infra-red pictures.

archival processing Procedures during processing aiming for the most stable image possible.

artificial light General term for any man-made light source. Artificial-light film, however, normally refers to tungsten illumination of 3200 K.

ASA American Standards Association, responsible for ASA system of speed rating. Doubling the ASA number denotes twice the light sensitivity. Now replaced by *ISO*.

aspheric contour A shape not forming part of a sphere. In lenses this is difficult to manufacture because most grinding/polishing equipment functions with spherical action.

auto-bracketing A rapid series of pictures taken by the camera automatically, each giving a slightly different exposure.

autochrome Early colour transparency (plate) system, using a mosaic of additive colour filters.

autofocus System by which the lens automatically focuses the image (for a chosen area of subject).

Av Aperture value. Auto-exposure camera metering mode. You choose the aperture, the meter sets the shutter speed. (Also known as aperture priority mode.)

B setting See *bulb*.

bag bellows Short, baggy form of bellows used on view cameras for wide-angle lens. Allows camera movements otherwise restricted by standard lens bellows.

barndoors Set of folding metal flaps fitted around front of spotlight. Controls light spill or limits beam.

barrel distortion Aberration by which the image of a square is more magnified at the centre than at its edges – forming a shape like the cross-section of a barrel.

baryta paper See *fibre-based paper*.

baseboard camera Camera with fold-open baseboard, which supports lens and bellows.

between-lens shutter Bladed (or 'leaf') shutter positioned between elements of a lens, close to

aperture.

bleacher Chemical able to erase or reduce image density.

blue-sensitive Emulsion sensitive to the blue region only of the visible spectrum. Also known as 'ordinary'.

bounced light Light which is reflected off an intermediate surface before reaching the subject. If the surface is relatively large and matt surfaced the resulting illumination will be soft in quality.

bracket In exposure, to take several versions of a shot giving different exposure levels. See also *auto-bracketing*.

brightness range The difference in luminance between darkest and lightest areas of the subject or image. Combined effect of lighting ratio and subject reflectance range.

bromide paper Printing paper with predominantly silver-bromide emulsion.

bulb Also 'brief'. The B setting on a shutter – keeps the shutter open for as long as the release remains pressed.

bulk film Film sold in long lengths, usually in cans.

burning-in See *printing-in*.

cable release Flexible cable which screws into camera shutter release. Allows shutter to be fired (or held open on 'B') with minimal shake.

capacitor Unit for storing and subsequently releasing a pulse of electricity.

cast Overall bias towards one colour.

CCD Charge-coupled device. An integrated circuit (chip) responsive to light and used to convert optical images into a stream of electronic data, recordable in analogue waveform or digital code form.

CdS Cadmium disulphide. Battery-powered light sensor cell, widely used in exposure hand meters.

characteristic curve Graph relating exposure to resulting image density, under given development conditions. Also known as H and D curve.

chlorobromide paper Warm-tone printing paper. Uses emulsion containing silver chloride and silver bromide.

chromogenic process Colour process which uses dyes chemically formed during processing to create the hues of your final image. Results contain no silver.

CI See *contrast index*.

CIE Commission Internationale de l'Eclairage. Originator of a standard system for precise description of colours.

circles of confusion Discs of light making up the image formed by a lens, from each point of light in the subject. The smaller these discs the sharper the image.

clearing time The time taken in a fixing bath for a film emulsion to lose its milky appearance.

click stops Aperture settings which you can set by physical 'feel' as well as by following a printed scale.

close-up lens Additional element added to the main lens, to focus close objects.

cold-light enlarger Enlarger using a fluorescent tube grid. Gives extremely diffused illumination.

colloidal silver A suspension of finely divided silver particles – e.g. coating the bottom of trays and deep tanks containing used developer, or covering the emulsion itself as 'dichroic fog'.

colour development A step in processing (or toning) in which coupler compounds become coloured where development is taking place.

colour separation negatives Black and white negatives of a scene exposed through blue, green and red tri-colour filters successively, and matched in image size and contrast.

colour temperature Way of defining the colour of a (continuous spectrum) light source, in kelvins. Equals the temperature, Absolute scale, at which a metal black body radiator would match the source in colour.

complementary colours Resulting colour (cyan, magenta or yellow) when one of the three primary colours (red, green or blue) is subtracted from white light. Also called 'subtractive primaries', 'secondary colours'.

condenser Simple lens system to concentrate and direct light from a source, e.g. in a spotlight or enlarger.

contact print Print exposed in direct contact with negative, therefore matching it in size.

contrast index (CI) A measure of contrast used by Kodak. Determined, in simple terms, by drawing an arc 2.0 (baseline) units long cutting the material's characteristic curve and centred on a point which is 0.1 units above minimum density. The slope of the straight line joining these two points is the contrast index. You give it a numerical form by continuing the straight line until it cuts the baseline, then quote the tangent of the angle made. Typically a film developed to a CI of 0.56 should print well on grade 2 paper, using a diffuser enlarger.

control strips Pre-exposed strips of film or paper used to test the accuracy and consistency of processing.

coupled dyes Compounds which have reacted to the (by)products of colour development to form visible colours.

covering power The area of image of useful quality that a lens will produce. Must exceed camera picture format, generously so if movements are to be used.

CPU Central processing unit. Solid-state electronic chip housed within camera. Used to compute exposure, focusing, etc., from data input by other electronic components.

cropping To trim one or more edges of an image, usually to improve composition.

cross front Camera movement. Sideways shift of lens, parallel to film plane.

CWA Centre-weighted average. Exposure measured by averaging out picture contents, paying more attention to central areas than corners.

D log E curve See *characteristic curve.*

D max Maximum density.

D min Minimum density.

darkslide Removable plastic or metal sheet fronting a sheet-film holder or film magazine.

daylight film Colour film balanced for subject lighting of 5500 K.

dedicated flash Flash unit which fully integrates with camera electronics. Sets shutter speed; detects film speed, aperture, light reading, subject distance etc.

dense Dark or 'thick', e.g. a negative or slide which transmits little light. Opposite to 'thin'.

densitometer Electro-optical instrument for reading the densities of a film or paper image.

density Numerical value for the darkness of a tone. The log (base 10) of *opacity.*

depth mode Automatic-exposure camera program which aims to preserve as much depth of field as possible in selecting aperture and shutter speed settings.

depth of field Distance between nearest and furthest parts of a subject which can be imaged in acceptably sharp focus at one setting of the lens.

depth of focus Distance the film (or printing paper) can be positioned either side of true focus whilst maintaining an acceptably sharp image, without refocusing the lens.

developing agent Chemical ingredient(s) of a developer with the primary function of reducing light-struck silver halides to black metallic silver.

diaphragm Aperture formed by an overlapping series of blades. Allows continuous adjustment of diameter.

diffraction Change in the path of light rays when they pass close to an opaque edge.

diffusion transfer process Any process by which a positive photographic print is made by physically transferring silver, or dyes, from the exposed material onto a receiving surface.

digital electronic recording Image information encoded into binary mathematical form – a string of pulses of either 0 or 1 values only, like a computer output. Images in digital form are relatively easy to manipulate, edit and re-record without quality losses. With suitable equipment digital forms of imagery can be converted to analogue, and vice versa.

DIN Deutsche Industrie Normen. German-based system of film speed rating, much used in Europe. An increase of 3 DIN denotes twice the light sensitivity. Now replaced by *ISO.*

dioptre Reciprocal of a metre. The dioptric power of a lens is its focal length divided into one metre.

dodging See *shading.*

dry mounting Bonding a photograph to a mount by

placing dry, heat-sensitive tissue between the two and applying pressure and heat.

drying mark Uneven patch(es) of density on film emulsion, due to uneven drying. Cannot be rubbed off.

DX coding Direct electronic detection of film characteristics (speed, number of exposures etc.) via sensors in camera's film-loading compartment.

dye-bleach processes A colour process by which three even layers of ready-formed dyes are destroyed (bleached) in certain areas. The dyes remaining form the final coloured image.

dye-image film Film in which the final processed image comprises dyes, not black silver.

dye transfer process Assembly colour print process. Three final-size black and white positives are printed from colour separation negatives (or from a colour negative printed through tri-colour filters) on matrix films. After gelatin-hardening development and hot water treatment the film's hardened gelatin forms relief 'printing plates'. You soak each positive separation in a complementary dye, Y, M or C, then squeegee them in turn onto a sheet of receiving paper to transfer their dye images. Excellent quality, but requires a high degree of control to achieve objective results.

easel See *masking frame.*

edge numbers Frame number, film type information etc., printed by light along film edges.

effective diameter (of lens aperture) Diameter of light beam entering lens which fills the diaphragm opening.

Ektaflex process Kodak amateur colour print process, utilizing dye-diffusion transfer. Exposed material is soaked in activator, then squeegeed to non-light-sensitive receiving paper. After a transfer period the sheets are pulled apart.

electronic flash General term for common flash units which create light by electronic discharge through gas-filled tube. Tubes give many flashes, unlike expendable flashbulb systems.

emulsion Mix of light-sensitive silver halides, plus additives, and gelatin.

EV Exposure value.

exposure-compensation dial Camera control effectively overriding film-speed setting (by + or − exposure units). Used when reading difficult subjects, or if film is to be 'pushed' or 'held back' to modify contrast.

exposure latitude Variation in exposure level (over or under) which still produces acceptable results.

exposure zone One of the 0–IX one-stop intervals into which the exposure range of a negative is divided in the zone system.

extension tube Tube, fitted between lens and camera body, to extend lens-to-film distance and allow focusing on very close subjects.

***f*-numbers** International sequence of numbers, expressing relative aperture, i.e. lens focal length divided by effective aperture diameter. Each change of *f*-setting halves or doubles image brightness.

false colour film Film designed to form image dyes which give a positive picture in colours substantially different to those in the subject – e.g. Infra-red Ektachrome.

fast Relative term – comparatively very light-sensitive.

ferrotype sheet Polished metal plate used for glazing glossy fibre-based prints.

fibre-based paper Printing paper with an all-paper base.

field camera Traditional-type view camera, often made of wood. Folds for carrying on location.

field image In still video photography, the option of recording only half the possible pixel information. This allows twice as many pictures to record on the same magnetic disc, but with poorer detail. See also *frame image.*

fill-in Illumination that lightens shadows, so reducing contrast.

film holder Double-sided holder for two sheet films, used with view cameras.

film pack Stack of sheet films in a special holder. A tab or lever moves each in turn into the focal plane.

film plane The plane, in the back of the camera, in which the film lies during exposure.

film speed Figure expressing relative light sensitivity. See *speed point.*

filter Optical device to remove (absorb) selected wavelengths or a proportion of all wavelengths.

filter factor Factor by which exposure should be increased when a filter is used. (Does not apply if exposure was read through lens plus filter.)

fisheye Extreme wide-angle lens, uncorrected for curvilinear distortion.

fixer Chemical solution which converts silver halides into soluble salts. Used after development and before washing, it removes remaining light-sensitive halides, so 'fixing' the developed black silver image.

flare Unwanted light, scattered or reflected within lens or camera/enlarger body. Causes flare patches, degrades shadow detail.

flashbulb Older type of flash source. Usable once only and ignited by simple battery/capacitor system.

flashing Giving a small extra exposure (to an even source of illumination) before or after image exposure. Lower the contrast of the photographic material.

flat A subject or image lacking contrast, having minimal tonal range.

fluorescence The visible light radiated by some substances when stimulated by (invisible) ultra-violet light.

focal length Distance between sharp image and lens,

focal plane Plane on which a sharp-focus image is formed. Usually at right-angles to lens axis.

focus hold See *AF lock.*

focus priority See *trap focus.*

fog Unwanted veil of density (or bleached appearance, in reversal materials). Caused by accidental exposure to light or chemical reaction.

format or 'frame' General term for the picture area given by a camera.

FP sync Camera shutter flash synchronization circuit designed to suit FP ('focal plane') flashbulbs. Since firing contact is made before the shutter starts to open, you will get no results if electronic flash is used on this circuit.

frame image In still video photography, recording full pixel information to give a fully interlaced video image. This takes up twice as much space on the magnetic disc as a *field image.*

gamma Tangent of the angle made between the base and straight-line portion of a film's characteristic curve. Once used as a measure of contrast.

gelatin Natural protein used to suspend silver halides evenly in an emulsion form. Permits entry and removal of chemical solutions.

glossy Smooth, shiny print-surface finish.

GOST Gosudarstvenny f Standart, the USSR standards organization responsible for GOST system of speed rating used in Eastern bloc countries.

gradation Variation in tone.

graduate Calibrated container for measuring liquids.

grain Clumps of processed silver halides forming the image. Coarse grain destroys detail, gives a mealy appearance to even areas of tone.

grey scale Set of tones, usually in steps from minimum to maximum density. Grey scales are available on paper or film base. They can be used to lay alongside subjects to act as a guide in final printing. Exposed grey scales act as process control strips.

guide number Number for simple flash exposure calculations, being flashgun distance from subject times *f*-number required (ISO 100/21° film). Normally relates to distances in metres.

halftone Full-tone-range photograph broken down into tiny dots of differing sizes, for ink reproduction on the printed page.

hard Contrasty – harsh tone values.

hardener Chemical which toughens the emulsion gelatin.

high key Scene or picture consisting predominantly of pale, delicate tones and colours.

highlights The brightest, lightest parts of the subject.

holding back Reducing development (often to lower contrast). Usually preceded by increased exposure. Also called 'pulling'. Term is sometimes used to mean *shading* when printing.

hot shoe Flashgun accessory shoe on camera; it incorporates electrical contacts.

hue The colour – blue, green, yellow etc. – of a material or substance.

hyperfocal distance Distance of the nearest part of the subject rendered sharp with the lens focused for infinity.

hypo Abbreviation for sodium hyposulphite, the fixing agent since renamed sodium thiosulphate. Also common term for all fixing baths.

incandescent light Illumination produced from electrically heated source, e.g. the tungsten wire filament of a lamp.

incident light Light reaching a subject, surface etc.

incident-light reading Using an exposure meter at the subject position, pointed towards the camera, with a diffuser over the light sensor.

infinity A subject so distant that light from it effectively reaches the lens as parallel rays. (In practical terms the horizon.)

ink-jet printer Equipment which prints an image – on paper, canvas, plastic etc. – by digital control of four-colour paint or ink sprays. It can give large-scale hard-copy images from *still video* recordings.

instant-picture material Photographic material with integral processing, e.g. Polaroid.

integral tripack Three-layered emulsion. Term still often applied to modern colour emulsions which may utilize many more layers but are still essentially responsive to blue, green and red.

internegative Intermediate negative – usually a colour negative printed from a colour transparency in order to make a neg/pos colour print.

inverse square law With a point source of light, intensity at a surface is inversely proportional to the square of its distance from the source: e.g. half the distance, four times the intensity.

inverted telephoto lens A lens with rear nodal point well behind its rear element. It therefore has a short focal length but relatively long lens-to-image distance, allowing space for an SLR mirror system.

IR Infra-red. Wavelengths longer than about 720 nm.

IR focus setting Red line to one side of the lens focus-setting mark, used when taking pictures on IR film. See page 80.

ISO International Standards Organization. Responsible for ISO film speed system. Combines previous ASA and DIN figures, e.g. ISO 400/27°.

joule Watt-second. Light output given by one watt burning for one second. Used to quantify and compare the power output of electronic flash (but ignores influence of flash-head reflector or diffuser on exposure).

kelvin (K) Measurement unit of *colour temperature.* After scientist Lord Kelvin.

when lens is focused for an infinity subject. More precisely, between this image and the lens's rear nodal point.

keylight Main light source, usually casting the predominant shadows.

kilowatt One thousand watts.

large format General term for cameras taking pictures larger than about 6 × 9 cm.

latent image Exposed but still invisible image.

latitude Permissible variation. Can apply to focusing, exposure, development, temperature etc.

LCD Liquid crystal display. Electronically energized black lettering, symbols etc. – e.g. used in camera's viewfinder or top-plate readout.

leaf shutter See *between-lens shutter*.

LED Light-emitting diode. Gives illuminated signal (or alphanumeric information) alongside camera viewfinder image, and in other equipment displays.

lens coating Transparent material deposited on lens glass to suppress surface reflections, reduce flare and improve image contrast.

lens hood, or shade Shield surrounding lens (just outside image field of view) to intercept side-light, prevent flare.

light meter Device for measuring light and converting this into exposure settings.

light trap Usually some form of baffle to stop entry of light yet allow the passage of air, solution, objects, according to application.

lighting ratio The ratio of the level of illumination in the most strongly lit part of the subject to that in the most shadowed area (given the same subject reflectance throughout).

line image High-contrast image, as required for copies of line diagrams or drawings.

linear perspective Impression of depth given by apparent convergence of parallel lines, and changes of scale, between foreground and background elements.

line pair (lp) One black line plus the adjoining white space on an optical test chart pattern.

lith film Highest-contrast film. Similar to line but able to yield negatives with far more intense blacks.

log Logarithm. In photography common logarithms, to the base 10; e.g. $\log_{10}$ of $10 = 1$ and $\log_{10}$ of $100 = 2$.

log E scale Range of exposures expressed on a logarithmic scale (base 10). Here each doubling of exposure is expressed by an increase of 0.3.

long-peaking flash Electronic flash utilizing a fast stroboscopic principle to give an effectively long and *even* peak of light. This 'long burn' allows an FP shutter slit to cross and evenly expose the full picture format, at fastest speeds.

low key Scene or picture consisting predominantly of dark tones, sombre colours.

luminance Brightness. The amount of light energy emitted or reflected.

M Medium-delay flashbulb. Flash sync connections marked M close the circuit before the shutter is fully open. Do not use for electronic flash.

macro lens Lens specially corrected to give optimum definition at close subject distances.

macrophotography See *photomacrography*.

magnification In photography, linear magnification (height of object divided into height of its image).

manual override The capability to operate an automatic camera in a manual, i.e. non-automatic, mode.

masking General term for a wide range of methods of selectively modifying tone, contrast and colour rendering of existing negatives or transparencies before printing or reproduction. Achieved through sandwiching a parent image with film bearing positive or negative versions made from it and having controlled tonal characteristics. Also achieved electronically, e.g. during scanning for photomechanical reproduction.

masking frame Adjustable frame which holds printing paper during exposure under enlarger. Also covers edges to form white borders.

mat, or overmat Cardboard rectangle with cut-out opening, placed over print to isolate finished picture.

matt Non-shiny, untextured surface finish.

maximum aperture The widest opening (lowest *f*-number) a lens offers.

ME Multiple exposure control. Allows superimposition of pictures in the camera.

microphotography Production of extremely small photographic images, e.g. in microfilming of documents.

midtone A tone mid-way between highlight and shadow values in a scene.

mired Micro-reciprocal degree. Unit of measurement of *colour temperature*; equal to one million divided by colour temperature in kelvins.

mirror lens Also 'catadioptric' lens. Lens using mirrors as well as glass elements. The design makes long focal length lenses more compact, less weighty, but more squat.

mirror lock (ML) Enables the viewing mirror of an SLR camera to be locked in the 'up' position whilst the shutter etc. is used normally. Used to avoid vibration; or to operate motor drives at fastest framing rates; or to accommodate some extreme short focal length lens.

mode The way in which a procedure (such as measuring or setting exposure) is to be carried out.

modelling light Continuous light source, positioned close to electronic flash tube, used to preview lighting effect before shooting with the flash itself.

moiré pattern Coarse pattern formed when two or more patterns of regular lines or textures are superimposed nearly but not exactly in register. Term derived from pattern effects when layers of moiré silk are overlapped.

monochrome Single colour. Also general term for all forms of black and white photography.

monorail camera Metal-framed camera, built on rail.

motor drive Motor which winds on film after each exposure.

MTF Modulation transfer function. A measure of the ability of an imaging system (lens, or recording medium, or both) to resolve fine detail.

ND Neutral density. Colourless grey tone.

neutral density filter Colourless grey filter which dims the image by a known amount.

nodal points Two imaginary points on the lens axis where it is crossed by the principal planes of the lens (given that the same medium, e.g. air, is on both sides of the lens). Rotating a lens about a vertical axis passing through its rear nodal point leaves the image of a distant subject stationary – a principle exploited in panoramic cameras.

normal (or 'standard') lens Lens most regularly supplied for a particular camera; typically has a focal length equal to the diagonal of the picture format.

notching code Notches in sheet film, shape-coded to show film type.

object The thing photographed. Often used interchangeably with *subject*.

one-shot processing Processing in fresh solution, which is then discarded rather than used again.

opacity Incident light divided by light transmitted (or reflected, if tone is on a non-transparent base).

open flash Firing flash manually while the camera shutter is open.

ortho Orthochromatic sensitivity to colours. Monochrome response to blue and green, insensitive to red.

OTF Off the film. Light measurement of the image whilst on the film surface during exposure – essential for through-the-lens reading of flash exposures.

pan and tilt head Tripod head allowing smooth horizontal and vertical pivoting of the camera.

pan film Panchromatic sensitivity. Monochrome response to all colours of the visual spectrum.

panning Pivoting the camera about a vertical axis. Following horizontal movement.

parallax Difference in viewpoint which occurs when a camera's viewfinding system is separate from the taking lens, as in compact and TLR cameras.

PC lens Perspective control lens. A lens of wide covering power on a shift (and sometimes also pivoting) mount. See *shift lens*.

PE Continental code for resin-coated paper. See *RC paper*.

PEC Photo-electric cell. Responds to light by generating minute current flow. Used in older, non-battery hand meters.

pentaprism Multi-sided silvered prism. Reflects and converts laterally reversed image on the focusing screen of SLR camera to right-reading.

PF Power focus control. Manual focusing performed electronically by pressing buttons or a lever on the camera body. (Like controlling electrically driven windows in a car.)

pH Acid/alkalinity scale 0–14, based on hydrogen ion concentration in a solution. 7 is neutral, e.g. distilled water. Chemical solutions with higher pH ratings are increasingly alkaline, lower ones acid.

photoflood Bright tungsten studio-lamp bulb. Often 3400 K.

photogram Image recorded by placing an object directly between sensitive film (or paper) and a light source.

photomacrography Preferred term for extreme close-up photography giving magnification of ×1 or larger, without use of a microscope.

photomicrography Photography through a microscope.

pincushion distortion Aberrations by which the image of a square is less magnified at the centre than at its edges – forming a shape like a 19th century pincushion.

pixel Abbreviation of 'picture element'. One of the hundreds of thousands of spots making up the picture in an electronic image.

polarized light Light waves restricted to vibrate in one plane at right-angles to their path of direction.

polarizing filter Grey-looking filter, able to block polarized light when rotated to cross the plane of polarization.

Polaroid back Camera magazine or film holder accepting instant-picture material.

polycontrast See *variable-contrast paper*.

positive Image with tone values similar to those of the original subject.

PQ Developer using Phenidone and hydroquinone as developing agents.

preservative Chemical ingredient of processing solution. Preserves its activity by reducing oxidation effects.

press focus Lever on most large-format camera shutters. Locks open the shutter blades (to allow image focusing) irrespective of any speed set.

primary colours Of light: red, green and blue.

printing-in Giving additional exposure time to some chosen area, during printing.

program, programme, or P Setting mode for fully automatic exposure control. The camera's choice of aperture and shutter settings under any one set of conditions will depend on its built-in program(s).

program back Data imprinting camera back with additional camera control features such as auto-bracketing, time-lapse, and exposure program display.

program shift 'Program' mode allows the camera to select both shutter and aperture settings, but the shift control allows user to bias it towards faster shutter speeds, or smaller apertures ('speed' or 'depth'). May also be biased automatically, when you fit either a wide-angle or a telephoto lens.

pulling See *holding back.*

push-processing Increasing development, usually to improve speed or increase contrast.

quartz iodine Compact tungsten filament lamp. Maintains colour temperature and intensity throughout its life.

rangefinder Optical device for assessing subject distance, by comparison from two separate viewpoints.

rapid fixer Fast-acting fixing bath using ammonium thiosulphate or thiocyanate as fixing agent.

RC paper Resin (plastic) coated base printing paper.

rebate Unexposed parts outside a film's picture areas.

reciprocity failure Breakdown of the usual reciprocal exposure relationship between time and intensity (twice the exposure time compensates for an image half as bright, and vice versa).

reciprocity law Exposure = intensity × time.

reducer Chemical able to reduce the density of a processed image. (Paradoxically the term 'reducing agent' is also applied to developing agents.)

reflected-light reading Measuring exposure (usually from the camera position) with the light sensor pointing towards the subject.

refraction Change in the direction of light as it passes obliquely from one transparent medium into another of different refractive index.

relative aperture See *f-numbers.*

replenisher Solution of chemicals (mostly developing agents) designed to be added in controlled amounts to a particular developer, to maintain its activity and compensate for repeated use.

restrainer Chemical component of developer which restrains it from acting on unexposed halides.

retrofocus lens See *inverted telephoto lens.*

reversal system Combination of emulsion and processing which produces a direct image of similar tonal values to the picture exposed on to the material.

ring flash Circular electronic flash tube, fitted around the camera lens.

rising front Camera front which allows the lens to be raised, parallel to the film plane.

rollfilm back Adaptor back for rollfilm.

rostrum camera Vertically set-up permanent camera system, over a horizontal bench or rostrum holding copy originals on paper or acetate. Used in audio-visual, animation and movie applications.

safelight Working light of the correct colour and intensity not to affect the light-sensitive material in use.

saturated colour A strong, pure hue – undiluted by white, grey or other colours.

second curtain sync Camera synchronization for electronic flash whereby contacts are closed just before the second blind of the FP shutter starts to close. With long duration exposures this means that flash records sharp detail at the *end* of exposure, and blur trails due to any movement record during the earlier part – e.g. moving objects in pictures 'head up' their blur, and do not record as if moving backwards.

secondary colours See *complementary colours.*

selective focusing Precise focus setting and shallow depth of field, used to isolate a chosen part of a scene.

self-timer Delayed-action shutter release.

shading Blocking off light from part of the picture during some or all of the exposure.

shadows In exposure or sensitometric terms, the darkest important tone in the subject.

sheet film Light-sensitive film in the form of single sheets.

shift lens Wide-covering-power lens in a mount permitting it to be shifted off-centre relative to film format.

shutter priority mode You set the shutter speed and the camera sets the appropriate aperture to give correct exposure according to the built-in metering system. Also known as *Tv mode.*

silver halides Light-sensitive compounds of silver and alkali salts of halogen chemicals, such as bromine, chlorine and iodine.

slave unit Flash unit which reacts to light from another flash and fires simultaneously.

SLR Single-lens reflex.

snoot Conical black tube fitted over spotlight or small flood. Restricts lighting to a small circular patch.

soft (1) Low contrast. (2) Slightly unsharp or blurred.

spectrum Radiant energy arranged by wavelength. The visible spectrum, experienced as light, spans 400–700 nm.

speed mode Automatic exposure camera program aiming to preserve as much freezing of action as possible in selecting shutter speed and aperture.

speed point Point on a photographic material's characteristic curve used to determine the speed rating of a film (or paper). For example, in current ISO and DIN systems two points (M and N) are shown on the material's characteristic curve. M lies where processed density is 0.1 above fog. N lies 1.3 log exposure units from point M in the direction of increasing exposure, and development time is picked which makes N correspond to a processed density of 0.8 greater than M. When these conditions are satisfied the exposure at M is the numeral value from which the speed rating is calculated.

spot meter Hand meter, with aiming viewfinder, to make spot exposure readings.

spot mode Narrow-angle exposure reading of the subject with a TTL meter. The small area measured is outlined on camera's focusing screen.

spotting Retouching-in small white specks or hairs – generally on prints – using water colour, dye or pencil.

still-life General term for an inanimate object, set up and arranged in or out of the studio.

still video (SV) International term for still (as opposed to movie) systems in which optical images are sensed and recorded electronically rather than by traditional chemical photographic methods.

still video compatible Camera designed to accept chemical film but adaptable, usually via a special replacement back, to record images in still video form.

stock solution Chemical stored in concentrated liquid form, diluted for use.

stop bath Acidic solution which halts development, reduces fixer contamination by alkaline developer.

strobe Inaccurate general term for electronic flash. Strictly means fast-repeating stroboscopic lamp or flash.

subject The thing being photographed. Term used interchangeably with object, although more relevant to a person, scene or situation.

subtractive colour processes Processes which represent subject colours by superimposed yellow, magenta and cyan images. Each of these layers subtract unwanted quantities of blue, green or red respectively from white light.

supplementary lens. See *close-up lens.*

SV See *still video.*

sync lead Cable connecting flashgun to shutter, for synchronized flash firing.

synchro-sun Flash from the camera used to 'fill-in' shadows cast by sunlight.

T setting 'Time' setting available on some large-format camera shutters. Release is pressed once to lock shutter open, then pressed again to close it.

tele-extender Supplementary lens system fitted between camera lens and body, to increase focal length. Also reduces the lens aperture.

telephoto Long focal length lens with shorter back focus, allowing it to be relatively compact.

tempering bath Large tank or deep tray, containing temperature-controlled air or water. Accepts drums, tanks, bottles or trays to maintain their solution temperature during processing.

thermal printer Machine producing hard-copy images from electronic (*still video*) recordings. It uses a dot-matrix head to heat a sandwich of dye and plain paper, transferring dots of colour.

tinting Applying colour (oils, dye, water colours) to a print by hand.

TLR Twin-lens reflex.

toning Converting a black silver image into a coloured compound or dye. The base remains unaffected.

transparency Positive image on film. Includes both slides and larger formats.

trap focus Autofocusing mode by which the camera shutter remains locked until an object moves into the lens's zone of sharp focus.

TTL Through-the-lens camera reading, e.g. of exposure.

tungsten-light film Colour film balanced to suit tungsten light souces of 3200 K.

Tv mode Time value exposure mode. Used on some cameras to designate *shutter priority mode.*

uprating Increasing your film's speed setting (or selecting a minus setting on the exposure-compensation dial) to suit difficult shooting conditions. Usually followed up with extended development.

UV Ultra-violet. Wide band of wavelengths less than about 390 nm.

UV filter Filter absorbing UV only. Appears colourless.

value Term used in the Munsell colour system. It refers to a colour's luminance factor or brightness.

variable-contrast paper Monochrome printing paper which changes its contrast characteristics with the colour of the exposing light. Controlled by filters.

view camera Camera (usually large-format) in which the image is viewed and focused on a screen in the film plane, later replaced by a film holder. View cameras are primarily used on a stand. See also *field camera.*

viewpoint The position from which the camera views the subject.

vignetting Fading off the sides of a picture into plain black or white, instead of having abrupt edges.

warm tone A brownish black and white silver image. Often adds to tonal richness.

watt-second See *joule.*

wetting agent Detergent-type additive, used in minute quantity to lower the surface tension of water. Assists even action of most non-acid solutions, and of drying.

white light Illumination containing a mixture of all wavelengths of the visible spectrum.

wide-angle lens Short focal length lens of extreme covering power, used on relatively large format to give a wide angle of view.

working solution Solution at the strength actually needed for use.

X Electronic flash. Any flash sync socket and/or shutter setting marked X is for electronic flash. (Also suits flashbulbs at exposures $\frac{1}{8}$ second or slower.)

zone system System embracing subject brightness range, negative exposure, development and printing, to give you control over final print tone values. Ideally allows you to pre-visualize and decide the tonal range of your result at the time of shooting.

zoom lens Lens continuously variable between two given focal lengths, whilst maintaining the same focus setting.

zooming Altering the focal length of a zoom lens.

Picture credits

Cover: Chris Alan Wilton/The Image Bank.
Fig. 1.2 Bert Hardy/BBC Hulton Picture Library. 1.3 Dr Jeremy Burgess/Science Photo Library. 1.5 John Downing/*Daily Express*. 1.6 Annie Morris, London. 2.13 Carl Zeiss, West Germany. 2.24 Chris Harris/*The Times*. 2.25 Ilkay Mehmet/*Daily Telegraph*. 3.17 Shell Research Ltd. 4.2 Kodak Ltd. 4.8 Dick Swayne, Godalming. 4.26 Simon Marsden, London. 4.27 Jon Barnes, London. 6.1 Susie Weeks, London. 6.2 Cecil Beaton/Sotheby's. 6.17 Tim Imrie/Anna Tait Associates, London. 6.20 Andrew Heaps, London. 6.23 Jon Barnes, London. 6.35 Dr Gary S. Settles, Stephen S. McIntyre/Science Photo Library. 8.1 Patrick Eagar, London. 8.2 Monique Cabral, London. 8.3 Sue Parker, Tintern, Gwent. 8.4 Bobby Collins, Studio 77, Southsea. 8.8 Michel Tcherevkoff/The Image Bank. 8.9 Charlie Waite/Landscape Only. 8.12 Philip Fraser-Betts, Centremark Design and Photography, Chelmsford. 8.14 Laurie Campbell, Edinburgh. 8.16 Chris Smith/*Sunday Times*. 8.18 Laurence Gould/Colorific Photo Library. 10.39 Tim Stephens/Faber and Faber. 11.1, 11.2, 11.3 Lorry Eason, London. (All other pictures by the author.)

Index